MOVEMENT MAKERS

MOVEMENT MAKERS

HOW YOUNG ACTIVISTS UPENDED THE POLITICS OF CLIMATE CHANGE

Nick Engelfried

Reconnect Earth Action

Previous versions of some parts of this book appeared in earlier, usually abbreviated form on WagingNonviolence.org. Check out their excellent website for more inspiring stories of grassroots movements resisting oppressive institutions and power structures.

*For the countless young people who have given their
time, energy, hard work, and imaginations to make the
youth climate movement what it is today*

Contents

PART THREE
Preparing for the Next Wave 203

Acknowledgments

It would be impossible to adequately thank the many people without whose help *Movement Makers* never could have come together. First, I am deeply indebted to each of the young activists, educators, and others with expertise in youth climate activism who took time out of their busy schedules to talk with me about their work. Even those individuals whose stories, due to limited space, did not make it into the final version of *Movement Makers* provided important insights into the trajectory of youth climate movement evolution over the past two decades and more. Some quotes that appear in this book have been lightly edited for concision or clarity, but always with the intent of preserving their essential meaning. Any mistakes in the book are mine alone.

Nor could I have completed this project without the support of family members. I want to thank my parents, Tina and Steven Engelfried, for believing in me; my sister, Rose Engelfried, for lending her help as a friend, confidant, and my primary editor throughout the writing process; and my partner, Carolyn Stewart, for her understanding and reassurances as I obsessed endlessly about this book's viability and my ability to complete it during the last two years.

Finally, I offer my endless gratitude and admiration to the thousands of young people—the vast majority of whom will never receive much public recognition for their work—who made the youth climate movement the vibrant, vital force it is today. I only wish there was space in these pages to acknowledge every one of them and give them the credit they so deeply deserve.

Introduction: When Youth Are "The Adults"

Early in the morning on September 20, 2019, a couple dozen young people arrived in New York City's Foley Square to prepare for one of the largest outpourings of public support for action on climate change in history. At noon, hundreds of thousands of people would converge in the park for an opening rally and march to the United Nations Headquarters a little over three miles away. Millions were joining similar demonstrations in cities and towns around the globe. Foley Square would soon fill with tightly packed bodies, the hum of voices, and the carefully controlled chaos that accompanies such massive gatherings. But for now, for a little while, only the organizers were on the scene.

Before almost any large activist event comes a moment when the leaders wonder if their efforts were worth it, whether the hoped-for crowds will show up. But this time there was no need to fear. High school students throughout the city were planning class walk-outs to join the rally and march. Activists young and old came from all over New York and beyond. When the first group of a hundred students showed up, march organizers got an intimation of how successful their recruitment efforts had been.

"From that point on, I knew it was going to get hectic," high school sophomore Rachel Lee told me in an interview months later. "Soon there were enough of us to shut down the street." When Lee introduced one of the rally speakers, the crowd extended farther into the distance than she could see.[1]

Lee belonged to the New York City chapter of the youth-led climate group Zero Hour, a participant in the multi-organization consortium that planned the massive climate march. In early 2019, she and other local activists learned New York would host a special U.N. summit meant to spur more ambitious government commitments to cutting carbon emissions. The September 20 mobilizations in the city and elsewhere were timed to fall just a few days before that official event—but to many observers, the summit itself felt like a response to an unprecedented flood of student-led climate activism sweeping the globe.

It was in August the previous year that a Swedish teenager named Greta Thunberg began skipping school to protest for climate action, sparking an international movement.[2] That November, young people from the U.S. organization Sunrise Movement generated headlines by calling for a Green New Deal at a sit-in in the Congressional office of House Speaker-elect Nancy Pelosi.[3] Student fossil fuel divestment activists were organizing at universities all over the country, and would soon disrupt a Yale-Harvard football match to protest the Ivy League schools' investments in polluting industries.[4] And now, on September 20, 2019, activists around the world were launching eight days of strikes and other mobilizations that represented a culmination of momentum from more than a year of youth-led climate organizing.

"Strikes are happening almost everywhere you can think of," Jamie Margolin, a prominent young activist from Seattle, told me in a phone conversation a few weeks before the 20th. "People are participating in literally every place in the world."[5]

I was interviewing Margolin for a story about the movement of school strikes for the climate for the online publication *Waging Nonviolence*. I had been writing about climate activism for years and spent more than a decade as a youth climate activist myself, so I was naturally interested in the recent upsurge of activity. However, my conversation with Margolin left me even more intrigued as to how this flood of youth-led action on behalf of the climate came to be. I learned that while the school strikes started in Sweden, their origins were intimately tied to developments in the United States—especially in Seattle, just a couple hours south of where I lived.

I was curious to see firsthand what Seattle's local youth climate movement looked like now. So, on an unseasonably warm Friday later that fall, I took a bus to the city to find out.

*

Seattle City Hall is an odd-shaped structure, built on a hillside in such a way that a patio which appears from the back to be on ground level actually looks down from above on the wide stone stairs leading to the front entrance. From this vantage point, I watched as a few dozen people began gathering on the steps below. There were children, young adults, and people of all ages up through retirees, but the group skewed young. School-age participants were missing class to be here. Some held hand-lettered signs with messages like "Business as usual is a death sentence" and "Fridays for Future." I was looking at Seattle's weekly climate strike.

Although this gathering wasn't large, I knew just a couple months earlier some ten thousand people had rallied in nearby Cal Anderson Park for the September 20 day of climate mobilizations.[6] The group who gathered in front of City Hall every Friday—a popular day for the school strikes sparked by Thunberg's activism—therefore represented the tip of a much larger movement. I meandered down to the building's front steps, hoping to learn what inspired some of the protesters to keep coming back week after week.

One of the first strikers I talked to was fourteen-year-old Zoe Schurman, a middle schooler with a shy expression and faint purple highlights in her hair. "The youth of today's future is on the line," she explained. "And adults aren't just doing nothing—they're actively continuing to burn fossil fuels and create further injustices.

If older generations aren't going to be responsible, then in times of crisis youth have to step up and be the adults."[7] It was inspiring to hear someone so young sum up the crisis their generation faces so clearly.

I also spoke with twelve-year-old Ian Price, the founder of Seattle's school strike. "I'm here because decision-makers like those in this building need to act," he told me, looking up at City Hall. Price first skipped school for the climate on Friday, December 14, 2018, making Seattle's one of the longest-running climate strikes in the U.S. He was moved to act after watching a YouTube clip of Greta Thunberg speaking at a U.N. climate conference. Price told his mother, Heather, that he wanted to protest on Fridays, and on the 14th he stood in front of City Hall with a sign that read, "It's Getting Hot: Climate Action Now." Heather Price waited nearby, keeping an eye on Ian's safety but otherwise not interfering.[8]

Unbeknownst to him at the time, Price was one of a scattering of U.S. students who had watched Greta Thunberg's speeches on social media and decided to take action, more or less simultaneously. On the same day as his first strike in Seattle, thirteen-year-old Alexandria Villaseñor sat outside the United Nations in New York with a sign that read "School Strike 4 Climate."[9] A week earlier, ten-year-old Zayne Cowie of Brooklyn began striking outside New York City Hall[10] and fourteen-year-old Kallan Benson organized a climate-themed hopscotch game outside the U.S. Energy Department.[11] Zane Kalmus-Kunde, age ten, and his older brother Braird started striking in Los Angeles around the same time.[12]

"We kind of embraced the fact that we were youth trying to make a difference," Zane Kalmus-Kunde told me in an interview for this book. "Greta is inspiring to me because even as a kid, she understands what climate change means for us and is acting more mature than a lot of politicians."[13] The strike movement grew, with some students skipping school every Friday and much larger numbers participating in occasional national or international days of action.

By early 2020, I was immersed in researching where the strike movement and other recent currents of youth-led climate activism had come from. At first my goal was to share what I learned in a series of articles for *Waging Nonviolence*. I spoke with high school climate strikers, college students campaigning for fossil fuel divestment, and young activists pushing a Green New Deal. The youth involved seemed to come from every race and culture, and spoke confidently about the intersections between climate disruption, racism, and other pressing social issues.

Slowly, I began to see how the movement that seemingly burst from nowhere in late 2018 had in fact built on over two decades of work by young people concerned about the climate. I was deeply familiar with some of those earlier efforts, having become a climate activist in my late teens in the '00s. Like many of the Generation Z members I was now interviewing, my own motivation as an activist stemmed from a deep sense of connection to a natural world increasingly under threat. I organized support for campus sustainability policies in college, then spent several years working to oppose large coal, oil, and gas projects in the Northwest. More recently I had turned away from fulltime activism to focus on my work as an environmental educator and writing about the efforts of others. Even so, I retained many connections in the climate organizing world.

I gradually came to see that to provide a full picture of how the modern youth climate movement came into existence, I needed far more space than was available in the short articles I was writing. This daunting task would require a whole book.

In May 2020, I spoke with Ian Price again. This was well into the first wave of COVID-19, so I connected with him and his mother over Zoom. As with most youth activists I talk to, little about

Price's appearance marked him as a likely movement leader. On the contrary, he seemed an ordinary adolescent with an unassuming demeanor and a tendency to fidget as he spoke. His hobbies are ordinary, too, for a young person in Washington State. He told me he enjoys skiing, and worries about the future of snow sports in a warming world. "The thought that when I'm older people won't be able to experience skiing like I have is heartbreaking," he said.[14]

During the tumultuous year that was 2020, climate change sometimes seemed eclipsed in the public consciousness by a string of other crises. First came the pandemic, then a long-overdue national uprising against racial injustice, then a high-stakes presidential election. But while COVID made in-person rallies hard to organize for a while, the youth climate movement adapted as best it could. Some students, like Price, posted photos of themselves holding signs on social media every Friday.[15] Others came up with creative ways to protest in small groups. In both the primaries and the general election, youth activists played a crucial role getting out the vote for progressive House and Senate candidates. All this occurred against a backdrop of unprecedented extreme weather events, which added urgency to climate activists' demands.

In 2021 and 2022, with a new Congress and president in office, it was time to see if the youth movement could translate grassroots momentum into policy wins. Young activists took on this challenge —sometimes more successfully than in other cases, but always in the context of a national discourse about climate that had been irrevocably altered by the last few years. I was by then thoroughly absorbed in writing this book, and I found myself trying to answer three broad questions: Where did the major strands of climate activism that burst onto the scene in late 2018 come from, and how did they spread so quickly? What was the relationship between modern youth climate organizing, and the efforts of an earlier generation of activists? And what, from the vantage point of the early

2020s, has been the effect of all this organizing on both government policy and the larger public consciousness?

The book now in your hands is divided into three parts, each loosely organized around one of the guiding questions above. While I sometimes touch on happenings in places like Canada or Sweden when they have direct bearing on developments in the United States, I have confined my focus mainly to events in this country. A comprehensive look at the vibrant international youth climate movement is beyond the scope of this project.

My research has involved interviewing well over a hundred current and former young climate organizers, culling through countless old news articles and blog posts, and drawing on notes and memories from my own years as a climate activist. I hope the resultant book serves as a repository of valuable lessons from more than two decades of youth climate organizing, a source of inspiration for those doing this work today, and a glimpse into the world of climate activism that will be illuminating for readers new to it as well as those with extensive personal experience.

The people whose stories appear in these pages include Jamie Margolin, the Seattle high schooler who started Zero Hour and helped inspire Greta Thunberg; University of Utah student Tim De-Christopher, who shut down an oil and gas auction with a creative act of civil disobedience; Chiara D'Angelo, who spent sixty-three hours chained to an oil drilling support vessel; young Indigenous organizers who galvanized massive protests against the Dakota Access pipeline; and many, many others. Their accomplishments may sometimes seem larger than life—but while indeed impressive, in the end they are simply ordinary young people who chose to take extraordinary action on the defining crisis of their generation.

In doing so they have, arguably, acted more like adults than many so-called grownups.

PART ONE

A Movement Rising

1

Generation Climate

SCHOOL STRIKES, ZERO HOUR, AND THE NEW CLIMATE MOVEMENT

It was the very worst kind of day for a protest. Pouring rain, the bane of all activists, began early and continued well into the afternoon. Even so, hundreds of teenagers gathered on the National Mall on July 21, 2018, sheltering under umbrellas and holding signs with messages like "Youth for Climate Action" and "This is Zero Hour."

For two hours, the youths listened to a lineup of their peers address them through a megaphone. Speakers included teen anti-pipeline organizer Tokata Iron Eyes of the Standing Rock Sioux Tribe, hip hop artist and activist Xiuhtezactl Martinez, and seven-year-old Havana Chapman-Edwards, whose message for children worried about the climate crisis was, "We've got this."[1] After the speeches, the young people marched: past the Washington Monument, Capitol Hill, and U.S. Supreme Court to Lincoln Park. It was still raining.

The weather likely depressed turnout. Yet, while not large compared to some protests in Washington, D.C., the action was part of the biggest climate mobilization led by young people in the U.S. in some time. It coincided with more than two dozen sister marches in cities throughout the country and as far away as Kenya. Two days earlier, over a hundred young people flooded Capitol Hill to lobby Congress for climate action.[2] The organizers of all this activity were almost all still in high school, a fact that caught national news media's attention. "As sea levels rise, ice caps melt and erratic weather affects communities across the globe, they [youth activists] say time is running out to address climate change," read a *New York Times* story.[3] "The forecast didn't disappoint," wrote Kristen Doerer of *Teen Vogue,* referring to the downpour. "But the young activists who took the streets didn't either."[4]

Many people helped make the day of marches a success, but the vision originated with sixteen-year-old Jamie Margolin of Seattle, who the previous summer began reaching out to students all over the country with the idea of starting a national youth-led climate organization. The result was Zero Hour, the entity behind the July 21 protests. In just over twelve months, a group of teens who began with almost no resources or funding coordinated a national event many well-established nonprofits couldn't have equaled.

There was a feeling at that march in the rain of something important happening. Even so, it would have been impossible to predict just how far the ripple effects would reach.

Origins of a climate leader

Anyone who interacts with Jamie Margolin soon realizes she has a lot on her plate. I first spoke with her during the conversation referred to in this book's introduction, in early September 2019. This was a little more than a year after Zero Hour's march on Washington, and Margolin was by then a high school senior. She had recently finished coordinating a training summit for young climate advocates in Miami, Florida. She was also finishing the manuscript for her book, *Youth to Power,* a compendium of advice for aspiring activists. And she was preparing for the eight days of climate strike events later that month, when millions of students would skip school to protest government inaction on the biggest crisis facing their generation. Margolin told me she saw these kinds of demonstrations as an opportunity to catalyze larger numbers of youth into becoming activists.

"A lot of people aren't initially attracted to the nitty gritty organizing work which is the vast majority of climate activism," she explained. "But if you say, 'Hey, do you want to join this exciting mass action?'—that attracts nearly everyone. It's a point of entry to the wider movement."[5]

I was curious how Margolin herself got involved in climate organizing at such an early age, and how the movement in which she was now a leader grew so fast. Zero Hour's 2018 marches were impressive for a day of action organized by teenagers, but drew hundreds rather than thousands of people. Now millions were preparing to take to the streets. Because Zero Hour was one of the major groups promoting the school strikes in the U.S., I had reached out to Margolin in hopes of learning more about her organization's relationship with the wider strike movement. Perhaps, I thought, her story could provide insight into where the flood of youth activism engulfing the world came from.

*

"I've been concerned about the climate crisis for as long as I can remember," Margolin told me during a second conversation later that fall. Growing up, she watched documentaries about melting ice caps and dying forests and realized this was the world her generation would inherit. "But doing something about it seemed like such a daunting task, I didn't know where to start."

For Generation Z, the imminent collapse of Earth's life systems has been normalized—if such a thing can be normal. Margolin described experiencing a sense of dread about the future that would rise to the surface periodically, only to fade into the ever-present background. Plenty of people from her generation will recognize the feeling. "Life happens, and you can't think about the climate all the time," she said. "But then I'd look around at the beauty of the Pacific Northwest where I live, and be hit by how soon it could all disappear."[6]

Well-meaning adults often tell young people they can make a positive difference for the environment, but rarely offer ideas commensurate to the scale of the challenge. A typical example is the popular children's book, *50 Simple Things Kids Can Do to Save the Earth*, updated in 2009 when Margolin was in second grade. Its suggestions for children who want to take action for the planet include recycling, picking up litter, and avoiding plastic bags. The book does touch briefly on simple forms of activism like writing to politicians, but the focus is overwhelmingly on individualistic solutions to problems rooted in society's large political and economic institutions.[7]

The advice offered to adults frequently isn't much better. A widely circulated blog post published on Earth Day 2015, when Margolin was in eighth grade, suggested readers "bring your own bags when you shop," "replace your lightbulbs," and "rethink your commute."[8] In the absence of more meaningful ways to have an impact, Margolin did what many people do when confronted by the enormity of the climate crisis: she tried to think about other things.

She devoted her time to school, friends, and athletics. Then, in 2016, she received an email from a Democratic Party group asking for volunteers to phone bank for Hillary Clinton. She decided to try it.

Despite later becoming disillusioned with Clinton's moderate politics, in 2016 Margolin saw in the presidential nominee a strong woman leader and the country's best hope for climate action. She began making calls and door-knocking for the King County Democrats. As a fluent Spanish speaker—Margolin is Colombian on her mother's side, Jewish on her father's—she became an important liaison to Hispanic voters.[9]

Clinton's loss to Donald Trump came as a crushing blow. But rather than despair, Margolin cast about for other ways to make a difference. She reached out to the local chapter of Plant for the Planet, a nonprofit founded in 2007 by nine-year-old Felix Finkbeiner of Germany.[10] From its original mission of planting a million trees in every country, the organization has branched into climate policy work. "Two weeks later I was at the State Capitol in Olympia, asking Washington's legislature to pass a climate bill," Margolin told me. She testified at public hearings, spoke at protests, and began thinking about ways to scale up her activism even more. "For a long time, I had the idea developing in the back of my mind of organizing a really massive mobilization."[11]

Then came the summer of 2017, when for the first time in Margolin's young life smoke from Canadian wildfires blanketed the skies above Seattle. It became hazardous to breathe outdoors.[12] The link between longer, drier fire seasons and climate change seemed obvious to Margolin—and when Hurricanes Harvey and Maria pounded the Caribbean and Gulf of Mexico later that summer, it only deepened her sense of worsening crisis. But too few people seemed to see what was going on.

"Most people I talked to weren't connecting the dots from extreme weather to climate change," Margolin said. "They would just be like, 'Oh, look, there's another big hurricane,' without questioning why this was happening. I knew I had to do something."[13]

In an Instagram post published on July 3, 2017, Margolin wrote, "If we have a #YouthMarchOnWashington where young people flood the streets and demand climate solutions, and then do a #sitin and essentially temporarily 'take over' the congress and senate, demanding our leaders to protect our earth....we can change the game in the #climatecrisis."[14]

An internet friend, fifteen-year-old Nadia Nazar of Baltimore, responded excitedly that she was interested. Soon after that, Margolin received similarly enthusiastic replies from Madelaine Tew of New Jersey and Zanagee Artis in Connecticut, friends she met at a teen political engagement camp earlier that summer.[15] This small but committed core organizing team began reaching out to their own online networks with the aim of making Margolin's ambitious vision a reality.

Growing the movement

Like Margolin, Andrea Manning knew about the climate crisis from a young age. However, for years the problem seemed remote to her. When it came up in school the focus was on melting ice caps and polar bears. To Manning, a Black high school student in Atlanta-area Georgia, such things felt far from her daily reality.

Then, during her senior year of high school in 2018, a friend asked Manning to help coordinate a local march for Zero Hour's July day of action. Manning researched the organization and was drawn to the way it discussed climate change. "The mission of Zero Hour," read the group's website, "is to center the voices of diverse youth in the conversation around climate and environmental justice."[16] Zero Hour's goals and messaging emphasized the needs of marginalized groups on the frontlines of the climate crisis, an approach shared by many other youth-led climate organizations started by members of Generation Z.

"Zero Hour helped me see how climate change affects real communities and racial justice," Manning said when I interviewed her in late 2019. My conversations with Margolin had inspired me to try to discover how Zero Hour groups took root and grew in communities all over the country—so I reached out to local leaders like Manning, then a freshman at the University of Georgia. She was on a city bus when we connected via Zoom, and spoke into her phone in the soft tone of someone trying to be heard without disturbing those around her.

"Zero Hour's message is about preserving a livable future, but also helping people who are affected by pollution and fossil fuel development right now," Manning told me. "We need to change the narrative so that when people think about climate change, they think of impacted frontline communities first. We're trying to cause that cultural shift."[17]

For Zero Hour's 2018 day of action, Manning and some friends organized a march through their city's Centennial Olympic Park. "National youth organization Zero Hour makes strides in Atlanta," read a *Georgia State Signal* headline.[18] Similar events drew dozens or hundreds of people in cities from New York to San Francisco to Seattle, who marched and rallied in solidarity with the flagship action in Washington, D.C. There were even actions in other countries.

On the morning of July 21, Zero Hour's national organizing team woke to images of protests already streaming in over social media from sister actions in the Eastern Hemisphere. "Seeing Zero Hour signs held up in the streets of London or Australia, I felt this pinch of it being reality now," said Sohayla Eldeeb of Florida, the organization's global outreach director. "We had started a worldwide movement."

Eldeeb, who immigrated to the U.S. from Egypt with her family as a young child, became concerned about the environment during annual summer vacations to visit relatives in the land of her birth. She was dismayed by the steadily worsening condition of the Nile. "In my grandmother's village, people depend on that river for their livelihoods," she said when I spoke with her in May 2020. "But every year I saw it grow more polluted."

The summer she was thirteen, Eldeeb and some friends installed garbage cans around her extended family's community to encourage safe waste disposal. Meanwhile, worries about pollution prompted her to learn more about global problems like climate change. In high school she landed an internship at Care About Climate, a nonprofit focused on youth outreach but led by adult mentors. A staff member put her in touch with the leadership of Zero Hour just as the new organization was getting off the ground.

"Zero Hour was still really small at that point and desperately needed people to help out," Eldeeb said. The group was in full event-planning mode, preparing for the march on Washington that July. Eldeeb took on the role of coordinating with students in the U.S. and beyond who wanted to organize solidarity events in their hometowns. She was in D.C. for the flagship protest.

Although the students didn't hold a sit-in on Capitol Hill as Margolin's original Instagram post had suggested, many met with their members of Congress two days before what they hoped would be a march of historic proportions. "I was picturing something like the Women's March," Eldeeb said, referring to the mobilization that brought hundreds of thousands of people onto the streets in Washington and elsewhere in January 2017. "As sixteen and seventeen-year-olds, we wanted thousands or millions of people to show up. Maybe that wasn't realistic—and then it literally rained on our parade. But it felt powerful to go through with our march anyway."

Not until the next day did the young people begin to realize what an impression they had made. Despite drawing smaller numbers of people than hoped, the teen-led nature of the march in the rain made for a good news hook. "We woke up and Zero Hour was on the front cover of the *New York Times*," Eldeeb remembered. "We were going wild with excitement. Getting your first big media feature like that feels amazing."[19]

Zero Hour went on to organize other youth-led mobilizations and a training program aimed at helping young people become ambassadors for socially just climate solutions.[20] When the school strikes for climate movement gained a foothold the United States in early 2019, it seemed natural Zero Hour would play a role spreading it in this country. After all, the organization started by Margolin shared strikers' goal of building a politically powerful climate movement led by young people.

In fact, as I dug deeper into the story of the strikes, I realized their origins were much more directly linked to Zero Hour than was apparent from most news coverage. Back in early 2018, as Zero Hour planned its debut day of marches, leaders like Margolin received messages from a scattering of young people outside the U.S. who were interested in what they were doing. Some ended up holding sister marches in their home countries, while others came up with new, innovative ways to advance the climate movement. Among them was a Swedish teenager with blond pigtails and an unusually blunt way of talking.

The Greta Thunberg question

Greta Thunberg is that rare phenomenon, a climate activist whose name is widely known to the general public even outside her own country. Anyone who is even slightly familiar with international climate politics will likely know that at age fifteen, Thunberg began skipping school to sit outside Sweden's parliament building and protest government inaction on the climate crisis; that her example spread on the wings of social media, inspiring thousands of students around the world to launch their own school strikes for the climate; and that this movement evolved into Fridays for Future, a campaign young people anywhere could join by skipping school once a week.

Some readers may even know details of Thunberg's personal life: that she was diagnosed at a young age as being on the autism spectrum, for example. She was an untalkative child, ate only very specific foods, and tended to think about certain subjects endlessly. "I can spend hours upon hours not getting tired of reading about [a topic] and still be interested to learn more," she told *Democracy Now*.[21] From early childhood, she trained this laser-like focus on climate change.

Mainstream Western culture offers distraction as a tool for coping with the overwhelming feelings called up by the climate crisis —something even Jamie Margolin experienced. As a consequence, young people who find they can't look away often feel isolated. This sense of aloneness likely contributed to Thunberg sliding into depression. It got to where she barely left the house and hardly ate. "I was so unhappy," she told the Swedish newspaper *Dagens Nyheter*. "If I managed to walk out of the door to the grocery store, that was something I would write in my diary and be proud of."[22]

What is less widely recorded is the influence youth climate organizers in the U.S. had on Thunberg's early activism. I was completely in the dark until Margolin casually mentioned during our first conversation that Thunberg—who was already famous by then—had contacted Zero Hour well before the 2018 march on Washington.[23] Statements from Thunberg and those close to her corroborate the role Zero Hour, as well as other youth-led activist campaigns like the March for Our Lives against gun violence, played in inspiring the school strike movement.

In the forward to Margolin's book, *Youth to Power,* Thunberg describes learning about Zero Hour's work and realizing she wasn't the only young person worried about climate change: "I remember feeling...as if no one my age saw what was going on around us or even wanted to make a difference—apart from people like Jamie Margolin." From Margolin and Zero Hour, Thunberg learned that in reality, "countless young people felt just like I did [about climate change]."[24] According to *Our House is on Fire: Scenes of a Family and Planet in Crisis,* a book co-authored by Thunberg and her family members, Thunberg arrived at her vision for a school strike during discussions with other Swedish youth about starting an organization akin to Zero Hour.[25]

On August 20, 2018, almost exactly one month after Zero Hour's day of marches, Thunberg launched her own protest outside the Swedish parliament. By early December, 17,000 students in two dozen mostly European countries were skipping school to follow her example.[26] She began traveling to high-profile climate events, including the U.N.'s 24th Conference of Parties (COP24 for short) in Katowice, Poland. There, her new fame earned her a speaking slot. "You say you love your children above all else," she told a room full of diplomats. "And yet, you're stealing their future in front of their very eyes."[27] Her words, broadcast over social media, caught the interest of early U.S. climate strikers, as described in this book's introduction.

Less than six months into Thunberg's school strike, young people were refusing to go to school on Fridays in countries from Mexico to India, Uganda to New Zealand.[28] Instead, they staged protests against inaction on climate change. This raises an important question: What was it about Thunberg's approach that succeeded in sparking a global mass movement around the climate crisis, when so many others fell short?

*

Thunberg certainly wasn't the first young person to call world leaders to task for their failure on climate change.

"We know that adults know exactly what challenges we have, and they know the solutions to these challenges, but we don't understand why there's so little action," thirteen-year-old Felix Finkbeiner, founder of Plant for the Planet, told the U.N. General Assembly in 2011.[29] Plant for the Planet later provided a pathway for thousands of young people, including Jamie Margolin, to get involved in climate work. However, the organization never had the reach of Fridays for Future.

One key to Thunberg's success was social media, which was more accessible through a variety of platforms in 2018 than 2011. But what led to her, rather than some other young person, harnessing Twitter, YouTube, and Instagram so successfully?

Thunberg's mother, Malena Ernman, is well-known in Sweden as both an opera singer and a writer of opinion columns about climate change.[30] But while Ernman's fame helps explain some of the initial media attention given to Thunberg's protest, it does not account for why people *stayed* interested, or why the strike movement spread to countries where Erman's name is little known. Something about Thunberg herself captured the world's attention. Perhaps it was that she differed sharply from people's mental image of what an activist should be like. An early *U.K. Guardian* story on the strike movement described her as "a diminutive girl with pig-tails and a fleeting smile—not the stereotypical leader of a climate revolution."[31]

Equally important was Thunberg's ability to speak with blunt conviction, a trait often associated with people on the autism spectrum. "I want you to panic," she told the European Parliament in April 2019. "I want you to act as if the house is on fire."[32] And at the R20 Austrian World Summit a month later: "Politicians one second say, 'Climate change is very important...and we are going to do everything we can to stop it.' And the next second, they want to expand airports, build new coal power plants and motorways, then they fly off in a private jet."[33]

There was at least one other key to Thunberg's success. Striking from school, her protest tactic of choice, was both attention-grabbing and easily replicable by young people almost anywhere. Ian Price and the other early U.S. strikers needed no special training to bring Thunberg's approach to climate activism to their own communities. This, combined with Thunberg's effectiveness as a messenger and Fridays for Future's efficient use of social media, allowed the strike movement to spread rapidly around the globe—including in the country more responsible than any other for creating the climate crisis.

Striking in the United States

About eight months after Zero Hour's first day of marches—and six months before the immense climate strikes which would take place around the world that September—hundreds of young people again rallied for climate action in the nation's capital.[34] "I am here because I believe we face the greatest threat humanity has ever faced, and that is climate change," Congresswoman Ilhan Omar, one of the speakers, told the crowd on March 15, 2019. "I am here because I know that my son and my daughters will bear the burden of this crisis."[35]

One of Omar's daughters, sixteen-year-old Isra Hirsi, was an organizer of the event, part of the first truly worldwide day of climate strikes. Such mobilizations, when thousands or millions of people joined the smaller numbers who protested every Friday, came to be known as "deep strikes." An estimated 1.4 million people in 128 countries participated in the March 15 deep strike day.[36]

The U.S. strike movement was by this time already a few months old—but the deep strike brought it to a wider audience. The young people who made it happen included Lana Weidgenant, a Johns Hopkins University sophomore who encountered a news article about the European strike movement in early 2019. "I thought, oh my gosh, the U.S. has to be part of this," Weidgenant said when I interviewed her in May 2020. "The United States is the largest historical emitter of carbon pollution, and we needed to bring the movement here."

Weidgenant connected on social media with a small group of younger students who were responding to a call from Thunberg for a global day of strikes. They included Hirsi, early strike leader Alexandria Villaseñor of New York, and twelve-year-old Haven Coleman in Colorado. Similar to Zero Hour in its early days, the team spread the word online, hung posters at schools in their disparate parts of the U.S., and contacted friends all over the country. Hirsi and Weidgenant took the lead organizing the Washington, D.C. event. Some local students skipped the whole school day to participate, while others staged class walk-outs that converged in front of the Capitol. "It felt like we were finally doing something that would get the attention of U.S. politicians," Weidgenant said.[37]

For the next deep strike event, on May 24, some 1.8 million young people and supporters joined protests and marches in the U.S. and around the world.[38] Then came the movement's biggest burst of activity yet: eight days of strikes and other protests from September 20-27, before and during the special U.N. Climate Action Summit whose stated purpose was to "boost ambition and accelerate [government] actions" to combat climate change ahead of the international COP25 talks that December.[39]

"This U.N. gathering was called in response to the worsening climate crisis and pressure from the strike movement," Jake Woodier, a climate activist from the U.K., told me when I interviewed him for *Waging Nonviolence* in early September that year. "This is a reversal from the past, when climate organizers planned demonstrations in response to official events set in stone long beforehand."[40]

New York, as the host city to the official U.N. event, played a pivotal role in climate strikers' plans. Responsibility for coordinating what became one of the largest climate protests in history fell to a collection of groups including the local Fridays for Future chapter, Zero Hour New York City, and Earth Uprising, an organization founded by Villaseñor. Greta Thunberg announced she would sail across the Atlantic in a solar-powered yacht to participate, then embark on a North America-wide speaking tour.[41]

"We put up flyers and stickers everywhere we could think of—bus stops, powerline poles, anyplace," said Rachel Lee, whose role in the march I described in the Introduction. As a member of the outreach committee, she participated in meetings alongside local strike movement celebrities like Villaseñor and New York Fridays for Future organizer Xiye Bastida. "It got to where I would often randomly come across flyers about the march posted by our group as I walked through the city," Lee said. She knew then they were doing a thorough job getting the word out.[42]

An estimated 7.6 million people worldwide participated in the September climate strikes, including nearly a quarter million in

New York City.[43] Many students who joined strike events were getting involved in climate activism for the first time.

"I had never been to a big protest before," said Lorena Sosa, who attended a September 20 rally in Orlando, Florida. She had become worried about the climate crisis after taking a high school environmental science class, and when she saw a friend's Facebook post about the day of action she was excited to be involved. "Standing in the crowd, I realized my fears about climate change were something we all shared and I felt hopeful we could unite as a movement," she told me. After attending the deep strike, she joined her local Fridays for Future and Zero Hour chapters.[44] For students like Sosa, the day of strikes served as a point of entry into the larger climate movement—just as Jamie Margolin had hoped it would.

One of the largest U.S. demonstrations on September 20 outside of New York unfolded in Washington, D.C. where close to ten thousand people rallied in front of the Capitol. One speaker, Reverend Lennox Yearwood of the Hip Hop Caucus, got the crowd chanting in unison. "We were so loud, I could hear our words echo off the Capitol building," said Zero Hour advocacy director Ethan Wright, one of the lead organizers. "I watched elected officials walk out onto the balcony to see what was going on."[45]

Other cities where crowd estimates reached well into the thousands included Boston, Denver, Minneapolis, Seattle, San Francisco, Los Angeles, and Portland, Oregon.[46] The truly massive, youth-led climate movement which Zero Hour tried to spark more than a year earlier had finally arrived. Now came the hardest part: translating this show of public support into policy.

In a nod to the newly prominent role of young activists as a force in global politics, the U.N. hosted a Youth Climate Summit on September 21 in New York, two days before the start of the larger Climate Action Summit where national delegations from around the world would discuss their ambitions for reining in carbon emissions. Among the hundreds of young people from 140 countries invited to the youth event were Thunberg, Margolin, and many other Zero Hour and global strike movement leaders.[47] Some stayed for the larger U.N. gathering to follow, which would set the tone for negotiations at COP25 in Madrid later that year.

A lot had happened since the previous year's COP meeting, when Thunberg castigated a roomful of diplomats in Poland. The question was, would it be enough to sway the direction of international climate talks?

Grassroots momentum, government failures

In December 2019, sixteen-year-old Zero Hour organizer Isabella Fallahi was at COP25, attempting to stage a peaceful protest during a panel where a Shell Oil executive was speaking. Fallahi had traveled from Indiana to Spain to try to influence events at the U.N. climate meeting—and what she had seen so far was discouraging.

That year's COP climate talks represented the twenty-fifth time the global community had come together with the goal of reducing carbon emissions through an international consensus process. Four years earlier, in a rare breakthrough at COP21 in Paris, almost every country in the world agreed to work toward limiting global temperature increases to "well below" two degrees Celsius (3.6 degrees Fahrenheit).[48] Most countries were now struggling to meet their domestic emission reduction targets, however, and the Trump administration had announced the U.S. would abandon the Paris Accords completely. Greta Thunberg's COP24 speech helped refocus international attention on the importance of the annual talks. But getting governments to follow through on their promises was an uphill struggle.

Most disturbing to young activists like Fallahi was the omnipresence of polluting corporations at COP. Companies from energy-intensive industries were represented on panels, met with negotiators, and even bankrolled much of the event itself. COP25 sponsors included military arms dealer Indra, large banks, and fossil fuel-dependent international utilities Iberdrola and Endesa.[49] "Nothing could get done because polluters were everywhere," Fallahi told me in a phone interview later that month. "I watched as they were invited into closed-door discussions with policymakers."[50]

Fallahi grew up in Indianapolis, capital of the U.S. state that consumes more coal than any other except Texas.[51] "Because of coal, we also have some of the dirtiest air in the country," she explained. She began developing asthma early in childhood, and it didn't take a medical degree to guess her illness was linked to poor air quality. By the time of Zero Hour's debut day of marches, Fallahi had organized for local climate activist campaigns and the Indianapolis Women's March. She joined the national Zero Hour team and was soon regularly speaking to crowds of hundreds or thousands—including in New York on September 20, 2019, where she shared the stage with Thunberg. The following day she attended the U.N. Youth Climate Summit, an event designed by diplomats who wanted to show they were on young people's side.[52]

"At the summit we met heads of state, ambassadors, and presidents," Mohammad Ahmadi, a Chicago-area high school student and Earth Uprising organizer, told me. "But most inspiring was seeing youth activists from all over the world come together and share what they were doing at home to build the climate movement."[53]

Collectively, young people at the summit had done more to advance the public conversation about climate change than over two decades of COP meetings—and there were times when U.N. officials seemed to have badly misjudged their audience. At one point, the event organizers showed a climate change education video produced by the makers of the Angry Birds movies. "The United Nations has a plan to help the Earth," announced the two-minute clip, "and they need all of our help before it's too late." The video went on to encourage viewers to recycle, eat less meat, and wear used clothing.[54] This was the stuff of *50 Simple Things Kids Can Do to Save the Earth*.

"We went to the U.N. to call for serious global action on climate change, and their response was to ask if we're recycling?" said Lana Weidgenant, who became Zero Hour's deputy partnerships director after helping bring the first global deep strike day to the U.S. "That felt really frustrating."[55]

Moments like this, which come across as patronizing regardless of intent, are unfortunately typical of how young activists are often treated by adults in power, even those who presumably mean well. "I was grateful to be at the U.N. with so many world leaders," said New Jersey high schooler Aurora Yuan, an organizer for her state's school strike movement. "But it felt like they weren't taking us as seriously as they claimed to be doing."[56]

The larger Climate Action Summit days later was even less productive. While many small, developing countries announced ambitious new goals for cutting emissions, major polluting economies mostly failed to deliver. The Trump administration barely participated.[57] When it came to strengthening world leaders' resolve for action ahead of COP25, the event fell disappointingly short. Sure enough, COP in Madrid produced no major breakthroughs.[58]

Fallahi went to Madrid to give a presentation on behalf of Zero Hour at another conference for young activists organized in conjunction with the main U.N. event. There, a diplomat impressed by her public speaking ability invited her inside COP, giving her access to the halls where representatives of the world's most powerful countries clinched deals affecting the global climate. She and other youth activists made plans for a silent, peaceful protest against Shell being given a platform on a panel. However, security guards prevented them from staging it. "They essentially said they would kick us out of the venue if we went ahead," Fallahi said.

Things came to a head the next day when hundreds of activists led by Indigenous youth occupied the main plenary room to demand rich countries pay for damages caused by the climate crisis. A line of guards forced them out and stripped many participants of the badges that let them enter the conference. International climate activist group 350.org called it "a crackdown with little precedent at the annual U.N. climate talks."[59]

COP25 was a reality check, a reminder that national and international government bodies change slowly and often lag far behind the energy of grassroots movements. The surge of youth activism that began with Zero Hour and became a flood with the school strikes jolted public engagement around climate to levels never seen before, but the real test was whether the movement could build the staying power needed to influence politics over the long term.

An ever-proliferating list of new youth-led climate groups seemed to at least be an encouraging sign. Zero Hour and the strike movement had shown how, armed with the tools of the internet, young people in the twenty-first century could launch activist organizations with a speed unimaginable in past decades. After COP25, Fallahi and a coalition of youth from around the world followed their example by starting Polluters Out, a group whose goal was to bar carbon-intensive industries from future U.N. climate meetings.[60]

"Polluters Out formed in direct response to the disaster that was COP25," fifteen-year-old Claire Hedberg of Virginia, who reached out to the organization after seeing a post about it on a Zero Hour Slack channel, told me in May 2020. "We're coming together to say it's time to ban polluters from all spheres of influence at the U.N." Soon after joining, Hedberg was coordinating media outreach for the new international campaign.[61]

Zero Hour also provided a pathway for Lena Rodriguez to get involved in climate activism and eventually start a fresh organization. The Las Vegas community college student (who doesn't use pronouns) told me in March 2020, "I've been an activist since age thirteen. It started with issues like mental healthcare access in the LGBTQ community." After coming across Jamie Margolin's organization on social media, Rodriguez realized "they were connecting climate to all the issues I cared about. I was fascinated." Upon reaching out to Zero Hour's leaders, Rodriguez discovered "just a tiny hole in what they were doing. No one organization can take on everything. I saw a need to educate people more on the background behind complicated intersectional issues."

Rodriguez founded Spark of Life Collective, an organization dedicated to producing educational toolkits on everything from the Tampon Tax to the Paris Climate Accords.[62] It was another example of how youth activists were making the climate movement their own, identifying areas where more work was needed and providing opportunities for even more young people to get involved. The rapidly evolving, dynamic youth climate movement stood as a counterpoint to the frustrating inertia at COP and other high-level policy meetings.

Thousands of young people and countless events contributed to developments that had brought things to this point. However, if you wanted to pinpoint a single place where it all began, Zero Hour's march in the rain in July 2018 would not be a bad place to start. This says something important about how modern social movements, and youth climate activism in particular, work.

Where social movements come from

Only a true cynic, or someone out to discredit youth organizing, would have called Zero Hour's 2018 day of marches a failure even at the time. The flagship action in D.C. drew hundreds of teen-agers to the National Mall to get involved in politics—no mean feat. Still, neither was it the huge event its young organizers had hoped for. A reasonable assessment might have been that the march and media coverage it generated would get the attention of some law-makers and remind a segment the public about the urgency of the climate crisis, but with minimal long-term consequences for national policy.

Political commentators, the media, and even activists themselves are quick to evaluate protests in such terms, judging an event's importance by how many people showed up and the next morning's news coverage. But the way social movements grow isn't so simple. Zero Hour's modest debut day of action put forward a vision for youth-led climate organizing that inspired Greta Thunberg and helped pave the way for much larger mobilizations.

Thanks to online news and social media, the actions of youth activists almost anywhere can have almost immediate ripple effects on distant parts of the planet. The route by which the school strike movement arrived in Seattle, in particular, illustrates this dynamic. It was from Seattle that Jamie Margolin launched Zero Hour. Yet, when Ian Price started the city's first climate strike, he did so without any prompting from Margolin. The two young Seattleites didn't even know each other then, and only later met face to face. The ball of inspiration had bounced effortlessly from Seattle to Stockholm and back again in a matter of months.

One way to understand the youth climate movement is to compare it to the intricate network of fungal hyphae and plant roots that twist through the soil in mature forests on the green mountains Jamie Margolin could see from Seattle. Strikingly colored mushrooms and flowers burst up from the leaf litter occasionally, attracting the interest even of casual passers-by. But what remains hidden is the web of complex relationships between plants and fungi, insects and microscopic organisms that nurture the whole ecosystem from underground. It takes an astute scientist, or someone deeply familiar with the workings of a forest, to parse out how the different life forms support and nurture one another.

Most media coverage of the climate movement resembles what a hiker who stops only to notice the biggest fungi and flashiest plants sees. In December 2021, my search for "'Zero Hour' climate" in the *New York Times* online archives turned up eight news stories that refer to the organization launched by Jamie Margolin. Of these, three briefly mention Zero Hour or quote its leaders in the context of larger stories about the effects or politics of climate change. Four focus on specific large activist events. Only one, "The Teenagers at the End of the World," by Brooke Jarvis, takes a nuanced look at the behind-the-scenes work of the climate movement.

Jarvis describes accompanying Margolin to an online meeting in February 2020, when leaders from Zero Hour and other youth organizations met over Zoom to plan a voter outreach project: "the screens showed everybody sweatshirted, lounging around in bedrooms with posters on the walls. One director absent-mindedly braided her hair. When Margolin's mother, Janeth, returned home from work, she didn't want to interrupt the call, but Margolin pulled her in for an on-camera hug anyway."[63]

Jarvis captures the cognitive dissonance one sometimes feels on realizing the people leading the youth climate movement are mostly ordinary teens and young adults. I have experienced this myself. Zero Hour's Ethan Wright, then a freshman at George Mason University, told me of catching a flight back to D.C. from the U.N. Youth Climate Summit just in time for another week of classes. "That's being a youth organizer," he said, laughing. "We do all this activism, then I'm like, I have to go home and do my Spanish homework."[64]

Social movement scholars know that for every Greta Thunberg, there are thousands of regular people working between job or school responsibilities to bring activists' goals to fruition. In this respect, youth climate activism is no different than any other uprising. Thunberg has been an effective leader partly because of her own skills as a communicator and her choice of an easily replicable protest tactic—but also because of the foundation laid by Zero Hour and the work of countless young people all over the world who brought the strike movement to their towns and cities. This is a much messier picture of how social change happens than the one usually painted by the news, with its focus on charismatic leaders and headline-generating events.

As the strike movement and its offshoots grew, they interacted with other climate activist campaigns which had been quietly gathering strength beneath the soil and preparing to burst into the open. Some of the groups involved spent years developing a sophisticated political analysis that helped inform the way climate strikers came to talk about their own goals. By the time strike activity hit its peak in late 2019, many of its leaders had embraced the idea of a wholesale societal transformation large enough to meet the scale of the climate crisis. They wanted nothing less than a Green New Deal.

2

No Time for Small Ideas

THE TRANSFORMATIVE FIGHT
FOR A GREEN NEW DEAL

One week after the 2018 midterm elections, 150 young people staged a sit-in inside soon-to-be-House Speaker Nancy Pelosi's U.S. Capitol office. Their protest in support of a Green New Deal—which would include funding for social services, massive investments in clean energy, and deep carbon emission cuts—took the political world by surprise. The weeks after midterms are traditionally a doldrum in Washington, D.C., when groups who gave their all for candidates catch their breaths and digest the returns. But there was nothing conventional about what the teens and twenty-somethings in Pelosi's office were doing.

"In politics, everyone plans through Election Day and not a day further," Will Lawrence of Sunrise Movement, the group behind the sit-in, told me in an interview for this book in July 2020. "But as soon as the election is over there's a battle to define what it meant and where we go next. At Sunrise, we realized if you keep organizing just a week longer than everyone else, you hit a vacuum of activity where you can command the narrative."[1]

Sunrise Movement planned to hold Democrats in the U.S. House of Representatives accountable to a vision for bold progressive change. The organization wasn't anti-Democrat; Sunrise had campaigned aggressively for progressives during the primaries, then helped the party take the House in November. But winning was only the first step. Young people sitting in at Pelosi's office wanted the Speaker-elect to establish a House committee tasked with drafting sweeping climate legislation to be enacted once Democrats regained control of the Senate and presidency. Many arrived with hand-written notes and photographs of people or places they feared losing. "Climate change threatens my family," said seventeen-year-old Laís Santoro of Pennsylvania, who brought a photo of the beach near her grandparents' home in São Paulo, Brazil. "If we don't act now, my little brother may never experience this place like I've been able to do."[2]

What really drove national media into a frenzy, though, was when a charismatic young congresswoman-elect stood in Pelosi's office to express solidarity with the protesters. "I want to let you know how proud I am of each and every single one of you," said twenty-nine-year-old incoming Representative Alexandria Ocasio-Cortez, fresh off of running on a campaign platform that included a Green New Deal.[3]

The concept of the Green New Deal—a massive investment in infrastructure and social programs meant to trigger a shift away from fossil fuels—wasn't new. The Green Party had been talking about it for years,[4] and in 2007 it entered the mainstream, even earning a mention in Barack Obama's 2008 campaign platform.[5] However, without a mass movement to propel it forward the idea made little real headway during Obama's time in office.

In 2018, with Republicans still controlling the White House and Senate, no one thought major climate legislation would advance in the next Congress. But Sunrise aimed to lay groundwork for a day when such progress would be possible. "The only credible approach to climate policy is to actually ask for the whole thing," Lawrence said. "It will take dozens of pieces of legislation over the course of years. We have to completely overhaul the electricity, agriculture, and transportation systems. We're talking about reinventing society."[6]

This philosophy—that addressing the climate crisis requires big, bold ideas equal to the scale of the challenge—was central to Sunrise Movement's approach. The action in Pelosi's office, which put a spotlight on this vision, had been in the works for months. Remarkably, though, many of the most important details came together only in the final seventy-two hours before the sit-in.

Being bold

A few days after the midterms, Sunrise leaders had been finalizing details for a protest where they planned to demand Pelosi support a federal green jobs guarantee. The action was to take place that Tuesday, at the end of a Sunrise training summit for students held in Washington, D.C. As organizers discussed how to amplify their message on social media, someone thought to call one of newly elected Congresswoman Alexandria Ocasio-Cortez's staffers. Would Ocasio-Cortez help tweet about the action after it was over? they asked. They were told she would get back to them.

Later that night the Congresswoman-elect's team reached out. Ocasio-Cortez liked what Sunrise was planning. In fact, she might be willing to attend the protest—an audacious move for a not-yet-sworn-in member of Congress, which Sunrise never expected. By Saturday her office had a new proposal: the jobs guarantee was a nice idea, but why not go even bigger? Ocasio-Cortez supported a Green New Deal modeled after economic spending packages from decades past that transformed daily life in the U.S. If Sunrise was going after Pelosi, why not pressure her on this?

On Monday, some of Ocasio-Cortez's staff dropped in on the Sunrise summit. "They saw we were pretty well organized, which helped them feel good about being involved," Lawrence told me when I interviewed him for this book. Later that day, the Congress-woman-elect herself stopped by, stood on a table, and gave a rousing speech. For most of the students her appearance was an exciting surprise. Very few knew what Lawrence and a core group of others did: that she would return to join them at the sit-in tomorrow.[7]

*

Sunrise chose to hold the Pelosi office sit-in—which ended with fifty-one activists being arrested and led out by police—at probably the most strategic time possible. Progressive energy was high after propelling major Democratic gains in the midterms, and lawmakers felt pressured to demonstrate their commitment to the ideals of the left. Pelosi and other leaders were deciding how to organize the new, Democrat-controlled House and Sunrise was going all in for action on climate change. By the end of the month, eighteen members of Congress had signed onto a resolution calling for a Select Committee on a Green New Deal.

On December 10, Sunrise's army of young people returned to Capitol Hill for another protest. This time around a thousand students flooded the offices of Pelosi and two other lawmakers: Rep. Steny Hoyer of Maryland, the second-highest ranking House Democrat; and Rep. Jim McGovern, incoming chair of the powerful Rules Committee.[8] Boston University student Bolaji Olagbegi was among the young activists who came from all over the country to participate.

A friend of Olagbegi's who belonged to Boston's Sunrise Movement organizing hub had been arrested at the November 2018 sit-in. His actions inspired Olagbegi to join this latest protest, and she arrived in D.C. in time for the pre-action training where each participant decided what their level of involvement would look like. The risks of navigating a racist justice system weren't equal. "Being Black, and concerned about what it meant for my family, I knew I couldn't get arrested at the sit-in," Olagbegi said. She could, however, be there to show her support.[9]

Morristown, New Jersey high school junior Ananya Singh was also at the December action, which fell on her sixteenth birthday. "Fortunately, my parents are really supportive of my activism," she told me in an April 2020 interview. "When I said I wanted to protest on my sweet sixteen, they understood."

Singh became a climate advocate at age twelve after attending Youth Empowerment Action Camp, a weeklong summer training program for young people. "Activism clicked for me in a way nothing else ever did," she said. She had first encountered Sunrise Movement at a 2017 climate march in D.C., and was pleased to see how the organization had grown since then. "Sunrise captured the hearts and minds of so many people. There was energy in the air at the sit-in that made you feel connected to something much larger than yourself."[10] By the end of the day Rep. McGovern, one of the protest's targets, announced his support for the Green New Deal committee.[11]

Sunrise continued to organize high-profile protests targeting leaders from both political parties. "We're here to demand Mitch McConnell look us in the eyes and tell us the $1.9 million he's gotten from fossil fuel CEOs is more important than my generation's future," seventeen-year-old Destine Grigsby of Louisville said during a sit-in at the Senate Majority Leader's office that

February. "Kentucky needs a Green New Deal to ensure we have clean water, clean air, and stable jobs."[12] Never before had the youth climate movement confronted so many of the most powerful people in Congress in such a visible manner over the span of just a few months.

Around this time, I began working on a story about Sunrise's work for *Waging Nonviolence.* The school strike movement was only just beginning to gain a foothold in the United States, but there was a feeling in the air that youth climate activism was gaining new ground around the globe. Sunrise's Capitol Hill sit-ins were one of the most obvious manifestations of this in the U.S.

I kept abreast of Sunrise's activities over the next several months, even as school strikes for the climate spread throughout the U.S. and reached a crescendo that fall. Sunrise seemed perfectly positioned to give political voice to the more generalized feeling of discontent with government inaction on climate change represented by the strike movement. But while high-profile protests in Washington, D.C. were important, I knew what members of Congress care most about are the opinions of voters back home. I was curious to see how Sunrise planned to engage members of Congress in their home districts—so I made another trip to Seattle, where an active Sunrise organizing hub was working to do just this.

Sunrise in the Northwest

On a cloudy day in December 2019, I joined fifty-odd people gathered in Seattle's Occidental Square, a short walk from the field offices of both Washington State's U.S. senators. Most members of the group were in college, but there were also several high schoolers, a few middle school students, and a scattering of older supporters. A couple organizers raised their voices to explain the plan. We would be marching to the offices of Senators Murray and Cantwell, where we'd ask them to commit to signing a Senate resolution in support of the Green New Deal.

Taking a page from the first Sunrise sit-in at Pelosi's office, protesters had been asked to bring a photograph or memento representing something special to them that was threatened by the fossil fuel industry. Offerings ranged from a picture of one of the Salish Sea orcas, to a voter's pamphlet symbolizing democratic freedoms. Twenty-year-old University of Washington-Bothell student Bee Elliott carried a photo of a mountain range in nearby Canada where glaciers are shrinking rapidly. "We have power as young people, and we're here to speak out about how important the Green New Deal is to us," she said when I asked what motivated her participation in the action. "Places like this that mean a lot to me are threatened by the climate crisis."[13]

Congressional leaders had not established the House Select Committee Sunrise asked for. However, soon after being formally sworn into office, Congresswoman Ocasio-Cortez introduced an official resolution in support of a Green New Deal. Among other things it set goals to "achieve net-zero greenhouse gas emissions through a fair and just transition for all communities and workers," "create millions of good, high-wage jobs and ensure prosperity and economic security," and "invest in the infrastructure and industry of the United States to sustainably meet the challenges of the twenty-first century."[14] This resolution, and an identical version in the Senate, became main vehicles for Sunrise to organize around going forward. Murray and Cantwell had so far declined to become co-sponsors, but Sunrise activists in their home state aimed to change that. I was here to see them in action.

I already knew a bit about how Sunrise came to Washington State. In early 2018, the student-run Cascade Climate Network hosted a conference at the University of Puget Sound in Tacoma, where national Sunrise Movement organizer Victoria Fernandez was a speaker. She invited students to sign up for Sunrise Semester, a fellowship program that engaged young people in electoral work leading up to the midterms. Twenty-one-year-old UPS student Lisa Grimm was among the activists who responded to the call. During her time in the fellowship, which she spent in the swing state of Pennsylvania, Grimm learned Sunrise was working to launch local organizing chapters, or "hubs," in congressional districts through-out the country. "The idea of building power locally made sense to me," she said when I interviewed her for *Waging Nonviolence* in February 2019. "I wanted to help keep the momentum going after I returned to school."

Grimm reached out through her activist networks to students all over Washington, who together launched Sunrise hubs in many of their communities. Their efforts were buoyed toward the end of 2018, when the Capitol Hill sit-ins attracted widespread attention. "After the Pelosi action, we saw interest in the Green New Deal skyrocket among students," Grimm said.[15]

Like Greta Thunberg's COP24 speech, which occurred around the same time, the Pelosi sit-in was a catalyzing event for large numbers of young activists. However, again like Thunberg's speech, it would have been far less effective if not accompanied by readily available ways for students to join the movement. Striking from school was an easy step high schoolers and middle schoolers could take to participate in Fridays for Future. Similarly, a network of local hubs offered young people a way to get involved in Sunrise Movement.

Sunrise Seattle's early actions included a public town hall on the Green New Deal and visits to Murray and Cantwell's district offices.[16] Now, in December 2019, they had returned to reiterate their ask of the senators. I lingered toward the back as the group in Occidental Square began marching. On our arrival at the building where both lawmakers have district offices, senatorial staff members herded us into a large conference room and told us to wait.

By the time I entered the room, some of the youngest members of the group had already assembled on a stage with a banner whose message to the senators read, "We need you to be brave." One was fourteen-year-old Zoe Schurman, whom I'd met a month earlier at Seattle's weekly climate strike. Her presence at the Sunrise action reminded me that for many young people, the school strikes and Sunrise's push for a Green New Deal were not just closely intertwined movements but part of the same effort. "We're skipping school today to share our concern about the climate crisis," Schurman told representatives from the senators' offices when they returned to hear the activists' message. "The politicians we're talking to have so much more power than us, and we want them to use it for good."[17]

"Our generation has grown up with crisis being the norm," added fifteen-year-old Kimaya Mahajan, who stood next to Schurman. "It might not even matter what our high school grades are or where we go to college, because our future could end up being nothing. Our senators will not be affected by climate change the way Zoe and I will be."[18]

The action ended with the senators' staff accepting the stack of climate-threatened mementos from students, but not making any promises on behalf of Murray or Cantwell. It was more or less what the organizers expected. What was perhaps most important was that Sunrise hubs all over the country were engaging with their representatives through similar actions, keeping the idea of the Green New Deal alive and building a youth-led movement to pass it.

Meanwhile, I was coming to better understand how the Sunrise organization operated at a nationwide level. Its hub model was designed to allow local leaders to take initiative while periodically participating in days of action and other coordinated protests. This interplay between local activism and high-visibility actions in D.C. was part of what made Sunrise powerful.

Where did it all come from, though? From the conversations I'd had with Sunrise activists, I knew many of the organization's founders had once been students at Swarthmore College in Pennsylvania, where they played a major role launching the national campaign to divest higher education institution endowments from fossil fuels company stocks. Later, they and other divestment leaders newly graduated from school looked for fresh ways to scale up the climate movement. In the process, they came up with the framework for Sunrise.

When I began researching for this book, I knew I had to speak with some of these impressive activists—and with the person at Swarthmore who perhaps more than any other helped influence them to become climate movement leaders.

A (very) brief history of the youth climate movement

Talking with social movements scholar and retired Swarthmore professor George Lakey gives one the feeling of being in conversation with a mind constantly in motion. White-haired and apparently not at all impeded by his eighty-plus years, Lakey exudes intellectual energy. "I was lucky," he said when I interviewed him about his time teaching at Swarthmore. "Student activism comes in waves, and I arrived at Swarthmore just when they were starting to get perky again."

During his own early adulthood in the 1960s, Lakey participated in Mississippi Freedom Summer and protests against the Vietnam War. He later co-founded organizations including the Movement for a New Society, Training for Change, and, in 2009, the Earth Quaker Action Team (EQAT). He taught about nonviolent social movements at University of Pennsylvania, Haverford College, and Temple University before coming to Swarthmore in 2006. Many young founders of Sunrise and the divestment movement regard him as an important mentor.

"Some of my students got interested in joining EQAT—in not just studying social change, but doing it," Lakey said. The organization's main project at the time was pressuring banks to end their financial support for mountaintop removal coal mining. "Soon students were sitting down in a bank with me, risking arrest. Not everyone on campus was delighted to think a professor would lead his students into jail," Lakey added with a good-humored laugh. "But I was absolutely not pressuring or even inviting them to join. They just saw the opportunity and took it."

Many of these students, who included Will Lawrence, were simultaneously enrolled in a seminar taught by Lakey where they gathered and analyzed information on historical nonviolent social movements. "It gave them a sense of what the technology of a campaign is like," Lakey explained. "That's how I think of it: a campaign is a social technology with its own character and demands. At the same time, some of them were going into banks and sitting in or standing up or otherwise being obnoxious—always strictly nonviolently, of course."[19]

It was an experience in organized, on-the-ground activism reinforced by academic research the likes of which few young people receive in college. Lakey's students studied 1950s and '60s civil rights campaigns, anti-nuclear power activism, and the apartheid divestment movement of the '70s and '80s, when young activists pressured their schools to cut financial ties to corporations doing business with the racist South African regime. For future Sunrise founders like Lawrence, the up-close look at social movement dynamics was eye-opening. "I realized the climate movement needed to find similar ways of building power locally," Lawrence said.[20]

One more key event shaped Lawrence's transformation into a dedicated climate organizer. During his freshman year in 2010, he and a small group of other Swarthmore students accompanied Lakey on a trip to West Virginia to witness firsthand the devastation wrought by coal mining. They felt a need to act, but the existing campus-based climate campaigns of the time didn't feel meaningful enough. Their solution was fossil fuel divestment.[21]

*

The surge of student-led climate activism that began in 2018 has sometimes been portrayed as a new phenomenon. But years before the climate strikes or Sunrise's push for a Green New Deal, there was the early fossil fuel divestment movement started by people like Lawrence. Prior to that came an even earlier wave of youth climate activism on college campuses. I was very familiar with these older phases of the movement, having become a climate activist in college in the early 2000s. The more I learned about modern groups like Sunrise, the more intrigued I became by how they both resembled and differed from the models of climate organizing I knew as a student.

In the first decade of the twenty-first century, student-led climate campaigns centered largely on transforming higher education institutions into clean energy laboratories. By deploying green technologies on campuses, the thinking went, young people could help bring them to scale while reducing local emissions. Activist trainings I attended in college focused on making schools bike-friendly, banning the sale of bottled water, and funding clean energy projects. There were also efforts to get out the youth vote, and occasional lobby days where students met their representatives in state capitols. However, these usually felt secondary to the goal of implementing campus-based solutions to climate change.

By 2010, this work was paying off. Announcements from schools committing to reductions in carbon emissions had become almost routine—and while some followed through more successfully than others, the idea of colleges as green energy trendsetters no longer seemed radical. If student activists wanted to continue pushing the climate envelope, they needed a new way of doing so. This was the dilemma facing Lawrence and other Swarthmore students when they returned from their West Virginia trip and developed the concept for a fossil fuel divestment campaign modeled partly after the anti-apartheid movement.[22]

In an example of the convergent thinking that sometimes occurs across social movements, national climate organizations like 350.org were inching toward a similar idea around the same time. The Swarthmore students found themselves on the cutting edge of a nationwide divestment movement that spread from colleges to municipalities, churches, private foundations, and other entities. By December 2015, these institutions had collectively divested over $3.4 trillion from fossil fuel stocks.[23]

Notwithstanding such successes, it was around this time that divestment as a strategy began to feel stale to some of the movement's own founders. "As the leading edge of the climate movement, it was no longer groundbreaking," Lawrence said. Like the earlier push for clean energy on college campuses, divestment lost some of its cutting-edge feel as it penetrated into the mainstream.

At the same time, a new presidential campaign cycle was heating up and the climate movement seemed unable to meet the political moment. This was the age of Donald Trump and Bernie Sanders, of rising populism on both the right and left. "We climate activists started hearing Bernie talk about taking on the fossil fuel billionaire class," Lawrence said. "And I thought: Hey, that's our message—only better."

After graduating in 2013, Lawrence and a small group of other recent college alums had launched the Divestment Student Network (DSN), which supported student activism through peer-to-peer mentorship. Founders included a handful of Swarthmore graduates, University of Massachusetts' Varshini Prakash, and University of California's Victoria Fernandez. Excited by Sanders' candidacy, these leaders now reached out to DSN's well-developed student networks about engaging in the 2016 election. They got mainly tepid responses.

"Something in the DNA of the divestment movement made people see it as not about contesting for political power," Lawrence said. For better or worse, students seemed to feel that even if they personally supported both divestment and Sanders-style progressive politics, these were separate projects belonging to different realms of work. "As a result, we were unable to meaningfully engage in the primaries at all."

In June 2016, Sanders dropped out of the Democratic primary. That November, Donald Trump took power in the White House. Rather than an era of progressive reforms, the election ushered in the opposite. A top priority for the new administration was dismantling Obama-era climate regulations.

By then, Prakash and Swarthmore alum Sara Blazevic had stepped back from DSN to explore launching a new climate organization focused on building political power. Lawrence, Fernandez, and a few other DSN staff joined them in late 2016. Perhaps DSN had served its purpose, they thought. Now it was time for a fresh brand of climate activism that could engage more effectively around elections.[24]

*

In 2012, when national organizations first began promoting divestment from fossil fuels, I was a graduate student studying environmental writing at the University of Montana. I was intrigued by what I heard about divestment, but was putting my activist energies into a campaign to stop new Montana coal mines and didn't pay much attention to the new movement at first. This changed the following year, a few months after I graduated, when a group of current UM students invited me to help plan a fossil fuel divestment campaign. It seemed like an exciting project, and I said yes.

By the time DSN formally disbanded in 2017, I had moved on from Montana and fulltime climate organizing. Still, I continued following developments around divestment and other climate campaigns. My first thought when I heard about the goals of the new Sunrise Movement was, *Well, good luck.*

In a final email to supporters that July, DSN leaders explained they were going on to start an organization focused on "uniting young people across America to make climate change an urgent political priority, create millions of good jobs, and elect climate leaders who will stand up for the health and wellbeing of all people."[25] It all sounded very familiar to me. Climate activists had been trying to influence elections since my own earliest days in the movement— and while these efforts inspired many students to get involved in politics for the first time, none succeeded in making climate a top-tier voting issue.

Nor was the rhetoric around clean energy jobs new. Before the 2008 election, "green jobs" became a climate movement byword. The slogan was supposed to emphasize how climate action could help working-class people, but it gained limited traction with the public. What I didn't foresee was that Sunrise would bring a political acumen largely missing from earlier waves of climate activism.

The Green New Deal, as it was envisioned by Sunrise and Alexandria Ocasio-Cortez in 2018, was about much more than jobs;

it was a matter of wholesale societal transformation. In addition, Sunrise's electoral interventions were unusually impactful, focusing resources on specific political races chosen for strategic reasons. After elections, Sunrise used highly visible protest tactics to advance policy and hold accountable the politicians they helped put in office.

"We wanted to bust down the false dichotomy between protesting in the streets and electing leaders," was how Lawrence put it. "This required an inspiring mass movement to capture the public imagination and make climate matter in politics. We were never under the delusion that there's no difference between the major parties, though. The modern Republican Party is a white supremacist organization dedicated to the destruction of democracy. Even a moderate Democrat is much better than that."[26]

The Sunrise approach to politics was far more comprehensive than anything I'd had contact with as a student, and undergirding it all was a carefully developed theory of how social change happens. From time to time, I heard activists refer to a "Sunrise training," a day-long event reproduced by hubs around the country for people new to the movement. Attending this training was, I'd been told, the best way to get a deep understanding of Sunrise's political philosophy. Clearly, I needed to experience it myself.

A vision for social change

Growing up in rural Pennsylvania's Marcellus Shale region, Jamie Ptacek saw the natural gas fracking boom unfold almost literally in her backyard. She watched, dismayed, as gas wells and pipelines crisscrossed the landscape. Later, while a student at Maine's Bowdoin College, she joined the divestment campaign there. She also spent four months in Talent, Oregon, interning for an organization fighting a proposed liquefied natural gas pipeline. A series of defeats left her demoralized.

"I felt beaten down by failure," Ptacek said in a Sunrise training she co-facilitated over Zoom for Seattle hub members, which I attended in August 2020. "I felt like these movements failed for the same reasons mainstream environmental groups have always failed." Ptacek took time off from activism to travel after graduation. In 2018, she moved back to Pennsylvania to organize for the midterms. "That's when I found Sunrise, and what felt like hope for the first time. This movement, in my opinion, is doing what every other environmental movement that came before it failed to do."[27]

Ptacek's words underscore something important about Sunrise: to many young people, it represented an entirely new approach to climate and environmental activism, and a break from the tired strategies of the past.

"Right now, things feel bleak," Ptacek said in the Zoom event, drawing from the script provided for Sunrise trainers. Much of the country was still in a state of semi-lockdown induced by COVID, anger at police shootings was boiling over, and the Northern Hemisphere was experiencing its hottest summer ever.[28] "But it's important to remember we've been in moments like this before." The image on Ptacek's laptop screen, which she had on share, flipped to a Great Depression unemployment line. "That crisis [the Depression] was met with the original New Deal, a sweeping set of legislation that led to the creation of dozens of administrations and programs that continue to form the backbone of our society."

Not that the New Deal was without problems. "It left a lot of people out and even furthered racist and oppressive systems," Ptacek quickly acknowledged. An example was redlining by the Federal Housing Administration. "It wasn't perfect, but it does show that even in a crisis, huge change is possible." In contrast, "for the past several decades, the solutions to climate change offered us were to use energy efficient light bulbs and start recycling. And we only saw politicians introducing watered-down legislation."

To illustrate this last point, Ptacek showed a video where Sunrise's Varshini Prakash dissects the only major attempt to pass climate legislation under the Obama administration, in 2009. Reasons for the eventual failure of that bill—a sprawling but not particularly ambitious carbon emissions cap-and-trade plan—were complex, but Sunrise believes part of the problem was green groups' reliance on multimillion dollar ad campaigns to sway public opinion. Polling suggests those efforts succeeded in shoring up support for climate legislation, but according to Prakash, "That support was too shallow to make a difference in the fight. Opponents [of climate action]...mobilized a smaller, far more intense opposition."[29]

In the end, a vocal minority of Tea Party activists and fossil fuel industry lobbyists drowned out the much quieter majority who supported climate action. "The good news," Ptacek said after the video, "is that Sunrise's strategy has been built directly from the mistakes of the environmental movements that have come before us."[30]

*

Sunrise describes its theory of how change happens as being based on three pillars: people power, political power, and political alignment. First and perhaps foremost is its belief that passive support from a majority of the U.S. population isn't enough to trigger change. "We already have a huge number of people on our side," said Chloe Yeo, another local Sunrise leader, during the Seattle training. "We just need to activate our passive supporters."

Sunrise seeks to accomplish this through acts of "moral protest": high-visibility actions that "present issues like climate change as simple, moral questions and force people to pick a side."[31] Examples include the late 2018 Capitol Hill sit-ins that motivated a wave of students to join and power the fight for a Green New Deal.

The significance of the second pillar, political change, is easy enough to comprehend. However, by working both to elect political candidates and get thousands of people in the streets, Sunrise distinguished itself from environmental groups who tend to choose one of these activities or the other. "The radical grassroots movements I knew as a student disdained any politician whatsoever and any effort to win an election," Will Lawrence told me. He credits the Sanders campaign with helping to bridge the gap between such protest movements and electoral politics. "Bernie showed the right kinds of candidates can popularize the vision of a social movement, even popularize the movement itself."[32]

The concept of political alignment, a paradigm that defines what is legislatively possible, is a bit harder to grasp. In any era, the dominant alignment dictates what national politics looks like and draws support from a wide array of groups who may have little else in common. It differs from a coalition, a more formal alliance of organizations who usually share broadly similar values. "Alignments set the terms for political debate and direct social and economic policy for as long as they remain dominant," Yeo explained, again using Sunrise's training script. "When a political alignment becomes dominant, it is able to define [what people think of as] common sense."

Last time the U.S. political alignment shifted in a progressive direction was when the Depression forced groups as divergent as civil rights organizations and pro-segregation southern Democrats to embrace programs that alleviate poverty. The diverse nature of these interests ensured the new alignment's success in the 1930s, but racist policies sanctioned during the New Deal provoked a much-needed response from the Civil Rights Movement. Backlash against civil rights, in turn, provided an opening for conservatives to bring large numbers of whites over to their side. This process culminated with the anti-welfare, anti-regulation alignment achieved under President Reagan in the '80s, which is still mostly intact today. "We call it the Reagan Alignment," Yeo said.

Sunrise has envisioned a new "people's alignment" based around the assumption that moral societies should work for the common good and that widespread poverty, systemic racism, and the collapse of Earth's life systems are unacceptable. Sunrise counts climate activists, the Movement for Black Lives, Indigenous rights groups, and political leaders in the mold of Ocasio-Cortez as among this paradigm's likely supporters. However, only when such things as the need for government intervention in the climate crisis become widely accepted as "common sense" will the new alignment be in place.[33]

*

Early on, Sunrise adopted a five-phase plan to achieve its goals. The first phases, "launch the movement" and "make climate matter in the midterm election" happened in 2017 and 2018. The third, "Make the entire country feel the urgency of the [climate] crisis," was arguably attained in 2019 with help from the strike movement. At the time of Sunrise Seattle's August 2020 training, hubs across the country were working on the fourth phase: "Win governing power." These efforts achieved mixed results.[34]

On the positive side, the 2020 election swept Donald Trump from office and added to the House Progressive Caucus.[35] Seattle high school sophomore Emma Coopersmith was one of the Sunrise volunteers who helped drive those victories, reaching out to 3.5 million young voters through phone calls and other forms of direct contact.[36] "We know the election's not going to win it all for us, but it's important," Coopersmith said when I interviewed her that September for a *Waging Nonviolence* story. "We're out in the streets —but we're also on the phones calling voters."[37]

Sunrise leaders knew they almost certainly needed unified Democratic control of the federal government to enact Green New Deal policies. Progressive hopes were high going into the election, but overall Democrats fared more poorly than widely predicted by polls. The party barely clung to its House majority and took the Senate only after January runoffs for two seats in Georgia. Victories by Democrats Raphael Warnock and Jon Ossoff in those races marked a moment of triumph for Sunrise, which placed over a million calls to Georgia voters and knocked on more than 8,500 doors in the lead-up to the runoff elections.[38]

"Our movement has been building toward this moment," Sunrise electoral politics director Shanté Wolfe said on a January 7, 2021 Zoom call celebrating the Georgia wins. "...[Now] it's time to push the Democratic establishment like hell and hold them accountable."[39]

The fourth phase of Sunrise's plan seemed to have achieved at least a degree of success. The fifth, "mass noncooperation," would be the most challenging of all.[40]

Striking for a Green New Deal

"Striking is how we can stop the worst of climate change and win a Green New Deal," Varshini Prakash said from the speaker's stage at the massive New York City climate march on September 20, 2019. "That's why Sunrise will be supporting and building the strike movement...We are going all-in on strikes."[41]

Over the last year, Sunrise had deftly built a new national public narrative around the Green New Deal and federal climate action. Since the collapse of the 2009 cap-and-trade bill, prevailing wisdom in the climate movement held that any attempt to move federal legislation forward was laughably naïve. But suddenly, people were talking seriously again about aggressive action from Congress.

As the strike movement exploded in the U.S., Sunrise and new organizations like Fridays for Future avoided the kind of counterproductive turf wars in which activist groups sometimes get embroiled. Instead, they began working together. While this made good sense, it wasn't inevitable. In fact, the approaches taken by Sunrise and early leaders of the school strikes were in some ways very different.

Sunrise's brand of climate activism has been a study in meticulously planned strategy and political analysis aimed at advancing a specific set of carefully articulated goals. Fundamental to its philosophy is the belief that a problem as huge as climate change demands an equally large response, a transformative set of progressive policies that will drastically reduce carbon emissions while bolstering the social safety net to ease the transition to a green, socially just economy. According to this view, previous climate policy campaigns failed largely because they were insufficiently ambitious and never inspired an enthusiastic outpouring of public support. The only remedy is to be bold and explicit about the kinds of changes that are needed, while supporting political leaders who do the same.

This approach differs dramatically from that of Greta Thunberg, who has mostly avoided endorsing specific policies or aligning herself with elected officials.[42] Deciding exactly how to curb emissions is the adults' job, Thunberg has always seemed to be saying—the task of youth is simply to point out the grownups' failure. As Fridays for Future chapters and strike organizations popped up around the world, some did choose to endorse specific policy proposals.[43] However, the core message of the school strikes as articulated by leaders like Thunberg remained profoundly and compellingly simple.

Still, at some point every movement needs to offer its own positive vision for the future, and Sunrise was perfectly suited to help with this task. At the same time, its leaders saw in school strikes for the climate an opening to initiate the final step in their five-phase plan.

"I gotta be honest with you...There are not enough of us here yet," Prakash told the crowd in New York. "There are four million people out in the streets today [around the world], but...If we want to win, we are going to need tens of millions of Americans to join us in the streets. If we are going to win, we have to bring society and even our economy to a standstill again and again." Such a vision of mass civil disobedience goes far beyond skipping school occasionally. "I want you to imagine striking not just for one day, but day after day," Prakash said. "Marching, demonstrating incessantly. Even shutting our cities and schools down to halt business as usual if we don't get what we came for."[44]

True to Prakash's word, Sunrise threw itself behind the strike movement. COVID-19 complicated this effort, derailing plans for another huge wave of coordinated strikes on Earth Day 2020. Even so, the idea was planted for a flood of civil disobedience that flowed seamlessly from the strike movement, and for anyone convinced of the need for mass protest it held undeniable attraction. However, all of this raises an essential question: Just how "non-cooperative" was the strike movement in practice?

*

Commentators and activists have sometimes referred to striking from school as "civil disobedience," a term implying protest that breaks laws or at least important societal norms. Thunberg's striking arguably does fall into this category. Thunberg didn't ask permission to skip class; her actions involved breaking the accepted social contract that says students in Sweden should spend their days in school. As Alexandria Villaseñor said in the U.S., "Why go to school if we won't have a future?"[45]

Striking didn't always take the form of civil disobedience, though. Many climate strikers sought permission from their school administrations to skip class, and their protests were often permitted rallies. There is nothing intrinsically bad about this, as minimizing the negative repercussions from participating in a protest often makes good sense. However, it is important to be clear about what terms like "civil disobedience," "disruption," and even "strike" itself really mean. "In the United States in particular, a lot of people don't understand what a strike actually is," said Nadine Bloch, a longtime climate activist in the Washington, D.C. area whom I spoke with while writing about the September 20 mobilization. "They're still talking about getting permits for protests, which isn't a true strike."[46]

Sunrise leaders who discuss mass disruption often have their eye on the number 3.5. This, according to social movements scholar Erica Chenoweth, is the percentage of the public whose sustained, active participation in a movement virtually guarantees success. "No movement who was able to mobilize this portion of the population has ever lost," Ptacek said in the Seattle Sunrise training, a statement borne out by Chenoweth's research.[47]

Here, "active participation" means more than voting, signing petitions, or posting on Instagram. It means getting into the streets, perhaps leaving one's comfort zone, and even engaging in the kinds of disruptive protests Prakash described. The mass demonstrations led by the Movement for Black Lives in 2020 in cities around the U.S. gave the public at least a glimpse of what this type of activism looks like on a large scale.

It remains to be seen how disruptive the youth climate movement might eventually become. What is clear, though, is that the climate strikes and Sunrise Movement both helped reshape the politics of climate change in the U.S. during the period of intense activity that began in late 2018. At least one more major prong of the new climate movement had a similarly important impact. It turned out the divestment movement which leaders of Sunrise had left wasn't past its peak after all. Instead, it underwent a reorganiza-tion and renaissance under a new cohort of young leaders, winning wide-reaching victories not only on college campuses, but in the board rooms of some of the world's largest financial institutions.

3

Money Talks

THE ONCE AND FUTURE DIVESTMENT MOVEMENT

The euphoria was palpable, even over Zoom, at the December 9, 2020 press conference where activists and New York lawmakers announced one of the fossil fuel divestment movement's biggest victories yet. After eight years of public pressure, the State Comptroller was moving to eliminate fossil fuel investments from New York's $226 billion pension fund.

"This will have enormous effects around the planet," renowned climate activist and 350.org founder Bill McKibben said at the all-virtual event. "It comes just in time to spur the next round of resistance [to fossil fuels]. I think what this demonstrates above all is the waning power of the fossil fuel industry to control events. They are being outpaced by clean energy and they are being stood up to by a huge and growing movement."[1]

The grassroots Divest New York coalition, which launched in 2012, spearheaded the years-long effort that pushed State Comptroller Tom DiNapoli to end the pension fund's investments in coal, oil, and gas. Coalition members included the New York State Sustainable Business Council, the Sierra Club's New York City and Atlantic chapters, 350.org, and dozens of other organizations.[2] But while climate activists of all ages shared in the victory, young people played a special role—especially in the campaign's final, decisive years.

"New York Youth Climate Leaders was instrumental in getting us to this moment," Divest New York's Jordan Dale said as he prepared to introduce the student-led organization's young executive director.[3] Though he was by then a freshman at Williams College in Massachusetts, Hridesh Singh grew up in Rochester and dove into statewide climate activism after attending the September 2019 strike in New York City.

"I'm somewhat speechless, honestly," Singh now told the journalists, environmental group leaders, and legislators assembled on Zoom. "The New York State Retirement Fund is the largest pension fund in the world and in the history of the fossil fuel divestment movement to make this sort of [climate] commitment."[4]

Prior to September 2019, Singh was a member of his high school's Climate Club and an alliance of Rochester-area students pushing Monroe County to adopt a carbon neutrality policy. However, the massive day of strikes inspired him to take his activism to the state level. Toward the end of 2019, he and other young activists launched New York Youth Climate Leaders (NY2CL), an affiliation of more than fifty student-led groups who made divestment their top priority.

"Unlike with some climate policy campaigns, the logic behind divestment is easy for most people to understand," Singh told me when we first spoke back in April 2020. "Companies like ExxonMobil, BP, and Shell are destroying the climate. Fossil fuel stocks are underperforming because of the success of renewables.

Investing in polluting industries means you're failing your duty to stockholders and fueling the climate crisis. It's simple for people to comprehend the significance of this, which is partly what drew me to divestment as a strategy."[5]

I had connected with Singh and other NY2CL leaders while working on a *Waging Nonviolence* story about how climate activists were navigating the COVID-19 pandemic. What I learned about the New York divestment campaign impressed me, and I kept tabs on NY2CL over the next several months. Their communications director, Albany-area high schooler Natalie Penna, would occasionally email me with updates. In August they won their first major victory: Comptroller DiNapoli committed to divesting the state pension fund from coal.[6] It was a harbinger of the much farther-reaching success to come.

The December announcement that New York would also divest from oil, gas, and fossil fuel-dependent companies in sectors like utilities and transportation represented one of the biggest milestones yet for a movement in the midst of a renaissance. After a few years of stagnation, youth-led fossil fuel divestment campaigns had come roaring back to life.

Reinvigorating a movement

Alyssa Lee was in her second year at University of California–Los Angeles in 2012, when the divestment campaign that began at Swarthmore ballooned into a national movement. She became interested in climate change as a freshman, after an activist from the small island nation of Tuvalu spoke at UCLA about the effects of rising sea levels. When Lee learned about divestment at a conference organized by the California Student Sustainability Coalition, the movement's approach made intuitive sense to her.

"I thought there's something very wrong with our higher education institutions when they try to teach us how to think and act in the world, but don't set a good example with the investments they make," she said when I interviewed her in February 2020.

Lee played a role starting UCLA's divestment campaign during the national movement's early heyday. After graduating, she accepted a job advising student divestment organizers for the New England-based Better Future Project. At the time, Better Future was one of several national and regional groups—including the Responsible Endowments Coalition, 350.org, and Divestment Student Network—supporting campus divestment campaigns that were scattered across the country. But over the next few years, each of these other organizations dissolved or shifted to different priorities. Meanwhile, a generation of student divestment leaders had grown weary of pushing against recalcitrant administrations.

"By 2017, a lot of campus campaigns had gone through two or three rejections and older students were becoming cynical," Lee said. Around this time, she realized she was the only campus organizer left in the country still doing fossil fuel divestment work fulltime.[7]

Lee and her colleagues wondered whether the college divestment movement had run its course, or if it merely required a new injection of energy to bring it back to life. According to Better Future Project Executive Director Craig Altemose, "We had gotten to a point where we either needed to shut down our divestment work or expand it by going national. It didn't make sense to go on campaigning in one isolated region as the rest of the country moved on."[8]

In 2018, Better Future began a series of consultations with students and alumni from colleges that now or formerly had divestment campaigns. "We found there were still lots of students working on divestment at their schools," Lee said. "But they were generally not being noticed beyond their campuses and had lost the feeling of being part of a larger movement."

Convinced there was lots of life left in these campaigns after all, Better Future hired additional organizers to start a new, national initiative called Divest Ed. The timing couldn't have been better. That July, Zero Hour held its debut day of marches. Months later, teenagers who'd been inspired by that effort during their final year of high school headed to college.

"We noticed an almost immediate influx of student energy and interest in climate activism and campaigns like divestment in the fall of 2018," Lee said. She attributes this uptick in enthusiasm partly to Zero Hour.

But as earlier chapters of this book have shown, Zero Hour was just the beginning. That November, Sunrise Movement held its sit-in at Nancy Pelosi's office. In December, Greta Thunberg's COP24 speech became a YouTube sensation. Thousands of young people watched these events unfold and wondered how they could contribute to the growing climate movement. For some, the answer was divestment. "Divestment is as effective a tool as it always was, but now it's happening against a new political backdrop," Lee explained in our early 2020 conversation. "Climate change is now a polling issue, the Green New Deal is a household term, and the climate strikes are almost inescapable."[9]

The challenge for divestment movement leaders was to channel the upsurge of student interest into actions that put pressure on college administrations.

*

At halftime during a November 2019 Yale-Harvard football game, 150 students and alumni from the two elite schools stormed down from the stands and unfurled a series of banners on the field. "Divest from fossil fuels," read one. "Nobody Wins: Yale and Harvard are complicit in climate injustice," said another. As 30,000 surprised football fans looked on, hundreds more spectators spontaneously decided to leave their seats and ran to join the protest. For about thirty minutes all eyes were on the climate activists.[10]

"It's our job as Ivy League students to mobilize our privilege in support of a world that's more just, ethical, and sustainable," Ilana Cohen, a Harvard student involved in the action, told me in an interview a couple months later. "We recognized the Yale-Harvard game was a unique opportunity to spotlight the role of these universities in the climate crisis."[11]

Cohen, who grew up in New York City, became aware of climate injustice when Hurricane Sandy slammed the coast in 2012, the year she was eleven. After the storm destroyed 300 homes and cut off power to hundreds of thousands in New York,[12] Cohen was confused as to why she and other students in more affluent neighborhoods returned to class within days, while lower-income schools remained closed for weeks. It was her first clear glimpse of a social order where already-marginalized people are hit hardest by extreme weather and have fewer resources to cope.

After Cohen discovered Zero Hour during her senior year of high school, she and a friend founded the new organization's New York City chapter. They went on to coordinate an event for the 2018 day of marches. Cohen was excited to get involved in divestment work at Harvard that fall, and participated in an organizing fellowship through Divest Ed. However, by the time she arrived at Harvard, the school's once-vibrant existing divestment campaign had dwindled to only a few active members. Cohen was part of a new cohort of students who revived it.

With the Yale-Harvard football game disruption, students from both schools sought to escalate divestment campaigns on campuses that had faced years of rejection from their administrations. "We knew what we were doing wouldn't be popular with everyone," Cohen said. "For most people, the point of a football game is to enjoy themselves and celebrate. But the disruption was worth it and necessary."[13] The protest, one of the highest-visibility actions in divestment movement history, ended with fifty activists being escorted off the field by security.[14] Few spectators had any idea how much careful planning went into the preparations for that moment.

Well before the football game, Yale and Harvard students researched legal repercussions and possible disciplinary actions from the universities. There were nonviolence trainings for everyone who planned to participate. Since the game was in Harvard's home field, students there helped raise money to cover transportation costs for those coming from Yale who might have to return to Cambridge for court appearances.[15]

Escalating tactics in this manner on college campuses required that participants learn a whole new set of skills not covered by a typical college education. To meet this need, a new student-led organization came together with the aim of guiding divestment groups and other student climate activist campaigns through protests that came with the risk of arrest.

Rebelling for the climate

In a socially stratified society like the U.S., not all young people have equal access to information about climate change. In better-funded school districts the topic is at least likely to come up, even if it is a side note on the curriculum. In contrast, students in more impoverished communities may make it through high school without hearing about the biggest ecological crisis of their time. This was the case with Ayisha Siddiqa, who grew up in a low-income part of New York's Coney Island. Even so, she sensed early on there was something very wrong in humankind's relationship with the Earth.

"I think I was aware of the problem subconsciously," Siddiqa said when I interviewed her in February 2020. "There are no more fireflies in New York. Animals that were present in my childhood aren't here anymore. I no longer see butterflies." From a young age she had a deep sense of foreboding about the future, the exact source of which was hard to pinpoint. This fear came into sharper focus during Hurricane Sandy.

Siddiqa is about the same age as Ilana Cohen and grew up in the same city, but their experiences during Sandy were radically different. "My neighborhood is mostly immigrants, Black and brown people who could not afford to live elsewhere," Siddiqa said. "Our community was completely destroyed." Nearly a decade later, heaps of rubble and boarded-up buildings would still attest to Sandy's damage on Coney Island.

Not until Siddiqa was a student enrolled in an ecology class at Hunter College did she encounter the science behind climate change. But by then, what she learned about the increasing severity of extreme weather didn't come as a surprise. "Dogs know when there's a storm coming," was how she put it to me. "I think humans know instinctively, too, that something big and dangerous is heading our way. Many of us just haven't acknowledged it yet."

Siddiqa studied political science in college. She became fascinated by the use of nonviolent civil disobedience—especially in activist campaigns spearheaded by young people. "Historically, from civil rights movements to the Salt March in India, civil disobedience has been led by students," she said. She participated in the planning body that organized the September 2019 New York City climate strike, but saw a need for the climate movement to escalate further. This drew her to get involved in Extinction Rebellion (XR), an international climate organization dedicated to disruptive protests against the causes of climate change.[16]

Extinction Rebellion's origins date to the fall of 2018, when a group of British climate activists put out a call for the public to join them in London's Parliament Square on October 31, for a protest they anticipated might draw a couple hundred people. When around 1,500 Britons showed up, the organizers realized they had hit a nerve. Extinction Rebellion went on to shut down bridges, blockade streets, and interrupt business as usual in London. XR groups soon sprang up around the world.[17] A coordinated day of action that January brought the movement to the United States, with a die-in in Washington, D.C., banner drops in Los Angeles, and a takeover of New York City's iconic Rockefeller Ice Rink.[18]

Siddiqa saw a special role for young people in spreading this more disruptive type of activism. "The wonderful thing XR brings to the table in the youth climate movement is civil disobedience," she explained to me.[19]

That May, Siddiqa and other young U.S. activists launched Extinction Rebellion University, a student-led branch of the larger XR movement. The organization supported a series of actions at Columbia University later that year, where students occupied the campus library and held a week-long hunger strike. Their demands included that the school divest from fossil fuels.[20] By early 2020, XR University was working with over fifty mostly Northeastern schools on nonviolent activism trainings and planning for escalated peaceful protests.

Still, while she believed in the XR movement, Siddiqa also saw limitations in it. Actions like street blockades sometimes seemed to negatively impact ordinary people while doing little to reach their intended targets. Perhaps this is less the case in the U.K., where the largest urban center is also the main seat of government and finance.

"When you block traffic in a city, the only people you're inconveniencing are those getting to and from home or work," Siddiqa said. "But at a university, you can affect actual decision makers. You can take over a college president's office or board of trustees meeting. And you're engaging people who the university relies on: students paying tuition." The key was to deploy XR's methods in spaces like college campuses where they were most effective.[21]

With the organizational savvy of Divest Ed and the nonviolent protest tactics of XR University, the divestment movement was roaring back to life. Soon, it was scoring new victories.

Measuring success

Assessing the real-world impact of movements like the climate strikes can be extremely difficult. Such mass street mobilizations attempt to influence decision-making bodies like the U.N. and Congress, which move at a snail's pace and often take years to respond to shifts in public opinion. Similarly, while Sunrise Movement's early protests changed the public dialogue about climate, the early effects on government policy were harder to quantify. An advantage to divestment as a climate movement strategy has been its ability to win easily measurable victories which advocates can use to construct a meaningful narrative of progress.

Every time a university, foundation, or pension fund divests from fossil fuels, it sends a message that the behavior of these industries is socially unacceptable—that coal, oil, and gas companies should be regarded as pariahs. This is not the same as directly harming a company's bottom line; developments on the stock market affect investors, not the corporations whose stocks are being traded, and evidence suggests divestment campaigns have little to no impact on company share prices. But while divestment may not by itself deprive the target industry of money, it does hurt the public image of the companies involved, especially when the decision to divest is well-publicized.[22] Done well, divestment campaigns create an environment where an industry's reputation is so tarnished that it becomes difficult to secure bank loans, backing from insurers, and government favors. Divestment has potential to be truly effective in this sense.

It didn't take long for the new wave of campus-based fossil fuel divestment organizing to start winning victories. In September 2019, the University of California system announced it would divest its $13.4 billion endowment and $80 billion pension fund from all fossil fuels.[23] Smith College in Massachusetts followed suit in October.[24] Schools that committed to full or partial divestment in 2020 included Georgetown University,[25] University of Pennsylvania,[26] Antioch,[27] Cornell,[28] Creighton University,[29] and University of Vermont.[30] In 2021, the list grew by over a dozen additional institutions including Columbia,[31] Tufts,[32] University of Southern California,[33] Rutgers,[34] University of Michigan,[35] Amherst,[36] and Princeton.[37]

When Harvard announced in September 2021 that it would allow remaining fossil fuel investments in its $41.9 billion endowment to expire—effectively divesting—the moment marked the culmination of one of the longest-running, most hard-fought divestment campaigns in the country. "This is what [the administration] told us for a decade they couldn't do, and today, the students, faculty, and alumni [who called for divestment] have been vindicated," student divestment leader Connor Chung told the *Harvard Crimson*.[38]

The experience of divestment activists at Georgetown, a Jesuit school in Washington, D.C., provides a typical example of the kinds of challenges students often face when engaging with reluctant administrations. The Georgetown campaign launched in January

2013, when the national divestment movement was young. Students used high-visibility tactics like sit-ins, banner drops, and walking into the university board of directors' meetings unannounced to get the administration's attention. In response, the board punted the divestment question to an advisory committee on socially responsible investing.[39]

Committees can, infamously, be tools for quashing good ideas—and divestment campaigners are all too familiar with this strategy. But in 2015, in the face of continued pressure from students, Georgetown's social responsibility committee put forward a proposal approved by the board of directors to divest from coal only. In 2018, the board added tar sands oil companies to the list whose stocks it would avoid.[40] Still, the ultimate goal of divestment from all fossil fuels remained elusive. "We got the occasional very short email from the committee claiming they were looking into it, but they didn't seem to be moving forward or taking action," Georgetown divestment organizer Sadie Morris told me in February 2020.

With the administration stonewalling, "Our campaign realized we needed to go back to our roots and engage the student body through more visible kinds of pressure," Morris said. She and other activists launched a drive to pass a campus-wide student referendum on divestment. Although nonbinding, a yes vote would have put pressure on the school administration—and the odds for passage looked good. Apparently wanting to avoid embarrassment, Georgetown's board of directors finally took action by preemptively voting to divest on the same morning students began filling out their ballots. "The administration clearly wanted to control the narrative and not be seen as caving to students," Morris said. Still, a win was a win, and no one was complaining.[41]

At Georgetown, Harvard, and dozens of other colleges and universities students were forcing administrations who were temperamentally resistant to change to reckon with their investments in the companies destroying the planet. But were these wins having their intended effect by making life harder for coal, oil, and gas corporations? The answer seems to be a resounding yes, at least judging by trends among large financial institutions, insurers, and other corporate players.

Shifting global finance

About seventy-five middle and high school students converged on a Chase Bank branch in Boise, Idaho on January 31, 2020, waving signs with messages about the climate crisis and a banner bearing Extinction Rebellion's hourglass-in-a-circle emblem. The youth briefly entered the bank before being repelled by security, then gathered on the sidewalk.

"We propped open the doors with buckets so they could hear us chanting from inside the lobby," said fifteen-year-old Shiva Rajbhandari, an organizer of the action. "Then we stood along the street calling out Chase for funding the climate crisis." The protest caused the branch to shut down for the day.

Rajbhandari's path to protesting at Chase began when he spoke during an open mic period at Boise's climate strike event on September 20, 2019. He drew the attention of a local Sunrise volunteer, who recruited him to join the town's hub. Through Sunrise, Rajbhandari met adult activists engaged in starting a Boise chapter of Extinction Rebellion, which had recently publicized an international call for organizers to start youth groups. Inspired by XR's bold message, Rajbhandari jumped at the chance. That January, he and a small group of friends organized an informational event about XR and the urgency of the climate crisis. A few dozen local high school and middle school students attended. "Everyone was so motivated, we decided to hold an action that next week," Rajbhandari told me in May 2020.[42]

The Boise Chase protest was part of a larger effort by climate activists to reach decision makers at one of the most powerful U.S. financial institutions heavily invested in the fossil fuel industry. At a local level, the action had its intended effect of focusing attention on the bank's climate policies. "So many people drove by us and honked their support," said middle school student Emma Palmer, another organizer. "I definitely felt like our voices were being heard."[43]

Palmer seemed to be right that the pressure on Chase would have a larger impact. Less than a month after the Boise action, the bank announced it was ruling out funding certain fossil fuel projects, including thermal coal plants and Arctic oil drilling.[44] That May, Chase's board of directors demoted former Exxon CEO Lee Raymond from a key leadership position.[45] Activists would continue pushing Chase to abandon its remaining fossil fuel investments, but these early signs strongly suggested they were making a difference.

Of course, those tentative actions weren't only due to the Boise protest, which happened in the context of the divestment movement and a national effort to cut off funding from fossil fuel companies. Chase, which invested $269 billion in coal, oil, and gas between the years 2016-2019, was a main target of climate activists.[46]

A database compiled by the Institute for Energy Economics and Financial Analysis shows that two major financial institutions—the European Investment Bank and World Bank—announced new policies to limit their involvement with coal in 2013, the year fossil fuel divestment truly became a national movement. They were joined by the French bank Agence Française de Développement in 2014. The next several years saw a dramatic uptick in such announcements from banks, asset managers, and insurers around the world: twenty-eight in 2015, eight in 2016, thirty-nine in 2017, twenty-four in 2018, forty-seven in 2019, sixty-seven in 2020, and fifty-three in

2021.[47] At least eighty institutions in the financial and insurance sectors have also restricted their investments in oil and gas since the beginning of 2017.[48] U.S. companies unveiling new policies to limit their involvement with fossil fuels included Citibank, Morgan Stanley, U.S. Bancorp, Liberty Mutual, and Markel Corporation.[49]

It is difficult to prove definitively that climate activism was a major contributing factor in these decisions, but the circumstantial evidence certainly suggests it. "Divestment has been more effective than we ever thought it would be in the beginning," Jamie Henn, one of the early architects of the fossil fuel divestment movement, told me. When we spoke in February 2020, Henn was transitioning out of his longtime job at 350.org to head up communications at a new organization called Stop the Money Pipeline. "Now we have national campaigns to get banks and asset managers to distance themselves from the same companies students have long been targeting."[50]

A university selling its fossil fuel stocks may not directly hurt the finances of fossil fuel corporations—but the inability to secure bank loans or insurance certainly does. Furthermore, banks and investors now openly discuss concepts like fossil fuel "stranded assets" that the divestment movement has been talking about for years. This idea, that investments in fossil fuels might quickly become worthless as the world transitions to renewable energy, seemed radical in 2012. Now market analysts worry about it in the pages of the *Wall Street Journal*[51] and *Forbes*.[52]

The founders of Sunrise Movement are likely correct that the mainstreaming of divestment means it no longer works well as a way to push the edge of the climate movement into groundbreaking new territory. However, as a force to put wind in the sails of other climate activist campaigns it works very well indeed. The steady drumbeat of colleges and universities announcing new divestment commitments reinforces the message that coal, oil, and gas companies aren't worthy of loans or political favors. This effect is further amplified when local governments, foundations, and pension funds get on board.

*

New York Youth Climate Leaders plunged into the fight to divest their state's pension fund from fossil fuels almost immediately after the organization's founding in late 2019. "New York prides itself on being ahead of the curve on climate policy," NY2CL's Natalie Penna told me in April 2020. "We're simply asking them to live up to that reputation."[53]

Penna's introduction to grassroots uprisings came during the National Women's March in 2017, when she joined a crowd of over seven thousand in the streets of Albany.[54] "It made me realize how ordinary people can make themselves heard," she said. In early 2019, she and a friend heard about the first day of global climate strikes planned for March 15 and found a strike event scheduled at the nearby State Capitol. When they realized no one was mobilizing students at their school to participate, they decided to take initiative. Penna went to school administrators to try to secure permission for students to walk out of class.

"I kept running into dead ends," Penna said. "It got to where I was like, this is going to happen whether you give us permission or not." On March 15, she and a few hundred other students left class and marched through downtown Albany to the Capitol.[55]

Soon afterwards, Penna got involved in Zero Hour and outreach for the September 20 day of strikes. She, Hridesh Singh, and others later launched NY2CL, which became a member of the Divest New York coalition. After years of unsuccessful efforts to get State Comptroller DiNapoli to act unilaterally, divestment advocates were shifting their focus to the legislature.[56] By spring of 2020, a bill to divest the state pension fund had majority support in the New York Senate and was short by a handful of votes in the State Assembly.[57]

Activists calculated the prospect of divestment legislation would prompt DiNapoli to act himself—and the strategy bore fruit that December. In the end, divestment advocates won even more than most had dared hope for. New York would not only shed its investments in drillers and miners of coal, oil, and gas, DiNapoli's office announced. It would also divest from carbon-intensive industries that base a large part of their business model on burning fossil fuels. No wonder spirits were high at the celebratory Zoom press conference.

"Look," said 350.org's McKibben. "Were it not for the pandemic, we would be assembling in Albany today for one hell of a party. And it would be a great pleasure to raise a bottle of good New York State beer with everybody here—except Hridesh, who I guess we'd have to give a Coca-Cola to."[58]

A last stand for fossil fuels?

Despite the positive energy, I experienced a strange sense of cognitive dissonance while listening to the New York divestment press conference. I had just been working on a story about the grassroots resistance to pipeline company Enbridge's Line 3 project, which would pump oil from the Canadian tar sands across the Minnesota border into the U.S. Activists led by local Indigenous organizers were marching, lobbying, and even standing in the way of oncoming bulldozers to stop construction. There was no obvious, urgent need for the pipeline—U.S. oil demand was down significantly because of COVID [59]—yet Enbridge was rushing to build it as though time were of the essence.

I couldn't help getting the impression that Enbridge was trying to complete one last major pipeline before movements like divestment made it nearly impossible to do so. The project's finances were already under scrutiny. A couple days after New York's divestment announcement, twenty young people in St. Paul blocked the doors to a Chase Bank while chanting "Stop Line 3."[60] That same day, activists in sixty cities throughout the U.S. visited financial institutions to deliver a letter signed by 158 organizations calling on them not to fund Enbridge's pipeline.[61]

Soon after the New York press conference, I hopped on a separate Zoom call with Hridesh Singh and NY2CL member Caitlyn Carpenter of Westchester to get their take on the connection between their work and what was happening in Minnesota. "New York's divestment decision sends a message to the world that fossil fuels are a thing of the past," Singh said. "It signals we must transition into a clean energy economy that doesn't work just for polluting industry executives, but for all people. That means stopping new fossil fuel infrastructure."[62]

"It seems completely counterintuitive to continue building oil pipelines when investors are abandoning fossil fuels and we're trying to sunset the industry," Carpenter added.[63] The increasingly large pools of capital fleeing the fossil fuel sector hardly inspired confidence in projects like Line 3.

Meanwhile, for the first time in a decade, people were talking matter-of-factly about federal climate legislation, a change brought on partly by Sunrise Movement and the school strikes. By early 2020, the COVID-19 pandemic had complicated the ability of these groups to hold large protests—but the youth climate movement continued to be a force in politics. Sunrise, Zero Hour, and other student-led climate organizations helped drive youth voter turnout that year to record-smashing levels, up by as much as 25 percent compared to the previous presidential election.[64]

The wider increase in climate movement activity had helped supercharge divestment campaigns, partly by absorbing young people into the movement at earlier ages than usually happened in the past. Millennial climate organizers tend to look back on their college years as the time when they became activists, but members of Generation Z were getting involved in high school or earlier. "Before joining Zero Hour, I'd never realized young people who cared about the issues I did could take our activism to the next level," Aditi Anand, a high school freshman from the Bay Area and Zero Hour's communications director, told me in May 2020. "I don't just mean people in their twenties or early thirties, but youth my age."[65]

Ava Stahl of Pittsburgh participated in Zero Hour's Getting to the Roots ambassador program, designed to train young people on how to educate their communities about the underlying causes of the climate crisis. When I spoke with Stahl in March 2020, the high school sophomore was Zero Hour's partnerships director and an organizer with her local Fridays for Future chapter. "Skills like public speaking that I learned through these experiences have given me confidence to try things that once seemed terrifying," she said.[66]

Students like Stahl and Anand who went on to college would bring grassroots organizing experience they could choose to draw from on behalf of efforts like divestment. "Many students who start working with us have previously attended or organized Zero Hour marches or climate strikes," said Alyssa Lee of Divest Ed. "We're now seeing students with backgrounds in climate activism who have heard about divestment even before they get to college."[67]

No longer were young people who wanted to do something for the climate—whether in high school or college—left only with the option of reducing their personal carbon footprint. "I was that kid always bringing my reusable dishes to the cafeteria because I worried about plastic waste," sixteen-year-old Anna Cerosaletti, NY2CL's operations director, said when I spoke with her in April 2020. During a family vacation to Western national parks the summer before sixth grade, Cerosaletti saw dry landscapes ravaged by devastating wildfires. She knew they were a preview of what the future in a world shaped by climate change likely held. Joining NY2CL in high school helped dispel her feelings of powerlessness. "I'd been trying to limit my own energy consumption, but it's so much more satisfying to be part of a movement influencing policy at a higher level," she told me.[68]

By early 2020, the new wave of youth activism had spread to nearly every corner of the country, mobilizing hundreds of thousands of people in a way my own generation of climate activists never managed to do. A small part of me couldn't help feeling envious. Why had today's young climate activists been so much more successful than those of us who were in college in the early 2000s, I wondered? Were they simply better organizers, was the political moment just right, or was there something else going on?

Many Generation Z climate activists *are* incredibly savvy. The broader upsurge in progressive resistance movements under the Trump administration, which included the Women's March and the March for Our Lives against gun violence, also likely played a role in inspiring new interest in climate organizing. Still, as I learned more, I realized these factors could not fully explain how the recent wave of climate activism arose and spread so quickly. Modern student organizers succeeded partly by building on years of less visible work done by those who came before them.

A breakthrough in my understanding came during my conversation with Lisa Grimm and other Sunrise Movement organizers in Washington State. As described in Chapter 2, Grimm explained that she first heard about the Sunrise Semester program at an event organized by the Cascade Climate Network. This caught my attention.

I had been part of the Cascade Climate Network (CCN), a regional organization with a presence on many Northwest college campuses, during my days as a student at Oregon's Pacific University. I'd lost touch with the CCN since then, and I didn't even realize it still existed until Grimm mentioned it. But her words made me consider how an older generation of climate organizations helped make it possible for groups like Sunrise to spread rapidly across the country by capitalizing on existing networks and communication channels.

My point is not to diminish the significance of what Generation's Z's climate activist leaders have accomplished. They are some of the most brilliant organizers I have ever met, without whom the movement could never have gotten to where it is today. Nor do I mean to suggest members of my own generation—or the constellation of overwhelmingly white, middle-class student climate groups I interacted with in college—were the first young people to think of challenging the power of the fossil fuel industry. We, too, built on earlier efforts, including the work of social and environmental justice organizers of color whom we all too often failed to recognize.

That said, the way modern youth climate organizations built on the foundation laid by their predecessors illustrates another important lesson about how social movements develop. Just as media narratives tend to focus on isolated activist events rather than behind-the-scenes organizing, the way they treat the relationship between past and present waves of activism is often somewhat misleading. There is a tendency to portray past campaigns as "failures" which are replaced by "successful" new movements. At times I have even found myself thinking this way.

An example of this kind of framing appears in an otherwise insightful *New Republic* article on the birth of Sunrise Movement, published soon after the late 2018 Capitol Hill sit-ins. The piece describes Sunrise founders as "refugees from more mainstream climate organizations,"[69] implying a process whereby activists flee and leave behind, old, unsuccessful groups and join or start new ones. This feeds into the media tendency to focus on individual founders of new campaigns, while overlooking the larger ecosystem of connections that nourishes the climate movement. It also encourages a perception that social movements replace, rather than build on one another.

This and the previous two chapters have described some of the means by which the modern climate movement led by members of Generation Z harnessed momentum from older organizing efforts like the early divestment and campus sustainability campaigns. However, the more I learned about projects like Zero Hour, Fridays for Future, Sunrise Movement, and Divest Ed, the more I became convinced that to really understand where they came from, it is necessary to take a much more in-depth look at the nearly two decades of youth-led climate organizing that preceded them.

Thanks to my own time as a climate organizer, I knew many people who were involved in this early work, some on a first name basis. As I began researching for this book I reached out, and was gratified by how many of them took time to respond to my requests for interviews. The next five chapters convey what I learned, while examining how pivotal events in the early climate movement paved the way for specific more recent developments. Occasional anecdotes from my own experience help give life to the narrative.

The pages ahead will often focus on events on college campuses, in national and state capitols, and at U.N. climate summits. However, as I considered where the story should begin, I realized it must start not in any of these places, but with some of the most marginalized and forgotten regions of the country whose inhabitants have been resisting fossil fuel extraction since long before the modern climate movement.

PART TWO

Tangled Origins

4

News From the Frontlines

EXTRACTION, WASTE, AND THE FIGHT FOR CLIMATE JUSTICE

High on a hill, sheltered from the wind by a rocky outcropping, a young boy named Evon Peter sat watching an amazing spectacle unfold far below.

It was not unusual for him to be up here alone. He was accustomed to spending hours on his own, exploring the creeks, tundra, and hills around the small Gwich'in community of Arctic Village in northern Alaska. "Every day was an adventure, an exploration of the land," Peter said when I asked about his childhood in an April 2020 interview for this book.

At an early age, Peter learned skills most people in the U.S. never acquire: how to place a fish net and cut through thick ice, how to set ground squirrel traps, when to hunt ducks and gather wild berries. On the tundra there were no fences, streets, or property boundaries. "It was an experience I can only refer to as true free-dom," he recalled.

On this particular day, the young Peter gazed down on what looked from so far away like thousands of ants pouring out of the Brooks Mountain Range and massing on the tundra. In fact, the animals were caribou, tired from the 400-mile trek to their southern wintering grounds. They would spend the next several months near Arctic Village. Some mornings, Peter would open the door of the cabin he shared with his grandfather and uncle to find dozens of caribou outside, and had to shoo them away to reach the outhouse. The big animals left tracks along streams and droppings on the snow. Their presence changed the landscape, yet they were as indelibly part of it as the tundra lichens. So were Peter's people, the Gwich'in, the land's original human inhabitants who rely on caribou for meat.

Centuries of colonization and attacks on Indigenous culture had not broken the Gwich'in relationship with the Porcupine caribou herd. "In the lower forty-eight states, the buffalo that provided for Native peoples were decimated during the genocide of those com-munities," Peter told me. "We Gwich'in are blessed to still have the caribou."[1]

The caribou are so important to Gwich'in culture that the ani-mals' calving grounds to the north—mostly within the coastal plain of what is now the Arctic National Wildlife Refuge (ANWR)—have been known for thousands of years as the Sacred Place Where Life Begins. Throughout the millennia it has sustained not only caribou, but the people who depend on them.

As Peter watched the great animals flood into the valley that winter, those essential calving grounds were about to come under threat as never before.

Protecting the Sacred Place Where Life Begins

Long before there was a national climate movement, there were many localized pockets of resistance to the U.S. fossil fuel industry, led by people living close to the point of extraction or pollution. Almost always, these were Indigenous nations, people of color, or working-class communities without easy access to the levers of political power. The Gwich'in, who struggled against seemingly impossible odds to protect the Porcupine caribou herd from the depredations of oil companies, are a typical example.

In 1988, when Peter was still a boy, leaders from all over the far-flung Gwich'in Nation came together in Arctic Village to confront the emerging threat of oil drilling. It was to be a historic gathering.

The Gwich'in homeland extends from what is now North-east Alaska to the Mackenzie River Valley in Canada's Northwest Territories.[2] The imposition of an international border by U.S. and Canadian authorities cut this vast region in two, and by the 1980s it had been over a century since members of the more than a dozen politically autonomous Gwich'in villages met in one place. But what was happening now necessitated such a step. The Reagan administration had recommended opening ANWR's coastal plain to oil drilling, a move that needed approval from Congress under the terms of the 1980 Alaska National Interest Lands Conservation Act. Leaders from every Gwich'in community met in Arctic Village to decide how to respond.

When I spoke with Peter decades later, he still remembered coming home from a night of duck hunting and lying down to rest on the logs outside the community hall where the historic meeting was taking place. Although too young to participate in the official proceedings, he joined the rest of the village for group meals and traditional dances organized in conjunction with the gathering. He could sense something momentous happening.

"It was imperative for us as Gwich'in people to protect the caribou and our way of life," Peter said. "The seeds of that understanding had been planted very early for me, but in 1988 it became more formulated—not only for me, but for the entire Gwich'in nation."[3]

By day, tribal leaders held discussions entirely in the Gwich'in language. Together, they arrived at a unanimous consensus: to present a unified front of opposition to any attempt to drill in the Porcupine herd's calving grounds.[4]

*

The Reagan administration's ANWR plans were unexpectedly derailed by political fallout from the 1989 Exxon Valdez oil spill, which turned public opinion against risky drilling ventures in places like the Refuge.[5] Threats to the Sacred Place Where Life Begins would resurface repeatedly in the years ahead, and the Gwich'in would be ready. But in the meantime, there were other battles to fight with the forces of colonialism.

Like many young Indigenous people, Peter found the U.S. education system alienating. He went to high school in Fairbanks, a bustling metropolis compared to Arctic Village's tiny population of about 100.[6] Though he never received his high school diploma, he later decided to pursue college at University of Alaska. "I knew if I wanted people to listen to what I had to say, I needed a Western education," he told me.

A couple weeks into his first semester, Peter was arguing with the professor in his philosophy class about intellectual assumptions based in Western ways of thought. Peter shifted his chair to near the front of the room, his back facing the wall perpendicular to the rest of the class, so he could move more easily between addressing the professor and other students. The arrangement unintentionally reinforced the feeling that the class was witnessing a conversation between two sophisticated intellectuals: the professor and their classmate Peter. He sat that way the rest of the term.

One day, after class, an older Native student came up and asked Peter if he would be interested in running for student senate. Indigenous voices were severely underrepresented in student government, and Peter obviously had the drive to be a force for change. Peter said yes, ran, and was elected.

He also became active in the school's Native student organization, which sent groups to Indigenous gatherings, advocated for including Native history in higher education, and organized protests. On Columbus Day the group erected a teepee in the student union. Although teepees were not regularly used by Arctic peoples, the organizers knew the symbolism would be recognizable to their non-Indigenous peers.

"We were doing what today would be called decolonization work," Peter said. He became more and more a spokesperson for Indigenous students at the university. Soon members of the media began seeking his perspective on contemporary statewide events.

Peter graduated in 1998, returning to Arctic Village a couple years later as director of the tribal energy program, a role in which he spearheaded a plan to install rooftop solar panels in the community and reduce reliance on fossil fuels. He also found himself back in the heart of the struggle to protect the Sacred Place Where Life Begins.[7]

*

Environmentalists accustomed to Western ways of thinking tend to see each fight as an isolated battle over oil drilling, pollution, or protected areas. Yet to Peter, the fate of the Porcupine caribou's calving grounds is inextricably linked with a host of intertwining problems. In the early 2000s, the George W. Bush administration launched a new push to drill in ANWR.[8] This latest threat to the Gwich'in was tied up with forced assimilation, climate change, and the privatization of Indigenous lands. When Peter decided to run for the elected tribal government, it was with the goal of addressing these inseparable issues.

Peter was elected chief of Arctic Village in 2000, at age twenty-four. His official duties included representing his people in state-wide, national, and international forums—and just like in college, he stood out as a gifted speaker. Soon he was participating in events organized by the Alaska Intertribal Council, Alaska Federation of Natives, and Indigenous Environmental Network. In 2007, he gave a keynote speech at Power Shift, an early youth climate activist summit in the U.S. capital. "We human beings are part of cre-ation—of what you can call ecosystems—but we...are disrespecting our [non-human] relations," he told thousands of listening college students. "There are consequences to that, and our [Indigenous] peoples have always known that."[9]

Soon after Power Shift, Peter decided to step back from the national speaking circuit to focus on empowering Indigenous com-munities back in Alaska. The immediate danger to ANWR had receded for the time being, and there was other work to do at home.

However, Peter's Power Shift speech left a lasting impression on thousands of young people just when what is now known as the youth climate movement was starting to take shape. His words were a reminder to student organizers that the movement they were joining was tied to larger struggles as old as the fight against colonialism itself.

Uprising on Black Mesa

Enei Begaye came of age thousands of miles from Arctic Village, the place where she would one day meet her future partner, Evon Peter. Growing up in the dry landscape of the Navajo Nation, it would have been hard to predict the chain of events that took her to the northern tundra. In some ways, the journey began when she was a Stanford student in the late 1990s.

"I thought college was a path that could help me make positive change in my community," said Begaye, who is Navajo and Tohono O'odham.[10] For decades her homeland had been targeted for coal, oil, and uranium extraction. Many Navajos lack electricity even today; but since the early '70s coal from their reservation has supplied some of the largest U.S. power plants.[11]

Begaye studied geology, environmental science, and land management at Stanford, hoping to become a more effective advocate for Navajo communities suffering the pollution costs of fossil fuel extraction. The environmental consequences of mining are numerous, but most concerning to Begaye was the depletion of the Navajo Aquifer.[12] Companies like Peabody were draining this precious water supply to wash coal and—perhaps most egregiously—transport it in slurry form through a 273-mile pipeline to Nevada's Mohave power plant.[13]

It wasn't long, however, before Begaye became disillusioned with the Western education she was receiving. "I realized the Indigenous worldview I grew up with had already taught me the concepts behind the scientific topics I was studying," she said when I interviewed her in April 2020. "The scientific terms for environmental phenomena describe forces I recognized as deities and part of my spirituality."

Frustrated with her classes, Begaye spent the summers working with other young people in Navajo country to confront problems caused by coal mining. She wanted to unite youth from both the Navajo and adjacent Hopi Reservations in opposition to the coal industry. This wasn't a simple task, as it required overcoming rancor stirred up between the two peoples by U.S. government divide-and-conquer tactics.[14]

Until the 1970s, Navajos and Hopis co-existed on 1.8 million acres of the vast area of land known as Black Mesa, which was managed jointly by the two tribes. This created complications for U.S. energy companies seeking to get at the area's rich coal seams, who preferred negotiating with one tribe at a time. In response, Congress passed the 1974 Navajo-Hopi Land Settlement Act, which partitioned Black Mesa and forced thousands of Navajos off coal-rich land now owned by the Hopis. The new law led to bad feelings between the tribes that still stung decades later, especially for those old enough to remember the era of division.[15]

"We young people didn't have all that historical baggage," Begaye said. Seeing a chance to move beyond the conflict, she and a small group of young Navajos and Hopis began building a multiethnic group opposed to coal mining, called Black Mesa Water Coalition. They soon attracted smaller numbers of white and Latinx youth who supported their cause.

"The work was really empowering," Begaye remembered, in contrast to her experience in college. Through Black Mesa Water Coalition, she began reconnecting with a traditional education that seemed more valuable than ever. "I started trying to unlearn the scientific way of knowing I'd realized wasn't the be-all, end-all. I was waking up and listening to elders again." She didn't finish senior year at Stanford.

To get more people involved, the Black Mesa leaders knew they needed to make their work fun. Their first major event was a Water is Life concert, with musical performances interspersed by speakers who talked about pollution issues. Black Mesa Water Coalition went on to organize runs, protests, and community meetings.

The organization's leaders also confronted the challenge of how to make a living while continuing to do good work. Early on, Begaye received funding from Stanford. Later she was employed by the Sierra Club, which was impressed by her work and wanted to support her activism. Not all the attention was positive, however. Like most places where resource extraction is an economic engine, Navajo communities were sharply divided between those who opposed coal's ravages on the land, and others who saw it as a necessary evil. Then there was the coal industry itself, already infamous for using violent tactics to suppress labor organizing. In coal country, speaking out loudly against the behavior of mining companies is risky.

Occasionally, after finishing a meeting in the house many of them shared, Black Mesa Water Coalition organizers would step outside to see a car with a camera sticking out the window drive slowly past before speeding off down the road. The message of surveillance was clear. "We weren't doing anything wrong," Begaye said. "But we were outspoken about a company with a lot of money. That made people angry."

When the house burned down under mysterious circumstances, arson was never proved—but it was hard not to suspect. By then, the fight for the Navajo Aquifer had become a defining aspect of the young people's lives and they took every opportunity to advance it. One of Begaye's friends emerged from the burnt house after losing almost everything, smoke and tears on her face. Camera-wielding news reporters asked her for a statement.

The journalists probably expected to hear something about how it felt to be suddenly homeless, or even an accusation of foul play. "We're having a concert this weekend," the young woman said instead. "You should all come. Water is life."[16]

*

Among the many Indigenous youth who came to regard Begaye as a mentor was fellow Stanford student Jihan Gearon. The two young Navajo women began organizing together through the university's Indigenous student organization when Gearon was a few years behind Begaye in school. They made a good team, but it was pure serendipity that led to them meeting again in Gwich'in territory years later.

It was 2003, and Gearon had just finished her Stanford degree. A professor recommended she look into the Climate Justice Corps, a project of the recently formed Environmental Justice and Climate Change (EJCC) initiative, which paired young activists of color with organizations advancing socially just solutions to climate change. She applied and landed a summer position working on community climate education with the Arctic Village Tribal Council.

Founded in 2001, EJCC was a coalition of more than two dozen groups who sought to draw attention to climate change's impacts on already-oppressed communities.[17] It grew out of the older environmental justice (EJ) movement, led by activists of color who built on decades of work by civil rights organizations. When discussing the EJ movement's origins, most scholars point to the 1991 National People of Color Environmental Leadership Summit, where activists drafted seventeen "Principles of Environmental Justice" to guide their work.[18] EJCC wanted to apply these principles to the emerging climate crisis.[19]

"Fossil fuel plants are disproportionately located in and pollute communities of color," Gearon said when I interviewed her for this book in April 2020. "Then there's the changing climate itself, from extreme weather events like Hurricane Katrina to the melting Arctic and its effects on Indigenous peoples. Those disasters were already being felt by the early 2000s, but so far it was mainly EJ communities who were affected."

Gearon was assigned to work with Gwich'in leaders on community climate education programs. The previous year, Begaye had moved to Arctic Village with her partner, Evon Peter, whom she met in the course of their mutual involvement in Indigenous rights organizations. Now she helped introduce Gearon to a landscape which so far had been less directly impacted by extraction than their homeland in Navajo country.

"It was such a different way of life," Gearon said. "Mostly subsistence living, no gasoline-powered vehicles. I loved it."

From Begaye and Peter, who was then still chief of Arctic Village, Gearon learned about the fight to stop oil drilling in the Porcupine caribou's calving grounds. As different as the tundra seemed from the desert of Black Mesa, Gearon easily understood the Gwich'in's struggle. Just as coal companies mined Navajo country to power Southwest cities, so the Sacred Place Where Life Begins would be sacrificed to fuel SUVs if oil companies got their way.[20] To a cynical observer, the resistance waged by small groups of Indigenous activists against some of the most powerful industries in the world would have looked hopeless. But over the next few years, Navajo and Gwich'in organizers won victories that once seemed impossible.

In 2005, thanks to advocacy from Indigenous-led organizations like Black Mesa Water Coalition, the Mohave coal plant and associated slurry line shut down. The event foreshadowed a wave of coal plant and mine closures in Navajo country over the next several years.[21] Also in 2005, the Bush administration's plan to drill in ANWR suffered defeat in Congress.[22] The fight to protect the Sacred Place Where Life Begins continues to this day, but it would not be until the Trump administration that an imminent threat to the caribou calving grounds arose again.

Meanwhile, in 2003, Begaye and Peter launched Native Movement, a nonprofit that trains young activists from organizations seeking to "dismantle oppressive systems for all, and that endeavor to ensure social justice, Indigenous Peoples' rights, and the rights of Mother Earth."[23] Native Movement has served an important function connecting the struggles of Indigenous organizers fighting fossil fuel extraction throughout the Western U.S. and beyond.

At EJCC, Gearon eventually took on a new role as coordinator of the same Climate Justice Corps that first sent her to Arctic Village. She later worked for the Indigenous Environmental Network, then became Black Mesa Water Coalition's executive director. Like Begaye and Peter, she inspired many other young people to get involved in climate work for the first time. Some were Indigenous youth fighting fossil fuel extraction on their lands. Others were youth of color from communities at the other end of the polluting industry pipeline: toxic waste disposal.

Brownfield resistance

In August 2002, fifteen-year-old Shadia Fayne Wood was at the U.N. World Summit on Sustainable Development in Johannesburg, South Africa. Wood, who is Arab American, had travelled from her small hometown in upstate New York with a delegation of young people of color organized by environmental justice groups. Though not yet old enough to have a driver's license, her activist resume was already impressive. It all started because people in her town kept dying from rare forms of cancer.

"I had a very real understanding from early on in my life that neighbors and kids I knew from school could get cancer diagnoses and die," Wood said when we spoke in February 2020. The reason wasn't hard to figure out: the town had a history as a toxic waste site.

When Wood was two, her mother joined the fight against a large corporation's plan to build a new landfill and waste incinerator within their school district, adding to the area's existing pollution woes. When attending meetings of a green-minded labor group, she left Wood in childcare provided by the organization where children learned about persistent organic pollutants and other ecological concepts. "When we all realized how this landfill would affect us, it was a radicalizing experience for our family and the larger community," Wood said.

Wood's older sister did her part by starting a chapter of Kids Against Pollution (KAP), an organization that gave children a voice in fights like the one their town faced. By the time Wood was old enough to join, the group had shifted its focus to state-level politics. Funding for New York's Superfund waste cleanup program was running dry, leaving little hope for restoration of toxic sites.

The adolescent Wood participated in KAP lobby days at the State Capitol, where young people asked their representatives to re-finance Superfund. One year, they made a model toxic waste site on the Capitol steps, complete with Tonka trucks and root beer cans representing barrels full of hazardous pollutants. In 2002, Wood and others set up a lemonade stand in a symbolic effort to raise Superfund money. "Our message for the adults was that we kids were doing our part, so why weren't lawmakers?" Wood said.

The Superfund campaign brought Kids Against Pollution into contact with EJCC, which invited Wood and other members to give a presentation at one of its early organizing summits. "I met and learned from so many movement elders there," Wood remembered. These included leaders from Black Mesa Water Coalition, Indigenous Environmental Network, the Southwest Workers Union, Harlem's WE ACT for Environmental Justice, and other grassroots organizations from across the country who together drafted ten new "Principles for Just Climate Change Policies."

Despite this early exposure to climate politics, it wasn't until after the U.N. Summit on Sustainable Development in Johannesburg that Wood herself got deeply involved in climate advocacy. At that conference, hosted by South Africa's post-apartheid regime, she began drawing new links between her own community's fight against toxic waste and worldwide struggles for social justice.[24]

*

Johannesburg wasn't the first place where environmental justice advocates tried raising their voices at a U.N. gathering. During COP6 in the Hague, Netherlands—two years before the South Africa event, and eighteen years before Greta Thunberg addressed COP24 in Poland—grassroots organizations convened a Climate Justice Summit to present a vision for fair policies to address climate change. The gathering stood in contrast to the official U.N. event, where more corporate-friendly, market-based solutions predominated.[25] Participation in the Climate Justice Summit by U.S. activists helped pave the way for the launch of EJCC the following year.[26]

In Johannesburg, activists worked to elevate the voices of communities at the front lines of climate change. During a meeting between youth activists at the summit and a group of business leaders, Wood witnessed an interaction that stuck with her for years. The conversation turned to Indigenous and other marginalized peoples —and one of the executives referred to them as "people," without the "s."

"No, it's peoples," said Clayton Thomas-Muller, a young member of the Mathias Colomb Cree Nation from Canada. The singular "people" implied a misunderstanding, he explained. The many, diverse peoples around the world who identify as Indigenous to their homelands are separate nations, not a monolithic entity to be treated with a one-size-fits-all approach.

"I felt something shift in the room in that moment," Wood remembered. "Maybe we were talking about an 's,' but it was really about more than that, because how we identify ourselves as peoples affected by climate change is something important that we bring into every space with us."

Less inspiring was what Wood saw while touring neighborhoods near the summit venue. "I had learned in high school that apartheid was over," she said. It didn't seem especially over in the slums of Johannesburg, where poor Black shantytowns were separated from affluent white communities by barbed wire. "I came to realize legal apartheid may have ended, but an economic apartheid still exists. Folks of color clearly couldn't access the same resources as white communities."[27]

The U.N. gathering was a whirlwind of such eye-opening experiences. Soon Wood was back in the U.S., engaged in what turned out to be the final stage of the Superfund campaign. In 2003, New York Governor George Pataki signed the Superfund/Brownfields Act, guaranteeing tens of millions of dollars to restore polluted lands around the state.[28] The signing ceremony took place in Utica, fifteen minutes from Wood's hometown. She and other local activists were invited. The Governor shook her hand.

It was a sweet moment in many ways. "But I thought, it shouldn't have taken half my life for this to happen," Wood said. The Superfund victory truly belonged to grassroots organizers in communities like hers, who worked many long hours for little or no compensation as they pushed back against polluting industries.[29]

Wood's experience in South Africa and with EJCC shaped her decision "to commit to prioritizing climate activism" in the aftermath of the Superfund campaign win. Her dive into climate work at the dawn of the new century came at an auspicious time. This was the era when a nationwide grassroots climate movement was just beginning to find a purchase in communities all over the U.S. On dozens of college campuses, young people led the way.

It all comes back to climate

Today, when the climate and environmental movements are often treated as nearly synonymous, it is easy to forget that as recently as two decades, ago climate change was widely seen as just one item on a long list of environmentalist concerns. At times, it didn't even seem like an especially high priority. Grassroots movements to conserve wild areas, clean up waterways, and protect endangered species had been a core part of mainstream environmentalism since at least the 1970s. Climate, on the other hand, was something of a second-tier concern through the beginning of the new century, despite evidence of Earth's warming having been well established by the '80s.[30]

"For years, discussions about climate were led mainly by scientists and academics," Kelly Lynch, a leader of the early youth climate movement, told me.[31] Maybe the sometimes-esoteric science of climate change was simply harder to grasp intuitively than the causes of deforestation or water pollution. Then, too, impacts like melting ice caps would have seemed far off to many environmentalists at the start of the 2000s. Not until 2006 did the Sierra Club, the oldest and biggest U.S. environmental organization, make campaigning for a "smart, safe, clean energy future" its number one priority.[32] Other large green groups began to shift their focus to climate around the same time.

"When I was in high school in 1999, the Sierra Student Coalition's campaigns were all about preserving wild deserts and roadless national forests," said Jared Duval, who directed the Sierra Club's student-run branch from June 2005 until September 2007. "By the time I took on a national role, climate work had become everything for us. We came to see it as an overarching challenge that could devastate everything we care about."[33]

Environmental justice groups led by people of color were by then already spearheading grassroots efforts to attack the causes of the climate crisis. With the founding of EJCC in 2001, the environmental justice community signaled climate was a top concern. The important role of programs like the Climate Justice Corps shows youth activism was central to the climate justice movement's work from its early days.

EJCC preceded by three years the formation of Energy Action Coalition (EAC), the alliance of organizations that became the main coordinating body for the national youth climate movement in the early 2000s, which the next chapter discusses at length. In 2004, Shadia Fayne Wood met EAC founder and former Yale student Billy Parish at the annual ceremony for the prestigious Brower Youth Awards for young environmentalists, where both were prize recipients. They soon got to talking about the new coalition.

Shortly after that, Wood joined the Climate Justice Corps at EJCC, which had recently become an EAC member. In 2006, the initiative hired her to coordinate its contribution to EAC's signature campaign, the Campus Climate Challenge. One of the hardest parts of the job, for Wood, was navigating tensions between the grassroots movement for environmental justice she knew, and the priorities of more mainstream environmental groups.

This book's early chapters touched on how modern youth climate organizations attempt to be good allies to marginalized groups who bear the brunt of fossil fuel pollution and extraction. To say these efforts have always succeeded would be disingenuous; the movement has continued to make mistakes, sometimes very serious ones, and its most admirable goals for diversity, equity, and inclusion are not always realized in practice. However, to the extent that climate campaigns led by young people have made progress in this area, it is mostly thanks to organizers of color who have pushed for change since the beginning.

"Working with EAC was amazing and also challenging," Wood said. "There was a sense from some member groups that we needed to cut carbon emissions before anything else, and a reluctance to look at issues of justice or race. It took young white people a long time to really hear what students of color were saying, that doing climate work collaboratively with frontline communities requires an anti-oppression framework."

At least Wood had a mentor to lean on: Jihan Gearon, her predecessor in the role of EJCC representative to EAC's steering committee. "In the early days, I'd sometimes go to EAC conferences and be the only person of color present," Gearon said. "It was mostly white people from extremely privileged backgrounds who didn't understand anything organizers of color like me were saying. They were the ones making up all the rules, all the policies, all the narratives."[34]

When I asked Wood about her years with EAC, she spoke of the coalition kindly but with an honesty that comes of hard experience. "There was an important generative process early on, with a lot of learning and stumbling," she said. "And by seeing what not to do, a lot of young organizers slowly learned how to do things better."[35]

A personal awakening

On a sunny day in early 2005, I sat with my political science class in a patch of lawn on Portland Community College's Rock Creek campus, waiting to hear Evon Peter talk about the Arctic National Wildlife Refuge.

I was seventeen, and had recently become a PCC student. My love of nature was nourished by a childhood spent catching beetles in the backyard and exploring forested parks near my family's home in Oregon. As an adolescent, I took up birdwatching. I became aware of environmental problems early in life, but came to see climate change as the biggest, overarching threat only in my late teens.

From a shy child, I grew into a socially awkward teenager. I was more interested in nature than politics, but by the time of the 2004 presidential election was aware enough to know that the winner's actions were a threat to life on Earth. George W. Bush had already pulled the U.S. out of the Kyoto Protocol, the only major international climate agreement at the time, and the administration's push to open ANWR to oil drilling horrified me. Bush's re-election was a rude wakeup call, just as the election of Donald Trump a dozen years later would be for members of Generation Z. I finally realized that to do something about climate change and the threats facing places like ANWR, I needed to learn something about politics. I enrolled in a political science class, thinking of it as a necessary but mildly unpleasant chore. I was amazed to find I enjoyed it.

I was fortunate to have a professor who brought the dry topics of government and elections alive in ways I'd never imagined were possible. Politics wasn't just the domain of old men in suits. It was also a story of ordinary people changing the system for the better, from the 1960s Civil Rights Movement to the early twentieth-century women's suffrage campaign.

When Evon Peter visited our PCC campus during a West Coast speaking tour, my professor had the whole class attend. "At first, when my people heard the government wanted to drill for oil in the Arctic National Wildlife Refuge, they couldn't believe it," Peter said, according to notes I took at the time. "They couldn't understand why anyone would want to put drills in that place just to get oil for gasoline that will give people cancer when it's burned."

At that point in my life, I lacked a sophisticated understanding of the intersections between fossil fuel development, colonization, and the struggle for Indigenous rights. Even so, I grasped the most important aspects of what Peter was saying. The fight over oil drilling wasn't just about caribou and polar bears. It concerned near-term threats to the Gwich'in's cultural survival. "I really enjoyed that," I said, going up to Peter after the talk. "It was wonderful." He murmured something polite in reply. It was a moment I'd remember poignantly when interviewing Peter for this book fifteen years later.

Experiences like listening to Peter's speech inspired me to get involved in the nascent youth climate movement that was then just starting to emerge on college and university campuses. That fall, I started an environmental club that made modest progress toward implementing a recycling program on my campus. The following summer, I attended one of the Sierra Student Coalition's week-long activist training camps. Only years later would I come to fully appreciate the challenging decisions being made behind the scenes at the SSC and larger Sierra Club as they pivoted their work to focus on climate. Still less did I understand what difficult conversations were happening as the mainstream environmental movement struggled to reconcile its white, middle-class history with an approach to climate activism centered on the needs of marginalized peoples.

There would be too many times in years ahead when the youth climate movement forgot the debt it owed environmental justice groups and leaders of color like Evon Peter, Enei Begaye, Jihan Gearon, and Shadia Fayne Wood. On the other hand, some of the movement's proudest moments would be when it harkened back to this legacy and the fight for true climate justice. The tug-of-war between these tendencies to honor or erase the contributions of people at the frontlines of fossil fuel extraction and pollution would be a defining aspect of the youth climate movement's evolution.

During the next decade, this internal struggle would play out hundreds of times as the new youth climate movement grew and spread to higher education institutions all over the U.S.

5

Moving the Elephant

BUILDING THE FOUNDATION FOR THE NATIONAL YOUTH CLIMATE MOVEMENT

In June 2004, a couple dozen leaders from U.S. environmental organizations with large student followings came together in Washington, D.C. for a gathering instrumental to the rise of a connected, truly national climate movement. Together, they laid a foundation that would contribute to the spread of campaigns like the school strikes a decade and a half later.

"Climate change was such a big issue, none of us felt we could make meaningful progress toward solving it by ourselves," said Billy Parish, the former Yale student who did more than anyone to bring the meeting about. "Making space to share ideas was critical." Despite the scale of the challenges they faced, participants would remember the main emotion that permeated the gathering as one of cheerful camaraderie. "It just felt really good," Parish said. "We had a lot of fun planning together."[1]

Some of the young people present belonged to groups like the Student Environmental Action Coalition (SEAC), which led a wave of youth campaigning around issues like old-growth forest logging in the '90s. Others came from age-diverse organizations with student-led wings, such as the Sierra Club and National Wildlife Federation. Many participants gave their time for free because they believed in the cause. The group made decisions by consensus, and everyone got time to speak. "It was a volunteer-led, co-creative process," recalled Kelly Lynch, then a SEAC campaign coordinator.

That the youth arms of many green groups were ahead of their older adult counterparts on confronting climate change seemed fitting. After all, Millennials would be more directly impacted by the climate crisis than any other generation then old enough to do something about it. "We wanted to give young people a voice on the climate issue," Lynch said. "We kind of already knew going in that we were going to form a coalition. It was mostly a matter of formalizing it."[2]

By the end of the three-day gathering, the leaders had a mission and bylaws for the new, youth-led Energy Action Coalition (EAC). A steering committee of representatives from member organizations served as its decision-making body. Parish became the coordinator and first paid employee.[3]

Over the next decade, EAC engaged thousands of students on hundreds of college campuses and convened some of the largest activist gatherings in climate movement history up to then. In the process, the coalition put in place organizational infrastructure and communication channels that played important roles in even bigger future mobilizations. All this activity owed itself to the sometimes-improbable series of events leading up to that first 2004 meeting.

From Energy Action to the Campus Climate Challenge

As I began researching the origins of the national youth climate movement for Part II of this book, I had a long list of prominent activists I hoped to talk with. One of the very first whom I emailed, however, was Billy Parish. The two of us connected on Zoom in January 2020. "In the early 2000s, more people were becoming aware of climate change," Parish told me during our conversation. "The issue was sort of entering the zeitgeist in a new way, but nobody really knew how to build a campaign around it."[4]

Parish in 2020 looked different from in photos and videos of his days in the early climate movement. Whereas he once had a thick head of curly dark hair, he now went bald. His jacket breast pocket bore the logo of Solar Mosaic, the clean energy crowdfunding company he founded in 2010. Yet, he spoke about developments from a decade and a half ago as though they were recent memories.

I knew that in 2002 Parish, at the time still a Yale student, won a grant to study community-based forestry in India, where he had an experience pivotal to his understanding of the climate crisis. On a hike in the Himalayas, he took in the sight of a glacier that feeds the Ganges River. Scientists were tracking the ice's steady retreat and millions of people's drinking water was at risk. It brought the human impact of climate change home for Parish as nothing had before.[5]

It would be easy, here, to skip straight from this scene to Parish's emergence as a climate movement leader. Some media accounts have done just that,[6] but such neat narratives miss the messy process of trial and error that goes into generating grassroots movements. After returning from India, Parish dropped out of school—temporarily, he thought—to organize a New England youth climate summit. Out of that gathering came a group called Eco Northeast.

"The idea was to work together on solutions to climate change in the region," Parish told me. "But it turned out what we actually needed wasn't a new organization. Eco Northeast became just another splinter group."

There was no shortage of organizations supporting youth environmental activism, Parish eventually realized. The problem was they tended to work in isolation, with no way to coordinate their efforts at the scale a problem like climate change demanded. "I didn't know any of this going in," he said. "I was just a kid who got freaked out about the climate and wanted to do something about it. But I slowly realized there was a whole landscape of existing groups whose purpose was to help young people campaign around environmental issues."[7]

Parish reached out to young activists involved in some of these organizations, like recent College of Wooster graduate Kelly Lynch of SEAC. As a student in 2000, Lynch had traveled to COP6 in the Hague, Netherlands, where she heard Inuit women warn world leaders about the melting Arctic. After graduation she moved to Philadelphia to volunteer with SEAC, a once-large organization that was now "a shell of its former self," with few paid staff and many chapters having gone dormant. Lynch worked to rebuild its activist network.[8]

Other organizers whom Parish and Lynch linked up with included University of North Carolina-Chapel Hill student Liz Veazey, who had recently won a campaign for a student fee to fund green energy on her campus. In November 2003, these three and other young leaders organized a nationwide day of action for clean energy with rallies and creative protests in sixty-five locations.[9]

"We set up a website showing where actions were planned all over the country," Lynch told me in a March 2020 interview. Anybody could RSVP online or register their own event, a template for internet-based activism that later became common, but which Lynch remembered "felt really new at the time."[10] Another, similar day of action the students organized in April 2004 drew 130 events.[11]

Around that same time, Veazey convened an organizing summit at Chapel Hill which attracted student activists from across the Southeast and beyond. As she recalls, it was Parish who suggested during the event that they formalize a coalition of youth-led groups working on climate campaigns. It was a good idea, others agreed. Months later they were in D.C. for the founding meeting of EAC.[12]

One of the new coalition's first projects was a third nationwide day of action, with 280 events across the continent in October 2004. "But we felt we needed to go beyond just doing joint actions, and take on a more long-term joint campaign," Lynch said.[13]

Soon they were making that vision a reality.

*

EAC's first major campaign, the Campus Climate Challenge, started with coalition leaders brainstorming what a coordinated, national effort to jumpstart the climate movement at colleges and universities could look like.

"Young people all over the U.S. and Canada had participated in our days of action," Veazey told me in February 2020. "We asked ourselves: What could we do to keep them engaged, assuming we had funding? The Campus Climate Challenge was something youth anywhere could join by starting a project that organized young people around clean energy." This might mean installing campus solar panels, retrofitting buildings for energy efficiency, or getting schools to commit to 100 percent renewable power. "We wanted to leave it open-ended and not prescribe what to do."

Campus-based clean energy projects would eventually come to seem like an insufficient response to the climate crisis to architects of the fossil fuel divestment movement and other, more recent student-led campaigns. However, in the early 2000s the Campus Climate Challenge represented a groundbreaking effort to engage students all over the country while focusing on changing institutions, rather than individuals' behavior. EAC supported the growth of a generation of climate advocates, while advancing college sustainability policies the coalition hoped might one day serve as models for state and even federal legislation. No single organization could implement such an ambitious effort on its own, so EAC members agreed on broad goals for the Challenge and divided up the work. "Each group put forward a proposal for how many campuses they thought they could bring into the campaign. Then we added them up," Veazey said.[14]

This division of labor had obvious advantages but also came with a risk: most EAC members had to pay field staff who worked directly with students, and there was a danger of competition for resources. "[W]e knew we couldn't fundraise for our collective campaign in the normal, organization-versus-organization model," Jared Duval of the Sierra Student Coalition wrote in his 2010 book, *Next Generation Democracy*. And so, "[b]efore we made a single funding ask, we collectively decided what our overall budget would be and how we would distribute funds...Organizations could only ask for donations to the whole campaign, to be divided up as agreed on, not for grants to support their individual work."[15]

This meant SEAC, for example, would fundraise on behalf of not just SEAC but the wider Campus Climate Challenge. "As a result, folks used to working for their own, siloed organizations instead began raising funds for a campaign each of us only had a piece of, but which was larger than the sum of its parts," Duval said when I interviewed him in February 2020.[16]

During the first full year of the Campus Climate Challenge, in 2006, EAC leaders reported bringing in over three million dollars, nearly triple the amount raised for all student organizing around climate issues in the U.S. in 2003.[17] However, they still needed to spread the campaign to hundreds of colleges and universities.

Soon this effort was getting an unexpected boost from a small liberal arts school in Vermont, where students were grappling with how to spark a mass social movement around climate change.

A new climate movement?

A class called "Building the New Climate Movement" caused a stir at Middlebury College in January 2005. Taught by economics and environmental studies professor Jon Isham, its purpose was to help students not only learn about activism, but actually do it.

About a year earlier, Isham had attended a two-day conference at Case Western Reserve University, where academics working on sustainability exchanged insights with those studying social movements. "It was a perfectly fine event," he told me in January 2020. But sometimes the conversations felt frustratingly academic. "At one point I stood up and said that if any of this means anything, we should be talking about building a climate movement—like a march on Washington. Well, people sort of laughed."

The next morning, though, a handful of colleagues wanted to discuss Isham's idea. They stayed in touch after the conference. Slowly, the outline for the new Middlebury course took shape.[18]

Isham's students, like sophomore Jamie Henn, soon realized they were participating in something unusual. Class readings included Saul Alinsky's *Rules for Radicals* and books on the Civil Rights Movement. The students divided into working groups tasked with finding an activist campaign to contribute to. Henn's group began working with Billy Parish, who had visited the class as a guest speaker. "Billy would come up to Middlebury and spend the night on someone's couch," Henn told me. "Then we'd meet at the student café and brainstorm ideas for scaling up EAC's work."

With input from Parish, the Middlebury students came up with a plan for a bus tour to promote the Campus Climate Challenge while gathering signatures from young people in support of fuel-efficient cars. It would finish in the nation's auto heartland, where activists would deliver their petition to major carmakers. They called it the Road to Detroit.

Simultaneously, Henn and others started a new climate group on campus, envisioning it as something different from Middlebury's existing suite of sustainability-related organizations. "We didn't want to be just one more club," Henn said. "We were a collection of students who wanted to work together on something bigger." It took a while to settle on a name—but they met on the last day of the week, and eventually "Sunday Night Group" stuck. The students organized speaker events, bike rides to the State Capitol, and a campaign to make Middlebury carbon neutral. Meeting attendance swelled past one hundred, five percent of the student body.

That summer, Sunday Night Group members departed from Vermont on the Road to Detroit, in a biodiesel-powered school bus with plastic jugs of vegetable oil strapped to the roof. They picked up Parish in Washington, D.C. What nobody realized was that when vegetable oil sits for too long in the hot sun, it makes a chemical reaction that slowly corrodes plastic. This only became apparent when a deluge of oil suddenly streamed down the bus windows, reeking of French fries.[19]

Despite such mishaps, the Road to Detroit continued over the next couple months and 15,000 miles.[20] In Tennessee, Henn and core Sunday Night Group member May Boeve split off to work on media support from the Greenpeace office in San Francisco. "That meant being on lots of phone calls and sending a lot of emails,"

Henn said. "I guess there were Google Docs back then, but certainly no Zoom meetings."

Henn and Boeve later headed for Detroit to prepare for the bus's arrival. With the help of mutual activist acquaintances, they connected with one of the area's most legendary figures: labor and civil rights champion Grace Lee Boggs, now aged ninety, who welcomed the students with open arms. When Henn and Boeve mentioned they had no firm place to stay, Boggs invited them into her home. They spent their nights there for the next few weeks.

Boggs and other local activists helped the Middlebury students make new connections between issues like pollution, race, and workers' rights. "We were just some white kids from Vermont come to talk about clean cars," Henn said. "To then be exposed to a revolutionary workers' ideology was mind-blowing."[21]

The experience stuck with Henn and Boeve as they returned to Vermont and tried to take momentum from the Road to Detroit to the next level.

*

Middlebury student Will Bates wasn't in Jon Isham's climate class. However, he joined the Sunday Night Group and in 2006 became one of the first core members to graduate. The leaders were already discussing what came next. "We cared too deeply about climate work to say that now we're done with school it's time to move on," Bates recalled years later.

There was talk of moving to Montana to fight coal mining proposals there. But then the students began strategizing with Middlebury scholar-in-residence Bill McKibben, who was also thinking about how to ramp up the climate movement. Like most people, McKibben was once a young person; in fact, he wrote *The End of Nature*, the first major book about climate change for a general audience, in his twenties, perhaps making him one of the first youth climate activists. By 2006 he was in his forties, but he would play an important part in the growing youth movement. He was increasingly convinced writing books on climate change wasn't enough.

McKibben and the students knew about the important role of civil disobedience in past social movements. Now McKibben had visions of a multiday march across Vermont, culminating with a sit-in at the Burlington federal building. To ensure their actions would result in the spectacle they hoped for, Bates called the police department and asked what it would take to get one of his alma mater's most distinguished faculty thrown in jail. "They said we could sit at the federal building as long as we wanted and never be arrested," Bates remembered with a laugh, when I interviewed him in February 2020.

Soon the group came up with a new plan: a march across the state ending with a perfectly legal rally.[22] That Labor Day weekend, around a hundred people began the trek from the Robert Frost Memorial in Ripton to Burlington, a distance of forty miles which they covered in five days. They picked up more people along the way, and toward the end the crowd swelled to a thousand.[23] All candidates running for federal office in Vermont were invited to speak at the rally, but only if they pledged to support cutting carbon emissions 80 percent by 2050. Newspapers hailed it as the country's largest-ever climate protest.

"Our first reaction was, that's so cool," Henn said. "But the next moment we were like, it's actually really depressing. If some college kids and a writer in Vermont could pull off the biggest climate event in history, clearly the larger movement had a long way to go."[24]

Building a youth-led movement on the scale of past social uprisings would require hundreds more skilled organizers taking action on campuses all over the country. Many of Energy Action Coalition's member organizations had training programs meant to empower such new leadership. But one, the Sierra Student Coalition, devoted more resources to this goal than any other.

Training the movement

If every EAC member had a niche, the SSC's was training high school and college students to become activists—especially at annual, weeklong camps so central to the organization's work that they became affectionately known as "Sprog," short for "summer program." "Sprog gives young people the chance to learn how to make a campaign plan, how to work with the media, how to develop strategic communications, how to lobby," said Jared Duval when I interviewed him about his time at the helm of the SSC for this book.

I experienced Sprog in 2006, a few months after Evon Peter spoke to my PCC class. That spring, I had visited a campus club fair hoping to find an environmental group I could join. There weren't any, but a political science classmate suggested I fill out the paperwork to start one. I did so, despite not knowing the first thing about running an organization. I was tabling for the new club a few weeks later when a fellow student named Nathan Jones stopped by. He ran a similar group on a different PCC campus and was also a Sprog trainer. We got to talking and he suggested I apply to participate in Sprog.

That summer, I arrived at a Mountaineers cabin in Washington State for Northwest Sprog. Jared Duval gave an opening night presentation on the Campus Climate Challenge. Over the next several days I learned many of the nuts and bolts of grassroots organizing.

I also met other young activists from throughout the region, some of whom I would work with on future campaigns. They included JP Kemmick, a Pacific Lutheran University student who earlier that year organized some friends to stand by their cafeteria garbage cans and ask students emptying their trays if they intended to consume the leftovers. When the cafeteria-goers said "no," Kemmick's team made a point about waste by helping themselves to the food. The sight of students eating garbage alarmed the administration, which called Kemmick in for a meeting. He emerged having been offered a sustainability internship and the school paid for him to attend Sprog.[25] Stories like this inspired me with ideas for my own activism.

At Sprog, participants like me and Kemmick learned to draft meeting agendas, write a press release, talk with elected officials, and identify campaign targets. What we didn't learn much about was intersectional, justice-focused organizing. Conversations about those topics had not yet entered the mainstream environmental movement in a large way, and would only be incorporated into the Sprog curriculum years later. How far the movement still had to go can be seen from an incident at an early EAC meeting where Jihan Gearon—whom I introduced in Chapter 4—proposed that anti-oppression trainings be required for EAC leaders.

"I thought other young people would understand the need for this kind of work," Gearon remembered. "But that isn't what I experienced." Much of the room was initially enthusiastic, or at least willing to support the proposal, but a single representative from one of the larger environmental groups kept blocking it. Most discouragingly, Gearon and the few other youth of color present were almost the only ones refusing to back down. Although the proposal eventually passed, the training itself still left Gearon feeling disappointed. "Some people were moved, but it wasn't turned into an opportunity for deeper learning," she remembered years later.[26]

Today it is standard practice to incorporate anti-oppression training throughout events like Sprog. A summary of major themes from the Sprog 2021 website included "identifying and confronting oppression, running campaigns for justice, [and] emphasizing anti-oppression as central to all environmental organizing."[27] As a result, Sprog continues to play a vital role in the more justice-focused modern climate movement.

"Training with the SSC is how I went from being interested in climate change, to becoming a climate organizer," Amira Odeh, a 350.org leader in Puerto Rico, told me in April 2020. As a student at the University of Puerto Rico in 2011, Odeh saw a Sprog flyer posted on her campus. She had been trying to start a campaign to ban bottled water at the school, but didn't know where to begin. She attended Sprog that summer. "Thanks to what I learned, our campaign went from ten people to sixty in one semester," she said. "That's when I realized the power of trainings."[28]

As a Sprog alum myself, I could relate. And even as students like me prepared to return to school in late 2006, conversations were underway at EAC about how to replicate some of the best parts of the SSC's signature program on an even larger scale.

Power Shift, Power Vote

In early November 2007, nearly six thousand young people[29] converged on the University of Maryland for what was by far the largest gathering of U.S. climate activists up to that time. This was the first Power Shift, an event which for many activists would come to define EAC's work more than any other. The weekend summit included trainings on activist skills, panels and speeches from movement leaders, and a Monday morning lobby day on Capitol Hill. Organizing the gathering was a monumental task.

"Considering how relatively inexperienced we were then, it was a beautiful, audacious thing to pull off an event that size," said longtime activist Ethan Nuss, who recruited for Power Shift as the Maryland Campus Coordinator for the Chesapeake Climate Action Network (CCAN).

Nuss had received his first taste of activism while a student at University of Kansas, where he organized demonstrations against the Iraq War. He dreamed of being part of a transformative social movement like those of the 1960s. "But to me, social change was purely historical, not something I could ever experience," he told me in January 2020. Soon after moving to D.C. for a job working on peace issues, he began hearing about something called the "youth climate movement." "I was like, how do I sign up?"

In his new role at CCAN, Nuss sought to give other young people the feeling of belonging to a movement. The idea for a national summit to energize and inspire a generation of youth activists had long percolated in the back of EAC organizers' minds, and in 2007 the moment seemed right. The Campus Climate Challenge was active at hundreds of schools, EAC was gaining name recognition, and Billy Parish had been featured in *Rolling Stone*.[30] Now EAC leaders threw their energy into putting Power Shift together. For Shadia Fayne Wood (introduced in Chapter 4) this meant lots of late nights at her house in D.C. that served as a crashing place for organizers. "It was Power Shift all the time," Wood said. "It was exhausting, but there was beauty in it, too. There's a lot of community in living that way."[31]

Among the most-anticipated moments of Power Shift was when Nancy Pelosi addressed students in a keynote speech. "I love the name Power Shift," the recently installed House Speaker told the massive crowd gathered in UMD's basketball arena. But as she discussed a modest clean energy bill advancing through Congress, someone started chanting, "We want more." Additional voices joined in, until the words reverberated off the stadium walls. Pelosi paused.[32]

"For a moment I thought, no, we're going to offend her," Nuss recalled. "But then I realized Speaker Pelosi needed to hear this. We sent her the message that young people want something aligned with what science says we need in order to have a future."[33]

Thousands of students returned from Power Shift ready to put skills they had learned to good use. "I've heard so many stories from organizers who say Power Shift set them on the path to activism," Liz Veazey said.[34] For Parish, the summit "was about giving students a sense they were part of something important. Just seeing that many people come together in one place was incredibly empowering."[35]

These words rang true for me. In early 2009 I convinced three other students from Oregon's Pacific University, where I was then enrolled, to go with me to the second national Power Shift, which drew twelve thousand students to the Walter E. Washington Convention Center in D.C. At one point, I looked down from an interior balcony above the main hall as thousands of people streamed by below.

For the last two years I had labored to organize actions, first at PCC and then at Pacific, which I hoped would make a small difference to the climate crisis. The work was difficult, the near-term positive results hard to discern, and I often felt alone. Now, at Power Shift, I was surrounded by literally thousands of young people engaged in the same struggle.

For the first time, I knew viscerally what it meant to be part of something vastly larger than myself.

*

Almost a year after Power Shift 2007, a group of students fanned out through the crowd descending on Hofstra University for the final debate between Barack Obama and John McCain. The young activists' goal: get as many audience members as possible to sign a card pledging to vote for candidates who would act on climate change. This was EAC's newest campaign, Power Vote.

"We mailed the filled-out pledge cards to EAC," said Hofstra student Laura Comer, organizer of the debate petition drive. "Someone entered all the contact info into a database and emailed it back to us in a spreadsheet, so we could remind students to vote. It was like magic."[36]

Power Vote was an attempt to channel energy from events like Power Shift into establishing climate activists as a force in national elections. EAC leaders set a goal of gathering one million Power Vote pledges from Millennials all over the country. Of course, not every school was in the fortunate position of hosting a presidential debate, but at scores of colleges and universities Power Vote volunteers canvassed their peers and got them talking about the election's importance. In November they cast their ballots. The results of this effort were mixed, and a reminder of how difficult it is to shape electoral politics.

Although Obama rode to office in 2008 on a wave of high Millennial voter turnout,[37] Power Vote played only a minor role in this victory. EAC organizations brought in around 300,000 pledges, far less than the million-pledge goal and too small a number to establish a national voting bloc.[38] To be sure, Power Vote got plenty of individual young activists excited about politics and spurred them to become involved in the election—but on its more ambitious goals it came up short. The reality was that while the youth climate movement had made impressive strides, it wasn't yet big or politically savvy enough to sway national elections. The only antidote would be many more years of hard work and painful experience.

Some more recent electoral interventions by climate activists, like those of Sunrise Movement, look superficially similar to Power Vote. However, there are important differences. Sunrise has engaged around elections in a much more targeted fashion than EAC did in 2008, utilizing student volunteers to make thousands of phone calls and send tens of thousands of text messages in specific, high-impact races where such efforts can tip the balance.

Contrast this with Power Vote, a broad campaign to get students everywhere to vote with the climate in mind. To be effective, such a sweeping approach needed to reach truly massive numbers of people—and mobilizing swaths of the electorate on this scale was a task the climate movement was not yet prepared for. It was a hard but important lesson.

*

Any shortcomings of Power Vote aside, 2008 put in office a president and members of Congress who had pledged to act on climate change. And, hard to believe as it now seems, there was a real sense that lawmakers might deliver. Climate activists hoped federal legislation would pave the way for countries including the U.S. to sign a new climate treaty at COP15 in Copenhagen in late 2009. The second national Power Shift, in February of that year, included a lobby day on Capitol Hill designed to take advantage of the moment. Coordinating the event was Laura Comer, fresh off of leading Power Vote at Hofstra.

Comer's activities in the early climate movement are a good example of how EAC hoped young people would climb a ladder of engagement opportunities and take on positions of leadership. Comer first got engaged in the Campus Climate Challenge at Hofstra, then participated in the Greenpeace Organizing Term, a months-long intensive experience with one of the country's major environmental groups. This led to attending a Power Vote organizer training and leading the campaign on her campus. Now, a few months after the election, she was coordinating the Power Shift lobby day for an EAC government relations fellowship.

In the weeks before Power Shift, Comer was almost constantly on the phone scheduling meetings between Congressional offices and the thousands of young people about to arrive in D.C. There were too many calls to possibly make all of them herself, so she turned to the kind of creative solution activists sometimes substitute for magic. A team of women volunteers worked through the list of numbers, all introducing themselves over the phone as "Laura Comer." "Even so, we could hardly confirm meetings fast enough," Comer told me. "That's how many people were coming."

An unseasonable snowstorm blew in the night before the lobby day, leading some students to head home early and some members of Congress to cancel appointments. But despite slightly fewer meetings than planned, the event represented a high-water mark for youth climate activists' engagement with federal lawmakers.[39] Unfortunately, it wasn't enough to usher in the change they sought.

Later that year, Democrats in Congress introduced the American Clean Energy and Security Act, or ACES, a bill riddled with concessions to polluters. It didn't represent a compromise so much as a judgement on the part of Congressional leaders that anything more ambitious had no chance of moving forward. Perhaps that assessment was miscalculated.

A decade later, Sunrise Movement blamed the defeat of ACES on environmental groups' failure to activate a vocal grassroots support base. Perhaps just as important was the inability of the bill's backers to unite climate organizations behind their cause. Some groups saw ACES as worse than nothing. "The giveaways and preferences in the bill will actually spur a new generation of nuclear and coal-fired power plants to the detriment of real energy solutions," read a statement from Greenpeace.[40]

Passing any climate bill would have been difficult, but without enthusiastic backing from the whole climate movement it was almost impossible. No one will ever know for sure if a stronger bill would have fared better, and it seems equally possible that the climate movement at the time simply wasn't big enough to push any meaningful legislation over the finish line. However, it should be no surprise that ACES failed. By late 2009, the bill's demise in the Senate appeared all but certain. It died the following year.

Hope and disappointment at COP15

In December 2009, Kelly Lynch directed an army of activists dressed as aliens from Planet B, who wandered the halls of COP15 asking to be taken to Earth's climate leaders.[41] The stunt captured the sense of optimism mixed with desperation many activists felt at this pivotal U.N. meeting, nine years before the one where Greta Thunberg first castigated heads of state. The warnings of climate scientists had grown ever more dire since Lynch attended COP6 in 2000, and now the new youth climate movement converged on what was being heralded as the most important COP gathering yet.[42]

"It was a hopeful time," Lynch said. "Obama was president and after years of inaction from the United States, COP15 was supposed to be where a binding global climate treaty would finally be signed."[43] True, climate legislation in Congress was all but dead, but activists still believed the Obama administration could deliver for them.

Nobody captured this feeling of hopefulness better than the recently founded 350.org, which grew from the efforts of Middlebury College students involved in the Sunday Night Group. After their 2006 march across Vermont, Sunday Night leaders including Jamie Henn, May Boeve, and Will Bates worked with Bill McKibben to launch Step It Up, a campaign that pressured presidential hopefuls to support cutting carbon emissions 80 percent by 2050. In April 2007, they organized a national day of action with small events distributed across the country. "We expected maybe a hundred actions," Bates said. "When we ended up with 1,400, it felt like a dream come true."[44] Presidential candidate John Edwards agreed to support the 80 percent goal at a Step It Up event,[45] with Hillary Clinton and Obama announcing similar pledges soon after.[46]

At COP13, two years before the crucial Copenhagen meeting, the Step It Up team connected with activists from all over the planet who came to Bali, Indonesia to participate in the summit. "We realized there was this incredible worldwide movement forming around climate," Henn said. "But it had never really united across the globe. We wondered if we could make that happen."[47] The result was 350.org, an international campaign named after the upper safe limit for parts-per-million atmospheric carbon dioxide. In October 2009, during the leadup to COP15, the new organization coordinated a global day of action with over five thousand events in the U.S. and 180 other countries.[48] The level of participation said something about how much climate activists' hopes rode on COP. Some groups were sober about the likely outcome, though.

"For eight years, the George W. Bush administration worked to stall the COP process," said Kyle Gracey, then the executive director of SustainUs, an organization that engages young people around U.N. climate gatherings. While other activist groups participated sporadically in past COP summits, SustainUs had been deeply immersed in the complex U.N. negotiations for years, and its leaders went into Copenhagen with a clearer view than most. "Obama was certainly better than Bush," Gracey said. "But he never promised to deliver what the science said we needed."[49]

Midway through COP, an estimated hundred thousand people marched through Copenhagen's streets in support of a strong climate treaty.[50] There were candlelit vigils and hunger strikes. Yet, in the final days of the conference, major economies forged an agreement that did little more than keep the COP process going. "There was a real sense something greater could have been accomplished, which made the blow even worse," Bates said.

The experience of Laura Comer—who bought a one-way ticket to Copenhagen after finishing her last exams at Hofstra—captures what many of the young people I've talked to about COP15 felt at the time. As the inconclusive talks were wrapping up, she stepped into an elevator where President Mohamed Nasheed of the island nation of Maldives was sobbing uncontrollably. "Before that, I'd still had faith in the U.N. climate process," Comer said. "But my community wasn't going to be the one underwater."

A photo of Comer crying on a train in Copenhagen, a candle and photo of President Obama in her hands, appeared in a story about the COP15 debacle at the top of the *Al Jazeera News* website. "I was like, why me?" Comer said of her reaction at becoming, if only for a moment, a symbol of the gathering's failure. "There I was, a white girl who'd been afforded opportunities as a climate organizer because I had the resources to pack up my life and head to Washington or Copenhagen. I was affected by climate change as a young person, but not to the same degree as lots of people."

Discouraged, and with conflicted feelings about the privilege she carried, Comer took a hiatus from climate work after COP15 and became a sixth-grade teacher for a few years, before returning to the movement as a Sierra Club organizer.[51] Her doubts mirrored questions many activists who had been at Copenhagen were asking: Where did the movement go next? What was the best use of their energy? And how to reconcile the movement's stated commitment to justice with the privilege key groups brought to the table?

In hindsight, COP15 turned out to be not an ending, but a turning point. After a period of regrouping, the climate movement emerged ready to escalate its use of nonviolent tactics and eventually coalesced around a strategy of challenging the fossil fuel industry directly. The next few chapters will treat these developments at length. First, though, it's worth reflecting on the fate of Energy Action Coalition and other groups at the vanguard of youth climate activism in the '00s.

Things we know now

All activist organizations reach a peak in their influence, and EAC's probably came in 2009, the year of COP15 and the second Power Shift. While future Power Shifts would continue inspiring thousands of young people, the role of the coalition as a center of climate movement gravity declined as other groups rose in prominence. The Campus Climate Challenge was gradually eclipsed by divestment campaigns, the Green New Deal, and school strikes for the climate. As for Power Vote, the campaign saw reprises in future elections but never again united most youth climate organizations behind it as in 2008. Over time, EAC became less known for running campaigns and more closely associated with the Power Shift summits. Meanwhile, calls for a radically new approach to anti-oppression work within the coalition grew louder.

"A few women of color organizers pushed us to incorporate anti-oppression in EAC in a way that was critically important," said Liz Veazey, referring to leaders like Jihan Gearon and Shadia Fayne Wood. "We didn't appreciate enough what they were doing at the time, but they helped me and hopefully a lot of other white organizers come to better understand our privilege."[52]

Veazey transitioned to a backseat role at EAC when she started grad school at University of Oregon in 2010. By then, many other founders had already moved on. Billy Parish stepped down as coordinator in 2007, going to work with Black Mesa Water Coalition for a while before founding the clean energy startup Solar Mosaic.[53] Kelly Lynch remained a fulltime activist.[54] In 2015, Veazey briefly took EAC's helm again as interim executive director, at a time when funding was drying up and the coalition's viability seemed uncertain. One of her main tasks was to recruit a new long-term director. She succeeded when EAC hired Lydia Avila, a leader Veazey described to me as "amazing."[55]

The daughter of Mexican immigrants, Avila grew up outside Los Angeles and majored in environmental studies at UCLA. After graduation in 2010, an internship with the Sierra Club brought her to Texas to work with farmers, ranchers, and shrimpers on a successful campaign to defeat a proposed coal plant. "Moving to Texas was a culture shock, but also one of the best experiences I ever had," Avila said when I spoke with her in March 2020. "After we won, I thought, how can I ever do anything else? Organizing works."

In 2011, Avila attended the third national Power Shift as a trainer. "Being surrounded by ten thousand young people fighting for the climate was unbelievable," she said. "I left knowing I wanted to be part of the organization who made that happen." A few years later, when a friend mentioned EAC was seeking an executive director, she applied.

Only after settling into her role did Avila learn of EAC's fraught history with marginalized communities, whose calls for change often felt unheard. "That was hard for me, as the first person of color to lead the organization. I'd had no idea." As though this wasn't enough, she had to contend with a proposal for addressing the coalition's other challenges by transforming it into a network.[56]

While coalitions have central decision-making bodies that steer an alliance of groups, networks are fundamentally decentralized. Rather than implementing campaigns from the top down, they create opportunities to collaborate. EAC was no longer prepared to plan campaigns as a coalition, but it could continue as a convening body for the climate movement, most obviously through the Power Shift gatherings. It rebranded as the Power Shift Network (PSN) and embarked on a year-long restructuring process. As part of the transition, Avila determined to make a clean break with the troubled past. The new network reconstituted its membership with organizations hand-picked for their commitment to social justice.[57]

Today, most PSN staff are people of color.[58] Other early climate groups have also diversified, though to varying degrees. "When 350.org started, they were a bunch of white college kids and Bill McKibben," said Jon Isham of Middlebury. "Today, if you look at the organization's messaging, who runs it, and the staffing, it's much more diverse. That's a dramatic transformation."[59]

When Zero Hour was getting off the ground in early 2018, nearly a decade after COP15, Jamie Margolin attended a PSN event for young climate movement leaders. She connected with organizers like Avila, who provided support and advice for Zero Hour's day of marches that July, a point I will revisit in Chapter 9. "Power Shift Network is doing the behind-the-scenes work that allows organizations like Zero Hour to win," Margolin wrote in a fundraising appeal for PSN later that summer.[60] With its diverse leadership and focus on marginalized voices, Zero Hour is an example of the kind of effort the network has sought to incubate.

The work of centering frontline communities in the climate movement is far from over. However, there has been real progress in at least some quarters. "Young people who came into PSN after its rebranding weren't influenced by the problematic parts of its history," Avila explained to me. "To them it was all new. Youth of color and students from all backgrounds found it an exciting, welcoming space."[61]

*

Radical changes in strategy, increased focus on diversity and inclusion, and the emergence of many new activist groups: all of this still lay in store for the youth climate movement at the conclusion of COP15 in 2009. Yet, at the time, most climate activists only knew the forces they were up against had proved to be even more powerful than they thought. "We have lost this battle," a COP delegate from Bolivia—one of the countries pushing for a stronger deal—said after talks in Copenhagen concluded, according to a blog post Kelly Lynch wrote soon after. "But we will win the war because of the strength of the youth."[62]

There could be little doubt now that a vibrant climate movement—an idea which made the academics gathered at Case Western laugh just a few years earlier—now existed in the U.S. and abroad. It hadn't won in Copenhagen, but nor was it going away.

In her post-COP15 reflection, Lynch recorded what another delegate from one of the African countries reportedly said about the new climate movement: "It takes a lot to get an elephant moving, but when you do it is hard to stop...[and] the elephant is [now] moving."

"The task ahead is to make the elephant move in the right direction," Lynch wrote. "And fast."[63]

6

A Stand Worth Taking

DIRECT ACTION AND A BRAVER MOVEMENT

On December 19, 2008, a twenty-seven-year-old University of Utah student named Tim DeChristopher walked into a Bureau of Land Management oil and gas auction and out-bid every company in the room, "winning" over $1.7 million worth of land he couldn't pay for.[1] His actions sent shock waves through a climate movement unused to such disruptive tactics, later inspiring young activists who were disillusioned by the failure of COP15. But when he first entered the auction, DeChristopher knew only that he wanted to derail a process threatening his generation's survival.[2]

Earlier that day, DeChristopher had joined a protest outside the building in Salt Lake City where the BLM was holding a controversial drilling rights sale. At issue were 150,000 acres near Arches and Canyonlands National Parks put up for auction by the outgoing Bush administration. Environmental groups had tried unsuccessfully to stop the auction in court. Now, activists gathered on the sidewalk holding signs.[3]

Protesting outside didn't feel like enough to DeChristopher. "I suggested to some people I knew that we go in the building," he said when I spoke with him in October 2020. "Maybe we could cause a disruption. They said, 'No, security won't let you in.' I said, 'Then let's make a statement by getting dragged away.'"

DeChristopher was prepared to risk arrest, but getting into the building proved easier than he expected. A security guard at the door asked if he was there for the auction. On replying yes, De-Christopher was directed to a desk where a BLM staffer inquired if he was a bidder. Again, he answered yes, thinking it was the only way to get in. The staffer gave him a bidding paddle marked with the number seventy.

Only in the auction room did DeChristopher realize a few other activists had gained entrance as observers, something he hadn't known was possible. Now he was surrounded by oil company representatives raising their paddles to bid on blocks of land. It was an efficient, strangely dispassionate process; had an alien anthropologist been watching, they would have thought mere numbers, not living pieces of Earth's crust, were involved. DeChristopher, who had led trips for at-risk youth in Utah's wildlands, abhorred the thought of drilling in such places. What worried him most, though, was the underground carbon these companies planned to extract and burn. As bidders lifted their paddles, he came up with a plan.[4]

DeChristopher began raising his own paddle to bid on parcels, driving up their price. Eventually, he started winning blocks outright. By the time BLM officials realized something was amiss, the university student had "bought" rights to 22,000 acres he had no ability to pay for. The room erupted in chaos as security escorted him outside.[5]

Another activist ran after the news reporters who were leaving for the day. Thanks to her quick thinking, a wall of media cameras greeted DeChristopher when he stepped out of the building.[6] One reporter remarked that he seemed unrepentant about what he'd done. "Yes," DeChristopher said, smiling thoughtfully. "I think that would be fair to say."[7]

The story of Bidder 70

By the time I interviewed DeChristopher for this book in October 2020, his story had appeared in hundreds of articles, TV segments, and interviews with prominent publications. There was even a documentary, *Bidder 70*, about him. During our Zoom meeting, he wore the same serious expression and warm smile I recognized from photos. All that was missing was the signature red bandana he used to wear around his neck.

DeChristopher's disruption at the 2008 auction was an example of what activists call "direct action," or sometimes "civil disobedience." Although often used interchangeably, these terms have slightly different meanings. According to Joshua Kahn Russell of the Ruckus Society, to take direct action is "to change our circumstances [ourselves], without handing our power to a middle person."[8]

On entering the auction room, DeChristopher didn't ask BLM staff to call off the oil and gas sale, which would have been pointless at this juncture. Instead, he acted to stop it himself, at least temporarily. His disruption caused the auction to be rescheduled, delaying it until the new Obama administration took office and cancelled it on a technicality.[9]

By bidding on land he couldn't pay for, DeChristopher violated the federal Oil and Gas Leasing Reform Act. Some activists would therefore consider what he did to be not only direct action, but civil disobedience. There are differing opinions on this point.

Russell classifies civil disobedience as "a specific form of direct action that involves intentionally violating a law because that law is unjust." Examples include lunch counter sit-ins during the 1960s Civil Rights Movement. By this definition, not every illegal protest is civil disobedience. Sometimes activists violate the law, but "the law being broken isn't the point [of the protest]. For example, we may be guilty of trespassing if we drop a banner from a building, but the violation is incidental: we aren't there to protest trespassing laws."[10]

Other activists use "civil disobedience" to refer to any protest involving illegal activity. Either way, not all direct action is civil disobedience. For example, a direct action tactic used by the Rainforest Action Network to protest banks' financing of coal has involved covering ATM screens with removable stickers that replace the usual withdrawal and deposit options with "Bankroll Climate Change" and "Invest in Coal-Fired Power Plants." The intervention doesn't damage the ATM and arguably violates no law.

By the time of the BLM auction, "I'd been building up a commitment to engaging in civil disobedience," DeChristopher told me. "I had been involved in climate activism for a couple years, mostly at the local level. I looked at how the national climate movement was operating and saw the contrast with historical social uprisings."[11]

In 2008, the U.S. climate movement's largest activist gathering to date—Power Shift 2007—focused on lobbying Congress. There had been no truly massive street mobilizations and not much large-scale direct action. This made climate activism very different from previous progressive movements, even within environmentalism.

One of the earliest examples of direct action for an environmental cause in the U.S. happened in 1982, when hundreds of residents of North Carolina's predominantly Black Warren County were arrested blocking construction of a toxic waste dump in their community.[12] Later in the '80s and '90s, activists affiliated with Earth First! blockaded logging roads and sat in trees to save old-growth forests. Greenpeace famously steered boats between whales and harpoon ships. But in the '00s, climate activists had yet to adopt similar tactics on a large scale. According to DeChristopher, "The movement's strategy was one of appeasement, appealing to people in power and trying to convince them we could have a world that's cleaner and greener but leaves existing social structures in place. It wasn't working. Successful movements have always had a big, radical vision that threatens the top of the power structure."[13]

Justice-focused organizations like EJCC wanted a radically changed society, but they were largely drowned out by the conciliatory approach of most mainstream environmental groups. "That messaging wasn't appealing to the broad swath of people who were marginalized under the existing system," DeChristopher said. "Climate activists needed to start confronting those in power publicly enough that people who could be our allies in a real climate justice movement would see we weren't just trying to appease their oppressors."[14]

DeChristopher wasn't the first person to come to such a conclusion. But the path by which he got there is a particularly compelling example of action in the face of despair.

*

DeChristopher was born in rural West Virginia, where his mother was an early opponent of mountaintop removal mining, or MTR.[15] The practice of MTR is just what it sounds like: it involves blasting the tops off mountains to reach underground coal seams. Although Appalachia has been coal country since the 1800s, MTR became common only in the 1990s. It later underwent a dramatic expansion under the George W. Bush administration.[16]

DeChristopher's family left West Virginia when he was eight, but the scars on the mountains informed his later activism. "Coal companies made our home so unlivable, my parents insisted we get out," he said. "When Utah lawmakers wanted to sell the state to fossil fuel companies, I felt it as a personal attack. I wasn't going to let them destroy another home of mine."[17]

In 2008, DeChristopher had perhaps the most fateful encounter of his life at the University of Utah's annual Wallace Stegner Symposium on conservation. One of that year's speakers, Dr. Terry Root of the Intergovernmental Panel on Climate Change, presented findings from the IPCC's latest synthesis report. Looking at Root's charts and graphs, it struck DeChristopher that the lines showing carbon emission cuts needed to avoid catastrophic climate change were far out of sync with those illustrating projections of actual pollution trends.

Agitated, DeChristopher went up to Root after the presentation and asked if he'd read the data correctly. Root answered glumly that he had. The reason she hadn't pointed out more explicitly how dire the situation is, was because she didn't want her audience to lose hope.[18]

*

Many people who confront the full implications of the climate crisis remain stuck in the first stage of grief: denial. Others get bogged down by despair. DeChristopher went through a time of mourning, as if for the death of a loved one. But if societal collapse caused by climate change was inevitable, it was time to ask what the world that rose from the ashes would look like. Would we recreate old, unjust systems or build something better?[19]

"Civil disobedience is one way social movements challenge those in power," DeChristopher told me. By the time of the drilling auction in Salt Lake City, he knew he wanted to help spark a shift toward direct action in the climate movement. But how?

Here, I saw a chance to ask DeChristopher a question that had intrigued me for years. I too had participated in direct action, I explained, though never with the consequences he faced. I knew that after the fact, activists tend to emphasize the spontaneous aspects of such protests rather than the painstaking planning that usually goes into them. A principled person suddenly deciding to take a stand makes a good story—but there is almost always more to it. Most direct action involves careful strategizing, research into legal repercussions, and training for participants.

DeChristopher had always implied publicly that posing as a bidder hadn't occurred to him until he entered the auction. But surely, I suggested, he must have had at least some idea beforehand what he was going to do.

"Not at all." DeChristopher smiled wryly. "I thought maybe I'd make a speech in the auction room and cause a disturbance. It was only when I got inside that I saw the opportunity to do something more impactful."[20]

In deciding to raise his bidder's paddle, DeChristopher joined a growing number of climate activists who were beginning to nudge their movement in a more radical, confrontational direction.

A new tide rising

On July 10, 2006, people flooded onto the only access road to Virginia's Clinch River coal plant, shutting down work for the day. Some sat in front of the facility's entrance. Others locked themselves to a coal truck to prevent it moving.[21] "It was a party in the street," remembered Brian Frank, a recent Evergreen State College graduate involved in organizing the protest.[22]

The two groups behind the direct action were the grassroots collective Earth First!, whose slogan is "No compromise in defense of Mother Earth," and the brand-new Rising Tide North America.[23] Originally a European movement, Rising Tide was founded in 2000 by activists at COP6 who were frustrated with the slow U.N. negotiation process.[24] Chapters spread across Europe, Australia, and the Americas. Rising Tide sought to bring a style of protest to climate organizing that more closely resembled the disruptive anti-globalization movement than the work of most large environmental groups.

Rising Tide's arrival in the U.S. was thanks to a loose network of organizers like Frank, many of whom got their start as activists outside the climate movement. When I interviewed him in May 2020, Frank told me he "hadn't been paying too much attention to climate change" when he graduated from Evergreen in 2001. "I was aware of the issue, but it wasn't my top concern."

Instead, Frank joined protests against sweatshops and global trade deals in college. He also got involved in Earth First!, whose priority in the Northwest was to stop old-growth logging. Mainstream environmental groups' approach to climate advocacy didn't appeal to him. But in 2005, he participated in Mountain Justice Summer, a program recruiting young people to work with communities affected by mountaintop removal mining.

In the hills and hollers of Appalachia, Frank encountered a resistance to fossil fuel extraction reminiscent of the more radical movements he knew.[25]

*

A small group of young people met in the entomology building at Virginia Tech University in December 2006. Surrounded by drawers filled with thousands of preserved insects—evidence of Earth's rich biodiversity—they discussed the next phase of Mountain Justice Summer, then entering its third year. They were accustomed to such makeshift quarters.

"[Our] meetings aren't parliamentary," wrote Mountain Justice organizer Willie Dodson of Virginia in a blog post soon after the gathering. "The campaign is not funded (and I mean seriously not funded). The people aren't so-called experts. Mountain Justice is a non-hierarchical, decentralized movement of people who believe in their own power."[26]

Dodson and others at the Virginia Tech meeting assessed progress they had made so far. Mountain Justice was founded in 2004, partly in response to a tragedy. At 2:30am on an August morning, a road building operation at a Virginia A&G Coal Company mountaintop removal mine had dislodged a thousand-pound boulder which rolled down the mountainside and crashed through the wall of a house as the family within slept, crushing three-year-old Jeremy Davidson to death.[27]

For locals fed up with the coal industry, this felt like the last straw. "[Mountaintop removal] is eco-cide and culture-cide, destroying not only some of Earth's most biodiverse temperate forest ecosystems, but also upheaving and displacing human communities where such mining occurs," Dodson wrote. Young Davidson's death seemed the ultimate symbol of how coal companies were treating mountain communities.

The first Mountain Justice Summer, in 2005, drew inspiration from the Civil Rights Movement's 1964 Freedom Summer. Appalachian volunteers hosted dozens of activists, many of them young people like Frank, who came from around the country to learn about mountaintop removal, participate in protests at mine sites, and strategize about how to build a national movement to stop the ravaging of Appalachia.[28]

Later that same year, Frank traveled to New Orleans to assist with relief after Hurricane Katrina. In the storm's wreckage he saw the impacts of extreme weather firsthand. "That experience and my time with Mountain Justice got me thinking that the movements I'd been involved in up to then felt a bit too narrow," he said. "I'd been missing the broader, encompassing issue of climate. A lot of other people in Earth First! were having similar thoughts, and we started talking."[29]

Some of the activists had been in contact with Rising Tide chapters abroad, and saw in this existing international organization a model for what they wanted to do. The Clinch River coal blockade was Rising Tide North America's debut action.[30]

Soon, local Rising Tide chapters began popping up all over the U.S. Many had ties to Earth First!, but while the two organizations often worked together, their relationship was complicated by problematic parts of the latter's history which Rising Tide sought to leave behind. These ghosts from the past were one reason people like Frank decided to form a new organization for climate-focused direct action in the first place.

Unrest in Cascadia

About the time that Rising Tide North America was getting off the ground, University of Oregon student Jasmine Zimmer-Stucky learned a cache of old Earth First! tree-climbing equipment was stored beneath the house in Eugene where she lived. The gear had once been used to stage tree-sits in Oregon's shrinking old-growth forests. Its presence in the basement of the Lorax, a cooperatively run, student-owned building, was a reminder of how one of the highest-profile direct action campaigns in environmental movement history collapsed.[31]

I first met Zimmer-Stucky during my own years in Oregon's climate movement. When I interviewed her over Zoom for this book, it was a sunny day in the small town in the Columbia River Gorge where she now lives. When she turned the phone's camera to show me her surroundings, I glimpsed blue sky and big conifer trees. It was the kind of idyllic Northwest landscape that reminds many of us environmental activists from the region what we're trying to defend.

On college field trips to Oregon's surviving pockets of old-growth in the '00s, I stared up in amazement at the canopies of ancient Douglas-firs with branches as wide around as the trunks of smaller trees. Zimmer-Stucky played an important role in relaunching the campaign to protect such giants, building on the ruins of what just a decade earlier had been a vibrant movement to oppose logging. "By the early 2000s, forest defense direct action in Oregon had effectively shut down," she said during our interview. "FBI persecution certainly played a role, but so did the types of evil things that accompany unchecked power within movements."[32]

In a series of post-9/11 operations widely known as the Green Scare, undercover FBI agents targeted Earth First! and other groups involved in the anti-logging protests for which Eugene was a hub, prosecuting activists accused of property damage as though they were dangerous terrorists. This operation contributed to the direct action campaign's downfall—but it might have survived, if not for unhealthy power dynamics tearing it apart from inside.

A culture of toxic masculinity permeated forest defense gatherings in the '90s and early '00s. Sexual assault became rampant. In a 2018 academic paper, Kiera James Anderson of Simon Fraser University explores how this dynamic played out at the Fall Creek tree-sit encampment in Willamette National Forest near Eugene. According to Anderson, "repeated acts of interpersonal [sexual] violence...at Fall Creek were representative of a wider pattern within anarchist-oriented environmentalist circles in Eugene as well as tree-sitting campaigns throughout Oregon and Washington."

A macho atmosphere that celebrated physically challenging tasks like scaling trees dominated at Fall Creek and proved a breeding ground for rape and assault. Victims who spoke out were ostracized. Schisms between activists who supported accountability and those refusing to accept it split the movement. Eugene's forest defense network eventually severed ties with the Fall Creek encampment, which dissolved soon afterward.[33]

By the late '00s, many Earth First! networks were making real if belated efforts to root out internal oppression. Even so, there was a tendency for the collective's gatherings to emphasize male leadership while undervaluing the contributions of women. The movement also never attracted people of color in large numbers. "Rising Tide wanted to avoid all that baggage," Frank explained to me.[34] The guiding principles for Rising Tide North America state that, "The 'natural' disasters caused by climate change amplify the injustices inherent in a capitalist, racist, and patriarchal society."[35] The organization sees combatting social injustice both within and outside the movement as essential to its climate work.

Similarly, Zimmer-Stucky and other young Eugene activists envisioned a new anti-logging direct action campaign which would move past the trauma of earlier years. "We asked around and found someone with the code to the Lorax basement door," Zimmer-Stucky said. "I think it was 'weed,' or something equally obvious. We walked in and realized we were looking at everything we'd need for a summer of forest defense."[36]

In July 2009, fifty people blocked a logging road in Oregon's Elliott State Forest with their bodies, the first such action in the region in years.[37] Some were part of Cascadia Earth First! Others, including Zimmer-Stucky, belonged to a recently formed local Rising Tide chapter concerned about not only the preservation of wildlife habitat, but deforestation's contribution to climate change.[38] Twenty-seven protesters, most in their late teens and early twenties, were arrested for "interference with agricultural operations."[39] Two years later a more elaborate action involving three road blockades and a tree-sit built on the 2009 protest. A reinvigorated forest defense movement that emphasized climate had arrived in Oregon.[40]

The rise of new direct action campaigns in the Northwest and Appalachia—not to mention Tim DeChristopher's disruptive protest in Utah—were signs of a nonviolent but more confrontational brand of climate activism gaining ground. At the end of 2009, this movement received an injection of energy from U.S. activists who were exposed to the tactics of climate organizers from around the world at COP15.

Copenhagen lessons

Three days before the conclusion of negotiations at COP15—where activists' hopes for a binding climate treaty crumbled—dozens of young people sat in the main hall of Copenhagen's Bella Center, where the talks took place, and began reading aloud the names of 11 million signatories to a petition in support of a strong climate treaty. They didn't intend to move, they said, "until a fair, ambitious, and legally binding treaty [is] reached."[41]

Things had grown increasingly tense in Copenhagen since world leaders started arriving several days earlier. Midway through COP, as prospects for a treaty dimmed, police corralled and arrested hundreds of climate advocates participating in mass demonstrations.[42] Activists reported being harassed even when not engaged in direct action. University of Maryland student Amy Dewan wrote of a friend being "bludgeoned in the face" by officers while attempting to cross a bridge to join a protest. "It showed how scared the elites are of us," Dewan said. "They simply would not let us assemble."[43]

It was in this atmosphere that the Bella Center sit-in unfolded. Knowing the likelihood of arrest was high, the young participants met beforehand and discussed what consequences they were willing to face. According to Vassar College student Moey Newbold, "The first level of involvement was to read names from the petition and leave when the police gave their dispersal warning. Other people decided to stay through a second warning, or until they were arrested."[44]

The group followed a similar process to that used in planning most climate movement direct actions. Having agreed on an objective—to remain in the Bella Center as long as possible—they assessed the likely consequences. Then each person decided how much risk they were willing to take.

For U.S. students like Newbold, protests where their freedom and safety might be on the line were unfamiliar. Young people from some other countries would have found the experience less strange. For the last few years, mass protests against a liquefied natural gas project in Rossport, Ireland had persisted in the face of police brutality and arrests.[45] In 2006, hundreds of people surrounded and attempted to shut down the Drax coal plant in the U.K.[46] Now, large numbers of U.S. young people came into contact with peers from these and other countries.

Nor was the impact limited to students physically present in Copenhagen. More than at any previous U.N. climate gathering, activists and reporters broadcast developments live on blogs, Twitter, and other social media. Thousands of people watched events at COP15 unfold in real time. I was among them; I had graduated from Pacific University that spring, and was trying to stay involved in climate activism while I searched for a job. I shared in the feelings of hope turned to despair so many activists experienced as talks in Copenhagen collapsed. About the only bright spots, it seemed, were acts of resistance organized by young people like those in the Bella Center sit-in. They provided a glimpse of the way ahead.

"It's important for us at home to build on the momentum from our friends in Denmark," wrote Louise Yeung of SustainUs, in a blog post published during COP15 from the organization's D.C. office.[47] Some of this activism would take the form of lobbying.

Newbold returned home to the U.S. and helped organize a last, desperate effort led by college students to pass the climate bill stalled in the Senate. Yet, it was increasingly clear conventional advocacy tactics would not, on their own, be enough to pass climate legislation in the United States.

As they searched for a new path forward, many young U.S. activists found inspiration in the example of Tim DeChristopher.

Becoming inconvenient

"This kind of event is not going to be enough to stand against the injustices we are on track for," DeChristopher said in a keynote address at Power Shift 2011 in Washington, D.C. "There's a lot about this movement that feels really good and is really convenient, but that isn't preparing us for what's ahead."[48]

This wasn't the typical up-beat, positive Power Shift speech. During Power Shift 2007 four years earlier, DeChristopher himself had been inspired by a YouTube broadcast of Billy Parish addressing Congress. Parish "was the first young person I'd heard speak about the climate with a voice of moral authority," DeChristopher told me. "Out in Utah, I realized other people felt what I was feeling and that there was potential for us to have a real movement."[49] But now the time had arrived for a different kind of truth-telling. "We're not going to meet [this challenge] in a way that fits into our school schedules," DeChristopher told Power Shift 2011 participants. "We're not going to meet it in a way that we can avoid sacrificing."[50]

The very fact that Energy Action Coalition invited DeChristopher to speak at Power Shift indicated a mood change in the wider youth climate movement. The previous national Power Shift, in 2009, featured Obama administration officials like Interior Secretary Ken Salazar and EPA head Lisa Jackson. The administration was pressing charges against DeChristopher, who was found guilty of violating federal oil and gas law in a widely publicized trial in March 2011.[51] He now awaited sentencing at a court hearing scheduled for that summer. The maximum punishment for his crime was ten years in prison.[52]

In the leadup to Power Shift 2009, DeChristopher recruited Utah students to attend the summit and the concurrent Capitol Climate Action, a nonviolent protest where more than two thousand people surrounded and blocked entrances to the coal-fired power plant that heated Capitol Hill.[53] Spearheaded by Greenpeace, it was one of the first examples of large-scale direct action in the U.S. climate movement.[54] However, although timed to coincide with Power Shift, the Capitol Climate Action was a separate event which not all EAC leaders embraced.

"We were told we couldn't do training or outreach in the Power Shift venue," said longtime activist Matt Leonard, then of Greenpeace, who played a major role organizing the illegal protest. "So, we rented a building across the street and each day thousands of youth came over from Power Shift for direct action trainings. I got screamed at more than a few times for that."[55]

Two years later, the wider climate movement had embraced at least the concept of direct action to the point where inviting DeChristopher to speak at Power Shift 2011 seemed natural. The former University of Utah student had plenty of experience addressing large crowds by then—partly thanks to a support network that used his story as a rallying point for climate organizing in Salt Lake City.

*

Riding home on a TRAX train after the fateful oil and gas auction, DeChristopher took out his phone and began calling friends who could help him figure out what to do next. Most were locals who shared his views on civil disobedience. "I told them, 'Hey, I just did this thing. Now we need a plan.'"

The first friend he reached happened to have a political blogger in the house. Within twenty-four hours, they had set up a bidder70.org website. In the days that followed, a loose network of University of Utah students and others from Salt Lake City's progressive activist community discussed how to capitalize on publicity from DeChristopher's upcoming court dates.

"It turned out what I thought about the need for a climate movement that's bolder and engages in civil disobedience resonated with a lot of people," DeChristopher said. One of the group's first projects was to raise $1.7 million in grassroots donations to pay for DeChristopher's auction winnings. When the BLM refused to accept the money, the activists used the funds to launch an organization called Peaceful Uprising to advance DeChristopher's vision for a confrontational climate movement.[56]

Rather than accept a plea deal in exchange for lesser penalties, DeChristopher was determined to bring his case to trial in a way that drew attention to the climate crisis. His support network got help from organizers with groups like Greenpeace and the Ruckus Society—including Henia Belalia, a San Francisco-based Greenpeace campaigner who later became Peaceful Uprising's executive director.

"We live in a country with a fine, long-standing tradition of civil resistance—of ordinary citizens taking action to contest and eventually transform unjust laws," Belalia wrote in a Greenpeace blog post. "As people concerned for the future, we stand with this courageous young man for acting on his belief, for standing up to create the just world he wants to see."[57] This message resonated with a growing number of people.

Peaceful Uprising was never just about the plight of one individual, though. "We had to walk a tricky line between capitalizing on the attention I was getting and translating that into a focus on the broader climate movement," DeChristopher said. Peaceful Uprising spearheaded direct action campaigns against polluting industries in Salt Lake City, like a Rio Tinto-owned coal-fired copper smelter.[58] Yet, in his Power Shift speech, it was the plight of communities in his home state of West Virginia to which DeChristopher returned. He encouraged the thousands of young people listening to picture what sustained mass direct action would really look like:

> [With] these ten thousand people [at Power Shift]...we could send thirty people onto a mountaintop removal site, shut it down temporarily, cost them a lot of money, and start to clog up the court systems of West Virginia. We could send thirty people the day after that, and the day after that, and the day after that every day for a year and...[President] Obama would be forced into a choice between ending the war against Appalachia, or bringing in federal troops to continue it...Until we force him into that choice...it's our fault, we condone [mountaintop removal].[59]

I wasn't at Power Shift 2011, but I watched DeChristopher's speech online. It was unlike anything I'd heard before. He seemed to be calling out the climate movement itself, equating its lack of courage with complicity in the climate crisis. What would I risk for a stable climate? I asked myself. My freedom, safety, future job prospects? What if I ended up in jail? What would my parents think? But how could those considerations matter when the stakes for the planet were so high?

Then again, I wanted to be reasonably sure any risk I took was worth it, not just an egotistical show of bravery. For better or worse, my solution was to start small. After graduating from Pacific University in 2009, I'd begun volunteering with groups opposing fossil fuel infrastructure projects in the region. I had a network of contacts at Portland activist organizations, including the local Rising Tide chapter. I also knew some Reed College students who were wrestling with the same questions about direct action I was. I sensed an opportunity to bring these groups together that was too good to pass up.

Small steps

On a spring day in 2011, I joined a small crowd of Reed students and twenty-something Rising Tide activists in Portland's Pioneer Square, to prepare for an action targeting two of the coal industry's biggest funders. There were murmurs of anticipation and a little nervous laughter from those who had never participated in this kind of protest before.

A couple Rising Tide organizers reminded us why we were here: Bank of America and Wells Fargo, both of which had downtown Portland offices, were then among the largest financiers of companies like Arch Coal, which was partnering with Australia-based Ambre Energy to build a giant coal export terminal on the Columbia River.

Although I had put the two groups involved in the action in contact, I did little of the work after that. The Reed students made our major prop, a multi-person cardboard coal train costume they now unveiled. Each of the five cars was about six feet long and meant to be worn by one person. "Ambre Energy Kills," read a message on the side of one. "No Industrial Sacrifice Zones," said another. Five students donned the costume and lined up, locomotive first. Our group headed down the sidewalk toward Bank of America.

Outside the bank, the security guard posted at the door looked flustered but made no attempt to stop us from going inside. As the coal train circled the lobby, the rest of us chanted, "B of A, stop investing in coal today!" Transactions ground to a halt while tellers and customers looked on. Our group was simply too large, loud, and flashy to ignore. One of the students read aloud a statement denouncing Bank of America's coal investments. Having made our point, we then exited the lobby and made for Wells Fargo.[60]

Our group of activists had no permits to engage in this protest. We hadn't notified the banks we were coming. And although no tense situations developed—some customers even smiled their support—things could have gone differently. Getting arrested at this particular action was unlikely, but we certainly could have been confronted more aggressively by security.

Things escalated slightly more during a day of action against the Canadian tar sands oil project which I participated in the following month. A friend had put me in touch with Ahmed Gaya of ForestEthics (now called Stand.earth), who coordinated the protest in Portland. On the day of the protest, Gaya, myself, and a few other people walked into a downtown Safeway and unfurled a banner in front of a shelf of Chiquita Brand bananas. Our message was that Chiquita should not use tar sands oil in its vast truck fleet.[61]

While two of us held the banner, the rest of the group acted out a humorous skit involving singing bananas. An incensed Safeway employee shouted and threatened to call the police while our security liaison calmly tried to engage her in conversation. Maybe the police did show up. If so, it was only after we left the Safeway, satisfied we had accomplished our objective.

Taken individually, these types of small, relatively low-risk actions cause minimal disruption to the companies involved. They could be dismissed as silly, even frivolous. However, I believed at the time—and still believe—this would be a mistake. Multiplied hundreds of times over, direct action protests targeting a large corporation hurt the company's image while elevating the urgency of the climate crisis.

Yet, while those of us in Safeway were never in much danger of lasting negative ramifications, some direct action has real, painful consequences for those involved. A stark reminder of this came on July 26, 2011, when a court sentenced Tim DeChristopher to two years in federal prison.

Final reflections

I learned about DeChristopher's punishment in an email from an activist organization which I read on my laptop at the University of Montana-Missoula, where I was starting grad school that fall. "Tim never ran from the punishment he faced, knowing that his sacrifice could stir something up in us, in our community, in our movement," Henia Belalia wrote in another blog post. "It has."[62]

In the years that followed, direct action—including large-scale protests involving hundreds or thousands of people—became much more common in the U.S. climate movement. DeChristopher's example wasn't the only reason, but it's safe to call him a contributing factor. However, when I interviewed DeChristopher for this book it had been years since he'd made a major speech. "I was blessed to have the opportunity to say things to big audiences and in big media venues for a while," he said. "I knew that wouldn't last, so I didn't hold back. But I never felt a need to stay in that role forever."[63]

While in prison, DeChristopher applied and was accepted to Harvard Divinity School, where he earned a graduate degree after his release.[64] He spent the next few years speaking at activist and faith gatherings about the moral implications of climate change, before gradually transitioning out of life as a public figure. "It got to where continuing on that path would have required an inappropriate level of self-promotion, and taking too much space away from new voices who need to be heard," he said. "With massive uprisings happening all over the country, the climate movement doesn't need me to talk about the value of resistance anymore."

This remark prompted me to ask for DeChristopher's thoughts on Sunrise Movement and the climate strikes. "Some of their direct action has been incredibly effective," he said. We talked about Sunrise's 2018 occupation of Nancy Pelosi's office, which DeChristopher observed had achieved "an unprecedented level of efficacy for that kind of protest."[65]

The divestment movement, too, has made good use of direct action—including some instances described in Chapter 3. In April 2021, I read about another example with particularly stark lessons for the climate movement. University of Michigan students had just won a stunning victory over a long-recalcitrant administration, prompting the school to divest its $12.5 billion endowment from fossil fuels.[66] Curious to learn how they did it, I reached out to the campaign's leaders and connected with some of them over Zoom.

"We were shut down by the administration early on," UM grad student Jonathan Morris told me. In 2015, divestment activists secured a meeting with UM administrators who, according to Morris, "basically told us if we cared about sustainability, we'd be better off picking up litter after football games."[67]

Rather than give up, divestment organizers decided to escalate. In March 2019, during the first global day of climate school strikes, hundreds of UM students and supporters held a sit-in at the university president's office.[68] They didn't expect arrests, partly because their demand was one they believed would be a soft ask: that the administration meet with students to further discuss divestment and other climate goals. To their surprise, the university responded by arresting ten sit-in participants.[69]

"That made the administration look really, really bad," said Sasha Bishop, another campaign leader. The university found itself put on the defensive and forced to explain why it would rather arrest students than meet with them about divestment. It was a classic case of those in power meeting nonviolent direct action with a show of force, only to have it backfire. "We emerged from the incident in a more powerful position of moral authority than before," Bishop said.

The students organized more direct action protests, including at a Board of Regents meeting in late 2019, where they blockaded the entrance to the parking lot outside to prevent cars from leaving. They made no secret of their plans beforehand. "In the days leading up to the meeting, we received emails from regents asking if we would allow the event to happen," Bishop said. "In that moment we students had more power than they did, a very rare experience for us."[70]

Under pressure from students, the Board of Regents voted to reject a new $50 million investment in fossil fuels. This set off a process of re-assessing the university's existing fossil fuel investments, culminating in a March 2021 vote to divest.[71] Student activists had triumphed in a campaign that once seemed unwinnable, using direct action to change power dynamics at the college. "You can try enticing decision makers into doing the right thing," said Noah Weaverdyck, another organizer of the campaign. "But in the end, they won't change until you make the status quo more uncomfortable for them than the position you want them to adopt."[72]

*

When done on a large enough scale, direct action can sometimes even force a U.S. president's hand, as DeChristopher foresaw in his Power Shift 2011 speech. "It wasn't until the very end of the Obama administration that we saw that kind of mass resistance in the climate movement," he said during our conversation. He was referring to the 2016 Standing Rock encampment against the Dakota Access pipeline, treated at length in Chapter 8. "If that kind of resistance had been more consistent throughout Obama's presidency, I think we would have seen more victories for the climate."

Mass direct action works partly because it forces those in power into a choice between granting the movement's demand, or responding with repressive violence. "Standing Rock was effective because it put Obama in that position," DeChristopher said. He believed such tactics likely would have worked under previous presidents, too. However, the ascension of Donald Trump changed things. "Trump is a rare kind of figure, who gets power from breaking taboos, who can brag about being as cruel and vicious to his fellow human beings as he can be and come out stronger for it. Civil disobedience doesn't work the same way with him."

Not that activists should abandon direct action when demagogues are in power. "We may need to be more selective about using it, though," DeChristopher explained. "And prepare for more severe consequences."[73] At the time of this writing, it remains to be seen whether direct action campaigns will again reach their full potential under the Biden administration. Sunrise Movement's vision for mass noncooperation, described in Chapter 2, provides one glimpse of what such an effort could look like—but so far it remains an ambitious vision to strive for, rather than a reality.

DeChristopher's own direct action didn't end after prison. In January 2020, almost seven years after his release from prison, he and three other people were arrested for climbing up a scaffold erected above a railroad to stop a New England coal train in its tracks.[74] When we spoke, he was facing felony charges for that protest. But in contrast to his first, highly publicized trial, he was working his way through the legal system "kind of quietly, because there're so many other people engaged in resistance who need attention."[75]

One critique of the focus placed on DeChristopher by the early climate movement would be that as a white male, he took a path closed to activists of color who would almost certainly have received less notice while facing even harsher consequences. His willingness to step out of the public eye more recently suggests he would agree with the need to pass the spotlight to more marginalized voices.

Yet, by the time DeChristopher went to prison, his actions and those of Peaceful Uprising, Rising Tide, and Mountain Justice had sparked a genuine shift toward direct action in the youth climate movement. That trend was about to accelerate during the fight over one of the most environmentally destructive extraction projects ever undertaken: the Canadian tar sands.

7

Tar Sands Wars

*THE MOVEMENT-SHAPING
FIGHT TO STOP THE KEYSTONE
XL PIPELINE*

Days before the inauguration of President Joe Biden, a couple hundred people gathered on the Cheyenne River Sioux Reservation for an anti-pipeline themed music festival. The event, organized by the Cheyenne River Grassroots Collective and International Indigenous Youth Council, drew attention to dangers posed by TC Energy's proposed Keystone XL tar sands oil pipeline, just as an administration widely expected to cancel the project was about to take office.

"We had local Indigenous artists perform and brought in others from as far off as Minnesota," said Joseph White Eyes, one of the coordinators. "It really raised our spirits how people came together."[1]

Keystone XL would have crossed under the Cheyenne River just outside the reservation, threatening tribal water supplies in the event of an oil leak. It was partly to prevent such a disaster that

White Eyes and others fought for years to stop the pipeline. Now their work was about to pay off. Hours after being sworn into office, Biden overturned the permit allowing Keystone XL to be built. In the process he put a cap on one of the longest, highest-profile campaigns in North American climate movement history.

"Keystone XL isn't just any project," veteran activist Matt Leonard told me soon after the rejection. "Its defeat is a testament to what movement building and direct action can accomplish."[2]

Opposition to Keystone XL spanned more than a decade and included large environmental groups, grassroots climate activist networks, rural landowners, Indigenous rights organizations, and tribal governments. Few environmental campaigns have touched so many people over such large swaths of the continent, or had as much impact on the larger climate movement. While a stroke of Biden's pen ultimately killed the pipeline, countless battles at the grassroots level paved the road to victory.

As they fought Keystone XL in court, in the streets, and on the White House steps, climate activists built a bigger, more aggressive movement that at least tacitly accepted the importance of direct action. Along the way, the fate of this pipeline and a specific polluting industry came to stand for something greater: a battle for the soul of the climate movement itself.

It all started more than a decade and half before Biden killed Keystone XL, with the birth of an international resistance to one of the dirtiest industrial projects in history.

The frontlines of tar sands extraction

If the continent-wide movement against mining the Canadian tar sands has a birthplace, it was probably the 2006 Protecting Mother Earth Summit in Minnesota, organized by the Indigenous Environmental Network. There, three women from the Deranger clan of the Athabasca Chipewyan First Nation approached IEN staff with a story about something horrific happening in their northern Alberta community.

"They told us about a project so large, so devastating that you had to see it to believe it," IEN anti-oil campaigner Clayton Thomas-Muller wrote in a reflection. "They spoke of a wild west of sorts, one of the last bastions of Earth where big oil was ramping up."

Fort Chipewyan's mostly Indigenous population had watched in dismay as some of the world's biggest oil companies began mining the form of low-quality petroleum known as bitumen from the Athabasca tar sands deposit in their backyard. The tar sands are a mixture of bitumen, sand, and finer sediment which stretches across an area roughly the size of Florida and is overlaid by one of the last great expanses of ancient forest in North America. The region is also home to a scattering of small, mainly Indigenous communities like Fort Chipewyan.

Extracting usable oil from the tar sands is an energy and water-intensive process that requires razing trees to reach the clay and sand beneath, then using toxic chemicals to separate the petroleum. Oil obtained this way has a carbon footprint at least 15 percent higher than conventional crude[3] and consumes 3-4 barrels of water for every barrel of fuel burned in the tanks of cars and trucks. Left-over water, contaminated with toxic chemicals, goes into tailings ponds that have a propensity for leakage, causing cancer clusters in downstream villages.[4]

The tar sands industry's base of operations was to the south of Fort Chipewyan in Fort McMurray, a town of 35,000 whose population more than doubled as workers streamed in to take advantage of mostly temporary jobs.[5] Oil field "man camps" became hotbeds for sex trafficking, especially of Indigenous women.[6] The situation was already dire when the Derangers came to IEN. According to Thomas-Muller, "They said that we needed to go up to Fort Chipewyan and help."[7]

Thomas-Muller, who belongs to the Mathais Colomb Cree Nation, grew up in inner-city Winnipeg, where he founded the organization Aboriginal Youth With Initiative. He later served as a youth spokesperson for the Assembly of First Nations,[8] and in 2002 traveled with other young activists to the World Summit on Sustainable Development in Johannesburg.[9] When IEN joined the Energy Action Coalition, Thomas-Muller represented it at EAC meetings. His work with Indigenous communities fighting the fossil fuel industry took him all over the North American continent, which IEN habitually refers to using the Indigenous name Turtle Island.[10]

Soon after the Protecting Mother Earth Summit, IEN organizers set out for Fort McMurray, where they toured the tar sands on foot, by car, and in a small plane. Although very familiar with oil companies' abuses of Indigenous land, Thomas-Muller described what he saw as being on a whole new scale: "To fly over endless clear cuts, open-pit mines and smokestacks surrounded by pristine Cree and Dene peoples' homelands was gut wrenching. When we drove through and walked in the tar sands the smell of bitumen filled our noses."

Convinced that the tar sands threatened Indigenous peoples' health and sovereignty, IEN made a plan with Fort Chipewyan locals to fight back. Their strategy centered on exercising First Nations treaty rights to challenge tar sands projects in court, in tandem with public pressure campaigns targeting oil companies, government officials, and investors.[11] Resistance to the tar sands spread across the continent.

Despite the essential part played by Indigenous organizers, the role of First Nations has often been left out of mainstream narratives about tar sands activism, which tend to start with U.S. environmental groups who didn't get engaged until years later. Defeating major tar sands projects required the participation of these big groups as well as grassroots activist collectives and lots of committed lawyers. However, it was Indigenous people who laid the foundation for success.

The collection of U.S. and Canadian organizations that emerged to oppose the tar sands wasn't a true coalition; there was no one decision-making body, and not all participants even thought of each other as allies. It was more an assemblage of groups who shared similar goals but sometimes took vastly different approaches to advocacy. Friction was inevitable. "We definitely argued," said Joye Braun of the Cheyenne River Sioux Tribe, who served as a mentor and role model for young activists like White Eyes. "There were lots of tears. For example, we faced a lot of white privilege and racism dealing with our non-Native peers."[12]

Yet, messy as it was and despite very real systemic issues, the tar sands resistance succeeded at uniting almost every major North American environmental organization behind a common goal of keeping bitumen in the ground. Along the way, it reinvigorated a climate movement grown too used to accepting defeat.

Superhero needed

On a July morning in 2009, a group of young people from the Avaaz Action Factory assembled outside U.S. State Department headquarters, around an inflatable wading pool filled with brown liquid that looked something like tar sands oil. An activist in a protective onesie climbed in and splashed around, becoming a "Tar Sands Monster." Nearby stood "Mother Earth" in a globe suit, "The United States" and "Canada" wearing their respective flags, and two scowling "business executives" representing Shell and the Royal

Bank of Canada. A canvas painted with trees and lakes depicted Alberta's vanishing forests in the background.

Then there was the star of the performance: "Super Climate Clinton" in a costume complete with cape, mask, and a wig that indeed resembled the Secretary of State. While hundreds of actual State Department employees streamed by on their way to work, a dramatized battle took shape.

It began with the Tar Sands Monster holding the United States, Canada, and Earth hostage in the oily pit. The moment called for a superhero, but Clinton stood by indecisively as the corporations distracted her. Avaaz activists Morgan Goodwin and Heather Kangas described what happened next in a blog post: "Once Clinton actually looked and saw the filthy destruction in the boreal forests, she rescued the trapped countries, beat the dirty Tar Sands Monster back and chased away the corporate executives. [The real] Secretary Clinton has the power to stop a major expansion of dirty oil production, but she needs to act quickly."[13]

Scaling up tar sands extraction required a network of new pipelines to connect Alberta mines to the U.S. energy market. However, any pipe crossing the international border needed a special permit granted by the State Department and approved by the President, affirming it was in the "national interest."

By 2009, it was already too late to stop the first major new tar sands conduit. TC Energy's Keystone pipeline—not to be confused with Keystone XL, a separate but related project—won approval from the George W. Bush administration in 2008 and was soon pumping tar sands oil through the Dakotas and Nebraska.[14] Climate groups had virtually no chance of stopping that project under an oil-friendly president.

But now another project, Enbridge Energy's Clipper pipeline from Alberta to Wisconsin, was up for consideration by Obama's State Department. Avaaz styled Clinton as a "climate superhero," inviting her to adopt that role in real life. The stunt captured the hopeful energy of Obama's early months in office. Still, as the deadline to approve Clipper approached, activists watched with trepidation to see what the administration would do.

They didn't have to wait long. That August, the State Department issued a permit finding Clipper was in the national interest.[15] Construction finished less than one year later.[16]

The Tar Sands Action

In early 2011, Matt Leonard was on his way to a potluck with the founders of 350.org, whom he expected would ask him to back off. He had been writing blog posts about the need for more direct action in the climate movement. "It was all friendly, but a lot of it was directed at the 350 crew," he told me in April 2020. "They were the emerging large climate group at the time who hadn't really embraced those tactics yet."

Leonard's own awakening to the power of direct action came in 1999. He had just finished high school and was living a "poor punk rock dirt bagger" lifestyle in Seattle as local activists prepared to protest the upcoming World Trade Organization meeting. That November, tens of thousands of people marched in Seattle's streets, shut down busy intersections, and locked arms to block access to the convention center where WTO negotiations took place. "The scale of the protests changed my perception of what was possible for activist movements to achieve," Leonard said.

Leonard went on to work for the Rainforest Action Network, Greenpeace, and other direct action organizations who were increasingly focused on climate change. He played a lead role organizing the 2009 Capitol Climate Action and attended COP15 that December. Like many activists, he emerged from the U.N. summit exhausted and uncertain as to what came next.[17]

"At 350, we had no plans beyond Copenhagen," said Will Bates of 350.org. He and other 350 leaders originally envisioned their organization as a temporary campaign that would quietly dissolve after securing a strong climate treaty at COP15.[18] If this sounds naïve, it is worth remembering that even very experienced activists underestimated the degree to which fossil fuel interests were embedded in U.S. and global politics. But while COP's failure was devastating, Bates and his colleagues remembered their social movement history. They knew setbacks were part of the package. "That we decided to continue as an organization was reflective of how deeply we'd grounded ourselves in history. Making social change is a slow, continuous process," Bates told me.

The Middlebury College students who ran 350.org decided to make it a permanent entity. This required implementing some changes—like separate email accounts for everyone. Until now, they had shared a single Gmail account.[19] They also needed a fresh target to campaign around. 350 held more international days of action modeled after its first one in October 2009. The next, about a year later, was even larger[20] but made less of a media splash; this tends to happen with annualized activist events, which seem a little less newsworthy every year. Going forward, 350 continued organizing occasional big days of action but increasingly channeled resources elsewhere.

In 2010, 350 and some Unity College students got their hands on one of the solar panels President Jimmy Carter had put on the White House in the 1970s, which somehow ended up on one of the Maine school's buildings after being torn down by Ronald Reagan. They took it on a biodiesel-powered road trip to D.C., essentially daring Obama to make a statement by putting solar back on the nation's most famous building. "As we expected (but secretly hoped wouldn't be the case), the White House didn't commit to...well, anything," 350's Jamie Henn wrote of the stunt.[21]

The solar campaign was a way to pressure Obama to act on climate in the face of Congressional gridlock. But the value of solarizing the White House was mainly symbolic, and while symbolism is important in any activist movement, it gets you only so far on its own. What 350 needed was an issue the president could act on himself, and which made a big enough difference for the climate to inspire people's imaginations. This was the state of things when Leonard and a couple other activists who believed strongly in direct action received invitations to a potluck with the organization's leaders.

"We had a productive conversation about escalating the climate movement," Leonard said. However, he still assumed the purpose was mainly to appease him and other guests. A few days later he got a phone call from 350.org, something about a pipeline from Canada and an idea for sustained civil disobedience. They wanted to know: How would he organize something like that? "I didn't think they were really serious," he remembered. "I thought it was just another way to get me to back off. But I wrote up a quick one-pager and sent it to them."

Not long afterwards, Leonard received another call. 350.org liked his ideas and wanted to hold a direct action protest pressuring Obama to reject the next major tar sands pipeline. Would he coordinate it?

"I hadn't expected to be the one responsible for making the action happen," Leonard recalled to me with a laugh. "I asked if I could re-write the proposal with a bit more intentionality."

He also said yes, he would organize the action.[22]

*

Stopping Keystone XL met all the criteria for a campaign that could push the President to take meaningful, unilateral action on climate change. If built, the pipeline would transport 900,000 barrels of oil per day on a 2,000-mile journey from Alberta to the Gulf Coast, solidifying U.S. dependence on the tar sands.[23] And a stroke of Obama's pen could stop it. "You don't often find perfect fights like that," Henn explained when I interviewed him for this book. "Hitting on that specific ask of Obama, to show climate leadership by rejecting a pipeline he had full authority over, was a breakthrough for us."[24]

It was also an opportunity for the kind of escalated protest which 350.org had yet to engage in, despite recognizing its value early on. Climate groups' experience with Clipper had shown conventional tactics like lobbying weren't enough to stop tar sands pipelines. Absent some dramatic new intervention in politics, Keystone XL would almost certainly be built.

In June 2011, prominent activists including 350's Bill McKibben, author Naomi Klein, and IEN Executive Director Tom Goldtooth published an open invitation to the Tar Sands Action, a multiday protest intended to change the terms of the Keystone XL fight. Every day for two weeks, a few dozen to a couple hundred protesters would sit in front of the White House until they were arrested. Each day, a new group would be led away by police.[25] People began signing up.

On the first day of the Tar Sands Action, seventy participants—including McKibben—marched to the White House and sat around a banner reading, "Climate Change is Not in Our National Interest: Stop the Keystone XL Tar Sands Pipeline." Soon the arrests started. First to be placed in handcuffs was a young woman from Wasilla, Alaska, hometown of oil-loving former vice-presidential candidate Sarah Palin.[26]

The organizers anticipated those being arrested would be brought to the police station and allowed to post bail. Instead, police took them to jail and kept them two nights. "People protest at the

White House all the time," Leonard said. "But dozens of new people getting arrested every day—the police weren't used to that. When they realized what was happening, they tried to deter us."[27]

Leonard, Henn, and others on the outside wondered what came next. Could the sit-ins continue or would future waves of protesters be dissuaded by the possibility of spending days behind bars? "The only thing we need is more company," McKibben assured them when they placed a call to the jail.[28]

The sit-ins went on.

*

Police soon gave up their strategy of intimidation as new waves of protesters arrived for the Tar Sands Action. "They released everyone after concluding we were going to flood their jails," Leonard said.[29] Soon, organizers were getting calls from the White House asking them to stop.

At a face-to-face meeting with McKibben, Henn, and other activists, Obama's team explained it was politically impractical to deny a major pipeline permit. What else could they do to make the protests go away? Nothing, the activists responded. They wanted Keystone XL stopped.

"The Tar Sands Action was just fifty or so people getting arrested at the White House each day," Henn told me. "This wasn't the revolution. Yet we made Obama feel really pressured. We realized we needed to do this sort of thing more often."[30]

The arrests generated a buzz among environmental organizations headquartered in D.C., many of whom were by then engaged in some type of tar sands work. Kendall Mackey, a recent University of Kansas graduate interning at the National Wildlife Federation, was inspired to check out the sit-ins after hearing IEN organizer Kandi Mossett speak. Mossett, who is Mandan, Hidatsa, and Arikara, was emerging as a leading young voice against tar sands development in the U.S. "We [Indigenous people] have done without [oil] and we can do it again, and in fact we will," she told a news reporter outside the White House near the close of the Tar Sands Action. "We don't have a choice. Oil will end."[31]

Mackey had helped organize an anti-tar sands lobby day for NWF, but Mossett made her want to do more. She stopped by the church where the Tar Sands Action held trainings for sit-in participants, asked if she could help out, and started volunteering. "I'd never been part of anything like it," she said. "It got me thinking about how nonviolent direct action can help movements build power."[32]

By the end of the Tar Sands Action, 1,252 people had been arrested in the U.S. climate movement's largest act of civil disobedience up to then.[33] In response, Obama pushed back the decision on Keystone XL's cross-border permit to an indefinite future date. Perhaps the administration hoped protests would fade with time.

Meanwhile, the president made one of his famous compromises. While continuing to review the section of Keystone XL that crossed into Canada, he would fast-track the southern leg between Cushing, Oklahoma and the Gulf Coast. Few people at the time could have predicted the move would trigger a direct action response more forceful than anything at the Tar Sands Action.

In the woods of North Texas

Just over a year after Obama greenlighted Keystone XL's southern section, twenty-two-year-old Maggie Gorry sat on a platform atop a forty-foot pole, preventing tractors owned by pipeline builder TC Energy (known at the time as TransCanada) from clearing a path through the Texas woodlands. Other activists watched from structures in nearby trees.[34] This human blockade traced its origins to a group of University of North Texas students who returned from the Tar Sands Action the previous year and begun talking with local landowner David Daniel about direct action to stop Keystone XL.

Daniel was one of many people along the pipeline's route whose property was to be condemned through eminent domain for its construction. He served as an official spokesperson for the Tar Sands Action and traveled around the South, speaking about Keystone XL's impact on property rights.[35] But when Obama fast-tracked approval of the southern leg, most large climate groups turned to the more winnable fight against the pipeline's northern half. To some Texans, this felt like a betrayal.

"Keystone XL was one project that ran all the way to the Gulf Coast," UNT student Cindy Spoon told me in March 2020. "But the national groups stopped talking about it that way once it became inconvenient for them."

Spoon attended the Tar Sands Action with some college friends, and was arrested on the second day of sit-ins. On returning to the university town of Denton, she got in touch with Daniel, whose land was a short drive from UNT. Daniel had vowed to build a treehouse in Keystone XL's path, if necessary, to block construction on his property. Spoon and other students offered to help. They went out to his land on weekends to build aerial wooden platforms connected by a catwalk. "It became more like a whole tree village," Spoon said.[36] Slowly, the idea of involving large numbers of people in a sustained protest called the Tar Sands Blockade took shape.

In late August 2012, soon after construction on Keystone XL began near the town of Livingston, the Tar Sands Blockade published an online call to action. "Your company is needed in Texas," activist Ben Kessler wrote. "Of some things we can be sure: [the blockade] will be difficult. It will be hot. Many of us will be arrested. Our resolve will be tested and our commitment strained.

The government and the corporations know this, and they will try to exploit it...What they aren't equipped to deal with is our joy, our resolve and our passion."[37]

Groups like Rising Tide North America—one of the few national organizations that put serious resources into fighting Keystone XL's southern half—recruited for the blockade. And people came. In late September, when TC Energy's tree-cutting crew arrived on Daniel's property, they were greeted by a banner hanging from the branches which showed a hand raised palm outward beneath the words "You Shall Not Pass." The *Lord of the Rings* allusion seemed oddly fitting; the machines ripping trees from the ground looked like some fantastical scene, a monster eating its way through the forest. A group of activists ascended to the canopy platforms, prepared to remain indefinitely.

This was no merely symbolic civil disobedience. Tar Sands Blockade protesters were prepared to block tree-felling equipment with their bodies, sometimes at great personal risk. Some who chained themselves to bulldozers were pepper sprayed and tased by the local Sherriff's Department.[38] In another incident, captured on video, a TC Energy earthmover ripped a tree from the ground as activist J.G. Genson approached to force the machine to stop working. Footage showed the operator repeatedly swinging the tree toward and away from Genson, who sat down to show he didn't intend to move. "It felt like he was aiming a loaded gun at me and would pull the trigger any second," Genson said. He had to leap to safety when the machine dropped the trunk dangerously near him.[39]

After eight days, TC Energy made the legally dubious move of bringing its machines outside the pipeline construction easement to skirt around the tree village. That night blockaders erected a pole in the bulldozers' new path, and Gorry climbed to the top. By the following afternoon it was clear she had stopped construction for the day. Tree-clearing equipment stood idle. "The only sound audible...is a wood-chipper and excavator moving slash piles of felled trees further away along the clear-cut scar," read a 1:00pm update on the Tar Sands Blockade website.[40]

The original plan was for Gorry to stay on her platform twenty-four hours—but when that time was up, she decided to remain another day. When she finally came down, having stopped TC Energy for forty-eight hours, she was arrested and later released on $11,000 bail. The Tar Sands Blockade raised money to cover her legal costs.[41] In the meantime, bulldozers made it around the tree village.

Protesters continued to harry TC Energy's advance toward the Gulf Coast, slowing but not ultimately stopping construction. Yet, their efforts weren't futile. "We had four goals for the blockade," Spoon said. These were: stop the pipeline, elevate the plight of landowners like Daniel, push the climate movement to embrace more escalated direct action, and legitimize resistance to fossil fuel infrastructure in Texas. Spoon felt they had accomplished all but the first.[42]

The Texas Tar Sands Blockade represented a dramatic early testing ground for the kind of sustained direct action that, within a few years, became much more common in the climate movement. It wasn't the only such experiment driven by opposition to the tar sands. Soon oil companies couldn't even haul the equipment used to mine bitumen across country without encountering a literal human wall of opposition.

All against the tar sands haul

Just after 1:00am on a warm August night, over 250 people streamed into the path of a 255-foot-long, twenty-one-foot-wide cylindrical structure nearly spanning an Idaho highway. The object, pulled by a huge truck engine, was a piece of water purifying equipment manufactured in South Korea and headed for the tar sands. It had been shipped across the Pacific and up the Columbia River and was being hauled to Alberta via Highway 12 when the blockade halted its progress through Idaho.[43]

Actually, calling this Idaho wasn't strictly correct. These forested mountains had always been Indigenous land, and even now remained legally under tribal control. The "megaload" had reached the Nez Perce Reservation. The night filled with traditional chants and songs as blockaders waved signs and the Nez Perce flag. Children sat in the road with their elders, illuminated in the glow of escort vehicle headlights. Police stood around trying to figure out what to do.[44]

The blockade was part of a battle that began a few years earlier, when companies like ExxonMobil subsidiary Imperial Oil proposed hauling what became known as the megaloads—giant pieces of equipment that served various functions in the tar sands— up Highway 12 where it follows the Clearwater and Lochsa Wild and Scenic Rivers. Activist Zack Porter described the route to me as "a hundred-mile stretch of tortuous terrain where semi-trailers routinely careen off the road."[45] Imperial planned to widen highways, fortify bridges, and build temporary on-ramps to accommodate the slow-moving loads, which blocked traffic both ways.[46] In April 2011, a test megaload meant to demonstrate how safe future shipments would be clipped a power pole in Kamiah, Idaho, cutting off electricity to 1,300 homes and businesses.[47]

As with the larger fight against the tar sands, it was Indigenous people who first sounded the alarm. After Exxon's plans became public, prominent Native activists like Winona LaDuke began speaking out about the implications the megaloads and tar sands development for the climate, protected waterways, and tribes like the Nez Perce who hadn't consented to have them pass through their land. It was a wakeup call for Porter, who was then a student at the University of Montana.[48]

Porter's feeling of connection to the natural world dated back to his childhood and adolescence in Boston. "Growing up, I felt most at home in the wild," he said when I interviewed him for this book in March 2020. His time in untamed landscapes helped him cope with crippling depression. "I don't know if I would be around today if not for places like that." After high school, Porter joined the Student Conservation Association doing trail work among the glacier-carved peaks of Washington's North Cascades. This led to a couple seasons as a wilderness forest ranger. By 2010, when Exxon's megaloads plans became public, he was a senior in University of Montana's Wilderness and Civilization program. By now school felt secondary to what he felt was his real calling: protecting wild places.

During his time at UM, Porter helped found a student group that successfully pushed the school to adopt a carbon neutrality policy. He also attended Power Shift 2009. On hearing about the megaloads, he "realized this was a chance to take all I'd learned about climate and wilderness issues and apply it to something with both local and global impact." After graduation, Porter became the unpaid coordinator of All Against the Haul, a Missoula-based organization formed to oppose the megaloads. The job involved working with local government leaders, the Nez Perce and Confederated Salish and Kootenai Tribes, nonprofits like IEN and the Western Environmental Law Center, and well-known Montana authors such as Rick Bass, Annick Smith, and David James Duncan.[49]

When a megaload bound for an East Montana oil refinery—a precursor to Exxon's planned Alberta shipments—arrived in Missoula in March 2011, activists from Northern Rockies Rising Tide flooded into the street to stop it.[50] Meanwhile, All Against the Hall organized community meetings in small mountain towns whose conservative residents might not believe in climate change, but didn't like the thought of ambulances being blocked for hours by megaloads. There were lawsuits and education campaigns. "We threw all we could at the wall to see what would stick," Porter said. But deep down, he never truly believed they could win. The forces opposing them just seemed too big.

At most, Porter thought, activists might delay the megaloads.[51] But in June 2012, Exxon shelved its Highway 12 plans in the face of mounting legal challenges.[52] The Nez Perce and Salish and Kootenai tribes, small town residents, and young climate activists had won. Porter was as shocked as anyone.

"It was stupefying," Porter said. "Victories don't come very often in this work. It was truly something to celebrate."[53]

*

Even rarer than victory in the climate movement is total, permanent victory. The vast majority of the 200 megaloads Exxon hoped to haul through the Nez Perce Reservation and Missoula never made it,[54] but in 2013 a company called Omega Morgan rushed one load through amid continued legal wrangling over whether such large shipments could use Highway 12. It was met by the August blockade on Nez Perce land, where nineteen people were arrested.[55]

The load was delayed again a couple nights later, in Missoula, during a protest organized by the Montana-based group Indian People's Action. A scattering of non-Native activists joined the predominantly Indigenous crowd that flooded into the street to prevent the megaload from moving. I was one.

Two years earlier, I had moved to Missoula to pursue a Master's in environmental studies. By then the campaign against Exxon's megaloads was winding down, and I devoted myself to other climate activist projects. Until now, I'd watched the anti-tar sands movement mostly from afar. This changed when Indian People's Action put out a call for an organized response to Omega Morgan's shipment. I joined meetings in coffee shops where Indigenous leaders and climate activists made their plans. That December, we learned three more megaloads were headed for our town via Highway 93, a route that skirted the protected Clearwater and Lochsa Rivers.

On a January night, tribal elders led a round dance in the middle of Missoula's Reserve Street as the first of this new set of loads sat waiting. The hope was that police would be reluctant to break up a spiritual ceremony. It worked, for a while. During a similar action two nights later, I glanced around at the seventy or so mostly Indigenous faces gathered under the glow of streetlights and was struck by the group's age-diversity. Teenagers looked away when I tried to make eye contact, understandably nervous of this tall white stranger in their midst. There were parents, some with children in tow, and quite a few elders. Some I knew from action planning meetings.

Among these local organizers was Dr. George Price, then a UM professor of Native American and African American Studies, whom I later interviewed about the megaloads for *Waging Nonviolence*. He helped me understand how the impact of the blockades went far beyond delaying each load for a relatively short time. "Many, mostly young, Native American people learned much about the issues facing our planet and became first-time public activists for the Earth during these protests," Price said. "They will be back again and again, in greater and greater numbers."[56]

From Fort Chipewyan to Nez Perce land, and from Texas to Montana, opposition to the tar sands shaped a new generation of activists who allowed no part of the industry's endeavors to go uncontested. Valiant as this resistance was by 2014, it seemed possible it would pale beside the response tar sands projects still had potential to stir up.

An Indigenous resistance

Joseph White Eyes was eighteen years old in 2013, when long-time Indigenous rights organizer Debra White Plume came to lead a nonviolent direct action training called Moccasins on the Ground on the Cheyenne River Sioux Reservation. It was part of a series of similar events put on throughout the Great Plains by White Plume's Owe Aku International Justice Project, to prepare communities for mass direct action should construction on Keystone XL's northern half begin.

"It was great seeing Indigenous people empowering Indigenous people," White Eyes said when I asked about his experience at Moccasins on the Ground. "There was no outside white influence telling us what to do. It was just us, creating our own plan to stop the pipeline." Presenters included White Plume, Winona LaDuke, Kandi Mossett, and other leaders of the tar sands resistance.[57]

Moccasins on the Ground took place in the reservation community of Bridger, mere miles from where Keystone XL would be built. An earlier version of the proposed pipeline route cut through the reservation, but tribal opposition forced TC Energy to alter its plans. The new path crossed beneath the Cheyenne River just outside the reservation boundary, but close enough to threaten local communities' water.

"We went over roles for a direct action: police liaisons, media coordinator, and those risking arrest," said Morgan Brings Plenty, who attended Moccasins on the Ground as a teenager. "I joined the media team because I knew about social media platforms."

Brings Plenty was in high school in 2010, when her family moved from Washington State back to the Cheyenne River Reservation where her mother, Joye Braun, grew up. They became concerned about the tar sands while in Washington and followed the controversy over the original Keystone pipeline. On returning to their ancestral homeland, Brings Plenty and Braun joined the fight against the next piece of TC Energy's pipeline network.

"Early on, it would sometimes be just the two of us standing on street corners with signs, talking to people about Keystone XL," Brings Plenty told me in February 2021. "You could tell some people didn't want to speak up or were afraid to, or just didn't know how." Gradually, partly thanks to the mother-daughter team, more tribal members got engaged.[58]

Braun began volunteering with White Plume's Owe Aku, and was instrumental in bringing Moccasins on the Ground to Bridger.[59] The direct action trainings were central in a broader effort to prepare for a civil disobedience response to construction on the northern part of Keystone XL, something like the Texas Tar Sands Blockade but many times larger.

The young White Eyes was inspired by older leaders like Braun and White Plume early on in the Keystone XL fight. To non-Indigenous readers this might seem counterintuitive; in mainstream U.S. culture, civil disobedience is often assumed to be the domain of the young and rebellious. The contrast with Indigenous movements where elders and youth inspire each other couldn't be greater. White Eyes himself went on to mentor an even younger generation planning to resist Keystone XL.

Since age eighteen, White Eyes had worked at a youth center where he developed skills that proved useful in direct action trainings and protests. "I knew the basics of how to watch over young people and make sure they're safe and comfortable," he said. He also attended advanced direct action trainings organized by IEN and the Ruckus Society. "I took what I picked up at those events and kind of created my own training manual for young people. We would hold mock actions, mock encounters with police, mock arrests, so we'd be prepared to deal with them in real life."[60]

By the late Obama era, an intergenerational direct action campaign-in-waiting lay ready for when and if work on Keystone XL's northern leg began. This organizing buoyed not only the resistance to a specific pipeline, but a broader pan-Indigenous opposition to large fossil fuel projects which would explode in its most dramatic form yet at the Standing Rock protests described in the next chapter. By then, the immediate danger from Keystone XL had receded.

In November 2015, Obama finally rejected Keystone XL's international boundary permit. It was the first time a U.S. president had stopped a major piece of oil infrastructure due to climate concerns. The victory was short-lived, however, as one of the Trump administration's first acts in office was to invite TC Energy to re-submit its application. The next four years saw a string of legal challenges delay construction until Trump's final months as president.

Despite a court ruling blocking it from building across streams, TC Energy began work on select segments of Keystone XL in 2020, when COVID-19 made holding large protests difficult. Even so, the youth-led Cheyenne River Grassroots Collective, of which White Eyes is a co-founder, blockaded entrances to construction camps and a pipeline storage site.[61] It was a harbinger of the direct action to come if construction started on a large scale. Organizations like 350.org stood by, ready to assist if and when local Indigenous leaders put out the call for a major mobilization.

Things never got to that point, though. On day one of his administration, President Biden rescinded Keystone XL's permit, halting all work on the project.

Toward a bigger, braver movement

"In the end, protests won't solve what ails environmentalism," wrote Ted Nordhaus and Michael Shellenberger of the

Breakthrough Institute, in a February 2014 *New York Times* op-ed criticizing the grassroots opposition to Keystone XL. The authors went on to argue that the strategy of challenging the fossil fuel industry directly, as the Keystone XL fight did, represented "not the beginnings of a new climate movement but the death rattle of the old one."[62]

Those words are a reminder that not every organization involved in climate work embraced the tar sands resistance and its focus on direct action. Breakthrough, a think tank skeptical of protest-oriented activist campaigns, was one example. However, among environmental groups with large grassroots followings the response to Keystone XL was remarkably uniform.

"[T]here is not an inch of daylight between our policy position on the Keystone [XL] Pipeline and those of the very civil protesters being arrested daily outside the White House," read a statement released by leaders of ten large environmental groups during the Tar Sands Action. Signatories included the heads of such staid entities as the Natural Resources Defense Council and Environmental Defense Fund, as well as groups like Greenpeace and the Rainforest Action Network.[63] Just a couple years earlier, some of these same organizations were at loggerheads over whether to support the ACES climate bill in Congress. Keystone XL brought them together as the drive for national legislation never had.

Of course, the tar sands resistance was not led solely by young people. "We don't want college kids to be the only cannon fodder in this fight," read the open invitation to the Tar Sands Action.[64] And as I saw in Montana, the age spectrum at tar sands protests—especially those led by Indigenous organizers—could be highly diverse. Even so, young people played a disproportionate role in the movement.

Youth were well represented in the crowd of thousands who encircled the White House in November 2011, in a follow-up protest to the Tar Sands Action. There were also lots of students among the 40,000 people at the Forward on Climate anti-tar sands rally on the National Mall in February 2013.[65] In March 2014, nearly 400 students were arrested in front of the White House in a protest called XL Dissent.[66] Young tar sands resisters in Cheyenne River Sioux country, North Texas, and elsewhere pioneered escalated nonviolent protest tactics, in the process helping to transform the U.S. climate movement into something bigger, braver, and less willing to give up.

In fact, Nordhaus and Shellenberger's analysis of the Keystone XL resistance could hardly have been more wrong. One can certainly disagree with the strategy behind the continent-wide campaign, but it's hard to deny it indeed foreshadowed the climate movement's future. For years, the largest climate protests ever organized in the U.S. were tar sands protests. These demonstrations against Keystone XL helped set the tone for even bigger street mobilizations that eventually arrived with the climate strikes. Similarly, lessons about the value of direct action from the Keystone XL campaign informed young people's decision to embrace such tactics in the divestment movement and Sunrise's push for a Green New Deal.

By the early 2010s, opposition to the tar sands was also galvanizing more localized battles against other fossil fuel projects, from fracking wells to coal mines. The next several years saw those regional campaigns take on an increasingly prominent role in the climate movement—a development I witnessed at close range.

8

Oppose All Pipelines

THE FOSSIL FUEL INFRASTRUCTURE RESISTANCE

People were already queuing up to testify on the evening of June 23, 2010, when a carful of Sierra Club staff and volunteers, including me, arrived at the Portland Building for a hearing on the fate of Oregon's only coal-fired power plant. While some of us joined the line for giving testimony, others handed out "Beyond Coal" T-shirts that distinguished us climate activists from members of the crowd sporting pins with the logo of plant owner Portland General Electric. This would to be a night of intense passion from both sides.

About a year earlier, I'd received a call from an organizer at the Sierra Club's Portland office inviting me to the kickoff meeting for a campaign to phase out the coal plant in Boardman, Oregon. I had just graduated from Pacific University into a recession and was living with my parents. I was twenty-three with plenty of spare time, and threw myself into the campaign. Soon I was carpooling up and down I-5 to public hearings on the coal plant's future.

Along with a small group of other young activists, I worked to engage environmental clubs at Oregon colleges and the odd high school in passing student government resolutions in favor of forcing the Boardman plant's swift closure. Young people who became invested in that effort would, our team hoped, go on to engage with decision-makers and participate in the all-important hearings. In the Portland Building, we presented the state Public Utilities Commission with resolutions from ten governing bodies representing over a hundred thousand students. "Letting PGE decide for themselves when to close the Boardman plant would be like letting me grade my own paper," McMinnville High School student Lindsy Gjesvold said in her public testimony.[1]

Beyond Coal in Oregon was the best-organized, most impactful activist campaign I had been part of up to then. However, it was far from a unique effort. Throughout the U.S., activists were beginning to focus on challenging individual fossil fuel projects as a strategy for addressing climate change. Over the next few years, this push for meaningful local victories drew energy from the escalating fight against Keystone XL. The continent-wide effort to oppose the tar sands was replayed on a smaller scale in communities all over the country, solidifying a grassroots power base that proved essential for later mass climate mobilizations.

Keeping it in the ground

The Beyond Coal campaign, launched by the Sierra Club and partner organizations in the early 2000s, was one of the first nationwide efforts to reduce carbon emissions by systematically targeting individual pieces of proposed or existing fossil fuel infrastructure. The idea wasn't completely new; in 2000, Amit Srivastava of CorpWatch observed that environmental justice campaigns against the oil industry represented "a major grassroots initiative to reduce production of CO2," with implications for the climate.[2] Still, nothing on the scale of Beyond Coal had been attempted before. What began as a defensive response to a wave of new coal plant proposals under the George W. Bush administration evolved by the 2010s into a push to retire existing coal-burning facilities. The campaign's early successes attracted interest from large donors including the Bloomberg Foundation.

Beyond Coal was not wholly or even mainly a youth-led initiative. However, young activists played important roles in many local battles. Some had firsthand experience with the effects of pollution. "I've had fragile bones since I was five," said Mabette Colon of Guayama, Puerto Rico, who at age sixteen began attending meetings and testifying at hearings for the campaign to close a coal plant near her community. "It seemed like every time I fell as a child, I would fracture something." Colon attributed this chronic health problem to cadmium leaking from the giant pile of coal ash at the plant.[3]

Coal's health effects also hit home for Talya Tavor, a Michigan State University student who awoke one day in the hospital after suffering an intense asthma attack. "The doctors said if I hadn't gone in for help, I likely would have had only days left to live," she said. "My lungs were so filled with pollution, I wasn't getting enough oxygen to survive."

Tavor, who grew up in Chicago, was diagnosed with asthma at age two. However, only when a Beyond Coal organizer spoke to her class at MSU did she connect her breathing problems to fossil fuels. She signed a petition and soon got a call from a volunteer with the student group working to close MSU's on-campus coal plant. "The following day I was standing in a courtyard, waving to strangers and asking them to join the campaign to clean up our air."

After her hospital visit, Tavor threw herself even more deeply into Beyond Coal at MSU, which gathered thousands of signatures, researched alternative energy, and built relationships with school administrators. In 2012, MSU adopted a plan to phase out coal combustion while increasing the school's reliance on renewables.[4] It was a major victory for the Sierra Student Coalition, which was contributing to the Beyond Coal effort by focusing on the more than 60 colleges then burning the fuel on their campuses.

"By then, the SSC had about hit our capacity for energy efficiency upgrade and clean energy purchase agreement campaigns," said Kim Teplitzky, a Temple University graduate involved in the formation of Energy Action Coalition. "That work was running out of room to expand, and we needed a new direction."

Teplitzky graduated in 2006, just as the first big chunk of funding for EAC's Campus Climate Challenge was being dispersed to members organizations. Members like the SSC used the money to hire for a slate of new organizing jobs. Teplitzky took a position coordinating the Campus Climate Challenge in Rust Belt states, then worked on Power Vote in 2008. The following year she became the coordinator for Campuses Beyond Coal. When I spoke with her in August 2020, she explained how resources from the well-funded, larger Beyond Coal campaign allowed student groups to "experiment with doing things most could never have afforded otherwise." The SSC sponsored basketball games at target schools, projecting its message on courtside screens. A Sierra Club-owned giant inflatable inhaler visited colleges for press events. Yet, perhaps the most important investment made by the campaign was in developing student leaders.

"We identified and trained student Beyond Coal leaders all over the country," Teplitzky said. "Many later got jobs with the Sierra Club or our partners and launched careers in activism."[5] An example is Tavor, who went on to work for the Climate Reality Project and the Audubon Society after school, then became a Sierra Club regional organizer.[6]

My own involvement with Beyond Coal left me impressed by what grassroots organizing could accomplish. In 2010, the Sierra Club secured an agreement to close Oregon's Boardman plant by 2020—later than we'd hoped for, but still a precedent-setting decision.[7] More than twenty campus Beyond Coal groups declared victory over the next few years.[8] While the fight against Keystone XL showed how to challenge fossil fuel projects at a national level, Beyond Coal provided a model of what winning looked like on a local or regional scale.

Meanwhile, seismic changes in the fossil energy industry itself were altering the landscape of projects with which activists had to contend.

The extract-for-export rush

In 2014, Cindy Spoon returned from the Tar Sands Blockade to Denton, Texas, a community reeling from the natural gas "fracking" boom. "Fracking wells were going up everywhere: next to elementary schools, on the UNT campus, right by parks and hospitals," Spoon remembered. None of this surprised her. In fact, organizing against fracking had been her gateway into climate activism.

Like tar sands mining and mountaintop removal, fracking is a form of fossil fuel extraction taken to the extreme. It involves injecting sand, water, and toxic chemicals deep underground to force out oil or gas that would otherwise be inaccessible. Harmful side effects include toxins leaking into groundwater, methane gas bubbling to the surface, even localized earthquakes.[9] Denton, located at the edge of the gas-rich Barnett Shale formation, was caught in the crosshairs when fracking activity ramped up in the early '00s. Resistance to the practice became a center of gravity for the town's progressive community, and Spoon was drawn in as a college student. Then Keystone XL intervened.

By 2014, oil was flowing through Keystone XL's southern leg and Spoon was back in Denton. For nearly two years she and other activists had lived and breathed the Tar Sands Blockade, facing down TC Energy workers, risking their own safety, and watching their friends be tortured by law enforcement. Now, like veterans after a war, they returned to a society that expected them to move on as though nothing had happened. "It was hard to readjust," Spoon said. Even so, she soon threw herself into a new conflict.

That fall, Spoon and other activists knocked on thousands of doors for a ballot initiative to ban fracking in Denton city limits. It passed, but the Texas legislature responded with a state law prohibiting local fracking bans.[10] In June, fracking trucks returning to Denton were confronted by activists who blocked the road with their bodies.[11]

The fracking boom unleashed a flood of new drilling activity from California to New England. Energy companies awash in gas began looking to export overseas. Coal corporations were also seeking to increase exports, but for different reasons. Competition from fracked gas and pressure from environmental groups had dimmed coal's domestic prospects, making international markets attractive. In what felt like a direct response to Beyond Coal's success at home, news broke in 2011 that Arch Coal planned to build a massive export terminal on the Columbia River near Longview, Washington.[12] Environmental groups planned to fight back.

As for me, I was about to start graduate school in Missoula. There, I would get embroiled in a campaign to oppose the new Eastern Montana mines which companies like Arch hoped to build to feed new shipping terminals like the one in Longview.

*

On May 21, 2012, I sat with a small group of University of Montana students in a hearing room in the Montana State Capitol, waiting for then-Governor Brian Schweitzer and other members of the state's Land Board to commence their monthly public meeting. We would each have only minutes to speak during the comment period on a proposed coal mining lease, so we divided up things to cover.

"It was one of my first times speaking on a stage like that," said Lowell Chandler, who was then a UM senior and a key organizer in the student-led Blue Skies Campaign, which I launched soon after arriving in Montana. Chandler lived next to the railroad tracks that pass through Missoula and extend all the way to the West Coast. He had noticed an increase in train traffic as coal shipments to existing British Columbia export terminals ramped up. "With that came increased diesel and coal dust pollution," he recalled, when we reconnected in July 2020 as I was writing this book. "But as an environmental studies student, I was also concerned about coal's climate impact."

Soon, even more trains could be shuttling between the coast and new export mines like Arch Coal's proposed Otter Creek project in Southeast Montana, where the company dreamed of extracting 1.3 billion tons of coal.[13] In late 2011, Chandler stopped by a table at UM where I was doing outreach for Blue Skies Campaign, whose primary mission was to rally opposition to the Otter Creek Mine. Now, at the hearing in the State Capitol, we waited our turn to address the Land Board. When the time came, Chandler spoke about life next to a coal train thoroughfare.

"After I finished, Governor Schweitzer called me back to the stand," Chandler recalled. "He proceeded to lecture me about how important the rail line was helping his ancestors get wheat to the market."[14] The Governor went on for a while as the room full of state officials, corporate executives, and wheat growers listened. He then asked Chandler a loaded question: "Should these farmers in this room be concerned that you'll also have a problem with them moving their grain?"[15]

"I think transporting coal, compared to wheat, is quite a bit different," Chandler replied. "Coal's dirty, and it's [carried in] open top rail cars...I think [farmers] should be concerned about the number of coal trains that'll be using the rail line and [their effect on] availability for freight transport of wheat."[16]

For a presiding official to call someone back to the stand during a public comment period was unusual—but Brian Schweitzer wasn't a typical politician. The bolo tie-wearing Democrat had gotten elected in conservative Montana by adopting a folksy persona and proudly supporting mining industries. I doubt he expected such a ready response from Chandler.

Nor were the Governor's settler forbearers the only ones with a claim on the landscape. "Arch Coal understands money," wrote Vanessa Braided Hair, a young member of the Northern Cheyenne Tribe, in a 2013 blog post for the National Wildlife Federation. "What Arch Coal doesn't understand is community. They don't understand history. They don't understand the Cheyenne people whose ancestors fought and died for the land that they are proposing to destroy. They don't understand the fierceness with which the people, both Indian and non-Indian, in southeastern Montana love the land."[17]

The opposition to mining which Braided Hair referenced spread from the Southeast Montana communities who were most directly impacted to the more populous western half of the state long before Blue Skies Campaign arrived on the scene. In February 2010, students from Missoula's Big Sky High School staged a class walkout to protest mining coal on state school trust lands.[18] "I had been trying anything I could think of to spread the word about why stopping the Otter Creek Mine was important," said Rachel Dickson, a Big Sky freshman who later came to UM and joined Blue Skies Campaign. "One time I baked cookies, and only gave them to people if they listened to me talk about coal."[19]

The month after the walkout, the State Land Board voted to grant Arch a lease for its Otter Creek Mine—though not before five young activists from Northern Rockies Rising Tide disrupted the meeting by rushing to front of the room and chanting until they were arrested.[20] Only a permit from the state Department of Environmental Quality now stood in the way of Arch's bulldozers.

My own early participation in the Otter Creek fight came to a head in August 2012, as I sat on a concrete jail floor after the first of five consecutive evenings of sit-ins organized by Blue Skies Campaign at the Montana Capitol. Nearly two dozen people, including well-known environmental writer Rick Bass, were arrested over the course of the week. Hundreds more joined support rallies.

Those of us arrested were allowed to choose between posting $340 in bond or spending the night in jail. As one of the protest's main organizers, I felt that if anyone stayed behind bars overnight, I should join them. Since the men's wing of the jail was overcrowded, our male contingent was put in the library. I fell asleep on a pad laid out on the hard floor, reflecting that I'd finally taken a small step into the kind of escalated protest I believed was necessary to counter the wave of proposed fossil fuel extraction projects then engulfing the country.

West Coast battlegrounds

In July 2015, Portland Mayor Charlie Hales returned from the Vatican where a select group of local government leaders had been discussing the climate crisis with Pope Francis.[21] Oregon's largest city has a longstanding green reputation—but after his trip, Hales became known as one of its most climate-friendly mayors yet. Never was this more evident than in December 2016, when he shepherded a ban on new fossil fuel storage terminals through City Council.

350 Portland organizer Mia Reback called the policy "a powerful message to other cities across the nation and the world."[22]

Hales wasn't always a climate champion. Early in his term he supported building a propane export terminal on the Columbia River capable of handling 72,000 barrels of gas per day.[23] A factor in his transformation from fossil fuel booster to opponent was pressure from climate activists, including some in middle school or younger. "Opposing fossil fuel exports got Charlie Hales on the map," said Jasmine Zimmer-Stucky, whom I introduced while discussing anti-logging activism in Chapter 7. "But public pressure was what moved him."

In 2011, Zimmer-Stucky took a job with Columbia Riverkeeper, a leader in the years-long fight against a suite of liquefied natural gas (LNG) terminals proposed in Oregon port towns. Although originally meant to receive gas imports, the projects' developers switched their business model to exporting after the fracking boom. When Zimmer-Stucky came on board, Columbia Riverkeeper was campaigning against LNG while also fighting a slate of newer export proposals for both coal and oil.

The Northwest had become a chokepoint for fossil fuel industries seeking to reach overseas markets. But while local activists tended to oppose coal, oil, and gas exports with equal vehemence, some national organizations were still touting the idea of gas—even when extracted by fracking—as a lower-carbon "bridge fuel." "Any environmental group would oppose oil exports," Zimmer-Stucky told me. "Opposing coal was easy, too. But gas always felt like the redheaded stepchild."

Efforts by 350 Portland and Portland Rising Tide to build a more unified narrative around fossil fuel exports culminated in a July 2013 protest on the Columbia. Activists announced plans to get upwards of 100 kayaks on the water during Summer Heat, a two-week series of actions around the country promoted by 350.org.[24]

Less widely publicized was that at the height of the "kayaktivist" protest, rappelers would descend off the I-5 Bridge above the river and unfurl a banner with the message "Coal, Oil, Gas: None Shall Pass." Zimmer-Stucky, who volunteered with Rising Tide when not at her Riverkeeper job, would patrol the water in a motor-boat to liaise between activists and police. Just before launch time she learned that leaders from the International Longshoreman and Warehouse Union wanted to get out on the river during the protest. The ILWU had come out against a proposed oil terminal in Vancouver, Washington and was an important ally to environ-mental groups. A fellow activist asked, would Zimmer-Stucky take them on her boat?

"I was like, okay," Zimmer-Stucky said, recounting the story to me. "They didn't know we were about to drop a banner with three people suspended on it off the bridge, though." Would the union representatives be put off by the illegal action? she wondered. "But when the rappelers came into view, Jared [Smith of the ILWU] started cheering. They all loved it." Zimmer-Stucky smiled. "The other part of that story is, Jared and I are now married. That action was one of the first places we spent time together."[25]

Over the next few years hearings about coal, oil, and gas ter-minals drew hundreds or thousands of people from a broad geo-graphic region. I caught a bus chartered by the Northern Plains Resource Council to transport Montanans to a coal export hearing in Spokane, Washington. In a room packed with activists wear-ing "Beyond Coal Exports" T-shirts, I listened to Eastern Montana ranchers and young Northern Cheyenne organizers explain how coal mining threatened their land and water.

Local leadership, often from rural areas, was at the forefront of the fossil fuel export resistance—but to bulk up their throngs of supporters, climate groups needed large urban areas. Portlanders flocked to hearings on oil in Vancouver, coal in Longview, and

LNG in Southern Oregon. "Portland did a great job supporting other communities," Zimmer-Stucky said. "Then Canadian pipeline company Pembina proposed building a propone terminal at the Port of Portland, and people in the city woke up to the fact that fossil fuel exports were coming to them."[26]

Backlash against Pembina, and Mayor Hales' initial enthusiasm for it, was swift. Among the youngest voices were a cohort of middle schoolers from Portland's Sunnyside Environmental School, who plunged into opposing fossil fuel exports after making a video about LNG for a class project. "I like writing, so I'd compose speeches or poems to read at protests," remembered Solomon Duke, one of the students who went on to speak out against Pembina and other fossil fuel projects. "Everyone had something to contribute."[27] Apparently realizing the propane terminal was inconsistent with the values of his constituents, Hales retracted his support.[28]

"When students brought a youth face to the campaign, that's when the tide started turning against fossil fuel exports in Oregon," Zimmer-Stucky said. "The moral authority they brought as young people was decisive."[29]

Following the money: Divestment and frontline communities

The divestment movement that exploded across the country in the early 2010s, and which Chapter 3 treated at length, was a direct outgrowth of work to stop on-the-ground operations of fossil fuel companies. Students at Swarthmore, where the national divestment campaign began, saw the impacts of mountaintop removal mining during a 2010 spring break trip to Appalachia's coal fields with their professor, George Lakey. Particularly important was their visit with Larry Gibson, a grizzled Appalachian in his sixties who refused to sell his land to coal companies.

Gibson took the Swarthmore group on a tour of his farm, leading them to the drop-off at the boundary between his land and a coal mining operation. Hundreds of feet below lay a lunar landscape where the green mountaintop had been carved away, leaving bare earth and piles of rubble. "Larry told us, 'I don't take you up here because I like you—although I do like you. I do it because I need you to do something about this,'" future divestment and Sunrise Movement leader Will Lawrence remembered. "We took that to heart."

The following year, Lawrence and fellow Swarthmore student Kate Aronoff attended a meeting with the Wallace Global Fund and Responsible Endowments Coalition (REC), to discuss funding for campus-based coal divestment organizing. Wallace Global was eager to support the work of student divestment leaders, and REC was involved in the discussions. 350.org was independently moving toward a similar idea. Lawrence had connected with REC at Power Shift 2011, but he and Aronoff—who had studied radical anti-capitalist social movements—arrived at this newest meeting with mixed feelings.

"We thought we were walking into the big, bad nonprofit industrial complex," Lawrence told me, laughing. "We went in and banged on the table—not literally, but you get the idea." The divestment movement was to be led by students and communities on the frontlines, Lawrence and Aronoff announced. Nonprofits and funders should play only supporting roles. To their surprise, the room agreed.[30]

Wallace Global, which had a long history supporting grassroots activism, provided essential funding for early fossil fuel divestment work. REC's role was to advise and serve as a sounding board for student leaders as they developed campus divestment campaigns. The organization helped students understand the arcane world of investment portfolios, a task former REC organizer Lauren Ressler described to me as "unpacking the obfuscating language used to hide what is basically high-level gambling."[31] Soon, stipended student fellows were organizing for fossil fuel divestment at Swarthmore and a half-dozen other schools. The movement grew in leaps when 350.org got deeply involved.

Lawrence, Aronoff, and other recent college graduates launched the Divestment Student Network in 2014 to support campus campaigns that were ready to escalate. There was a logical path for getting groups to this point, they came to believe. In early fall most campaigns concentrated on conventional tactics like gathering petition signatures. When that failed to convince school administrations, as it almost always did, students became open to direct action. DSN would "bring students along on a journey of radicalization," as Lawrence put it. By spring they would be ready for sit-ins and large protests.[32]

In 2015, DSN supported a month-long sit-in at Swarthmore that served as a pilot for a wave of similar campaign escalations the following year. Many students who risked arrest were doing so for the first time.[33] "It didn't become truly real to me until I was being put in a police car," said North Arizona University student and divestment organizer Michaela Mujica-Steiner, who was placed in handcuffs at an April 2016 sit-in.[34]

Despite the high stakes, a carnival-like atmosphere prevailed at many divestment protests. At Vassar College movie showings, sing-alongs, and an acapella performance kept spirits high during a multiday sit-in in the hallway outside the university president's office. "I have a lot of nostalgia for that time," said Sophie Cash, who participated in the protest as a freshman. "It was intense, but we also made it fun."[35]

I felt a special satisfaction that spring upon reading about the divestment sit-in at my own grad school alma mater. "I kept thinking, this sort of thing doesn't happen here," said Caitlin Piserchia, a lead organizer of a protest where students occupied the University of

Montana Foundation office lobby, chanting and singing so loudly that staff eventually gave up trying to maintain a semblance of control. "I realized that with enough people acting together, you can hold a space and there's not much the authorities can do."[36]

Divestment represented one way to channel momentum from campaigns against individual pieces of fossil fuel infrastructure, into attacking the political power of coal, oil, and gas companies at a national level. Another such effort was the September 2014 People's Climate March in New York City, by far the largest U.S. climate mobilization up to then.

"If it goes the way I'm hoping, there'll be tens or hundreds of thousands of people in the street," Phil Aroneanu of 350.org said when I spoke with him shortly before the march for *Waging Non-violence*.[34] The demonstration drew an estimated 400,000 people to New York, two days before a summit at U.N. headquarters intended to pave the way for a global climate agreement to finally be adopted at COP21 in Paris the following year.[37] Practically every large environmental organization and hundreds of smaller ones participated. I took a Greyhound bus from Montana to New York for the march, spending the night beforehand on a local activist's floor.

The next morning I witnessed anti-fracking organizers, coal mining opponents, campus divestment activists, and big green nonprofits come together in a public display of support for climate policy unmatched until the September 2019 climate strikes five years later. In the interval between these two huge mobilizations, the grassroots effort to oppose specific fossil fuel projects escalated in even more creative and inspiring ways.

Shell No

When Ahmed Gaya received an email from a Greenpeace organizer, asking him to speak out at a hearing against Shell Oil's plan to dock an Arctic drilling rig at the Port of Seattle, he couldn't have known he was stepping into what would become one of the highest-profile environmental campaigns in Pacific Northwest history. Gaya, who grew up in New York and attended Quebec's McGill University, had moved to Seattle in 2011 for a job with ForestEthics (now Stand.earth). On his first night in Washington State, he met his new employers at a high school in the community of Bellingham, where a public meeting on the proposed Cherry Point coal export terminal was unfolding. "The room was packed," Gaya remembered.

Over the next couple years, Gaya organized protests against fossil fuels in the Northwest through ForestEthics and Rising Tide Seattle. He had done similar work in Chicago after college, and was struck by the absence of large-scale direct action in his newest home city. "People told me Seattle was a notoriously difficult place to organize environmental direct action. There'd been the WTO protests back in 1999, but for ten years after that almost nothing."

This state of affairs would soon change, thanks to people like Gaya, and years later a milieu of hard-hitting climate campaigns in Seattle provided fertile ground for the rise of Zero Hour. However, a strong activist response to fossil fuel projects in the Northwest—let alone one involving direct action—was never guaranteed and came about only because activists worked for it. Gaya and a scattering of others organized a series of direct actions, including one where a protester suspended on a tripod stopped work at a Seattle rail yard used by oil trains.[38] By 2015, "Seattle had a reputation as the direct action fist of the Northwest fossil fuel resistance," Gaya said. The transformation set the stage for protests that spring against Shell's plan to use Seattle as a waypoint for the first offshore oil vessels to drill in Alaska waters.

"I thought, we needed a WTO protests-style response to this," Gaya told me in a July 2020 conversation. "We convened mass meetings and put out a call to organize autonomous actions. Hundreds of people showed up."[39]

Days after Shell's Polar Pioneer drilling rig arrived in Seattle, hundreds of people blocked the gates to the terminal where it was docked.[40] When the vessel left for the Arctic, a group of "kayaktivists" were arrested paddling into its path.[41] Anti-Shell protests spread to other Northwest cities where Shell was docking vessels related to its Arctic drilling expedition. In Portland, Greenpeace activists rappelled off a bridge and delayed Shell's Fennica icebreaker for forty hours as it tried to leave port.[42]

Another drilling support vessel, the Arctic Challenger, sat anchored in Northwest Washington's Bellingham Bay. Local activists staged a kayaktivist protest on the water, then met to plan how to escalate. "I was exhausted by then," said then-twenty-year-old Chiara D'Angelo, who had spent the last few days organizing protest activity nonstop. "I hadn't eaten, hadn't slept, and was emotionally and physically spent." Even so, when someone suggested attaching an activist to the Challenger's anchor chain, D'Angelo volunteered. She paddled out to the vessel on an inflatable dinghy, secured herself to the huge chain with climbing carabiners, and hung suspended above the water. "My legs started hurting after a few minutes," she said when we spoke in August 2020. "It only got harder from there."

D'Angelo grew up on Washington's Bainbridge Island, impressed by both the area's natural beauty and a realization that previous generations enjoyed "a state of wildlife abundance that's hard for us to even picture today." Now, love of the Northwest's land and waters kept her hanging from the chain despite intense physical pain. She described to me a key moment when a salmon leapt from the waves near her. "It jumped, jumped again, and kept jumping in the same place." To D'Angelo, this atypical behavior felt like a message about endurance directed at her. It was followed by an experience that sounds even more remarkable, at least from the standpoint of Western secularism.

In a vision that felt real as the ache in her limbs, D'Angelo suddenly seemed to glimpse the icy waters of the far north reaching down from the horizon toward her and joining with the sparkling Salish Sea. "My body still hurt," she said. "But I realized then that I would have to sacrifice being comfortable and stay as long as I could to protect what I love."

Visions and messages from animals may be difficult for some activists to accept at face value. However, when describing to me what motivated her to stay on the Challenger's anchor chain, D'Angelo emphasized not the warnings of climate scientists, but her Roma ancestors' traditional spirituality with its connection to nature. She descended from the vessel only after sixty-three hours, upon learning its departure was being postponed.[43] Her experience is a reminder of how the dimension of spirit has become increasingly important in the climate movement—especially in places where it overlaps with centuries-old struggles against colonialism by cultures to whom the strict dichotomy between science and religion is foreign.[44]

Stand with Standing Rock

"I never sugarcoat how I got to Standing Rock," Tasina Smith told me in a March 2021 phone interview. Smith, a member of the Cheyenne River Sioux Tribe, was twenty-three when she arrived at what grew into the largest sustained direct action against a piece of fossil fuel infrastructure in the U.S. to date. "I had gone down a bad path."

Smith grew up in a "very political" family, with a role model grandmother who participated in the militant American Indian Movement protests of the 1970s. Her grandmother's passing when Smith was in her early twenties had a destabilizing effect on the younger woman. She left home on the Cheyenne River Reservation for a job in the city, where she slid into drug and alcohol dependence. "I led a double life," she said. "I hid my addiction so well that no one suspected. But I wasn't healthy mentally, emotionally, or spiritually."

In July 2016, Smith had what she described as an "epiphany" and quit her addiction cold turkey. Like many people on similar journeys, she found strength in a search for new spiritual meaning. She had a friend who went shoeless in order to better connect with the Earth. "At first I was like, whatever," Smith said. But gradually the idea grew on her, "and I decided to ditch my shoes, too."

When she had been sober three weeks, Smith saw a newspaper story about youth from the Cheyenne River and neighboring Standing Rock Reservations who were organizing a multiday run to Washington, D.C. to protest the planned Dakota Access oil pipeline. If built, Dakota Access would cut under the Missouri River reservoir that supplies Standing Rock with drinking water. Smith recognized some of the young people's names from the Cheyenne River Youth Project where she worked prior to fleeing the reservation.

"Some of these kids came from backgrounds of domestic violence, rape, drug abuse, and alcoholism," Smith said. "Yet, they mustered up the resilience and courage to fight for a bigger cause. That inspired the hell out of me, and I instantly knew I needed to go home."

Smith made a visit to Cheyenne River, intending to return to her city job soon. She stopped in the reservation town of Eagle Butte to see her aunt, who pulled out her phone and showed Smith a message from another relative who was protesting the laying of pipe at Standing Rock, where Dakota Access had begun breaking ground. "I looked at her," Smith said. "And I was like, okay, let's go check this out."[45]

*

Earlier that year, veteran pipeline resister Joye Braun reached out to Cheyenne River Sioux youth working to stop the Keystone XL pipeline and asked them to join the fight against another oil project to the north.

"I'd been hearing for a while about how Dakota Access would affect Standing Rock," said Joseph White Eyes, whom I introduced in the previous chapter. "I kept wondering, who was going stop it while we focused on Keystone XL? But I assumed someone from up there would figure it out."

Braun's invitation changed everything. The Army Corps of Engineers had published a draft finding of no significant environmental impact from Dakota Access, despite threats to the Missouri.[46] Now Standing Rock elders were convening a meeting. "A group of us from Cheyenne River caravanned up in my grandmother's vehicle to participate," White Eyes said.

From that early gathering was born Sacred Stone Camp, a hub for direct action resistance that started with a small group of people pitching tents near the Dakota Access construction zone in April. Soon after that, White Eyes and other Cheyenne River and Standing Rock youth organized a 500-mile relay run to the regional Army Corps office in Omaha, documenting their journey on social media. They were so successful at generating publicity, they decided to organize an even longer relay that summer.

In July, the youth departed on a 2,000-mile run to the national Army Corps headquarters in Washington, D.C., where they secured a meeting with a Corps general. "We requested it be just young people who went in," White Eyes said. "Each of us talked about why stopping this pipeline was important to us." The government's response was underwhelming, though. "None of them really seemed interested in what we had to say."[47]

The runners couldn't convince the Obama administration to reverse a decision allowing pipeline construction beneath the Missouri, but by sharing their stories online they changed the terms of public debate over Dakota Access. "It was hard work," said Morgan Brings Plenty, who recorded moments from the run, collated them, and posted the footage on social media. "We were uploading content with two phones that barely functioned."[48] Nevertheless, videos where runners explained the stakes at Standing Rock went viral.

By the time the youth returned to Sacred Stone, the camp had grown to include hundreds of people. The next couple months saw more come from all over the continent, until at the height of the protest ten thousand people stayed at Sacred Stone and other encampments that split off from it. It was during this period of rapid growth that Tasina Smith arrived.

*

After driving to the protest encampment with her aunt, Smith decided to remain indefinitely. "I saw people there who I'd lost touch with since my grandma's passing," she said. "I realized I'd been selfish, leaving the reservation when all this was happening. Seeing everybody so unified in resistance to Dakota Access made me want to stay."

Smith shared a tent with her father, who joined her at Standing Rock as things were about to escalate. In mid-August she participated in a vigil next to the pipeline construction zone where participants sang and prayed over the din of machinery. She wore

Sundance ceremony regalia. "Eventually, a woman came up and asked me, do you want to actually stop this shit? I said yes, even though I knew I might be arrested."

Smith and three other women, all in Sundance dress, prepared to jump the fence into the construction zone and run to the bank of the Cannonball River where it meets the Missouri, just downstream of the pipeline route. Some wanted to wait until they had seven people, a sacred number—but amid the confusion, Smith ended up hopping early. "I took off running and the others followed. I was barefoot. I'm not normally a runner, but it felt like I was gliding, like I wasn't the one doing the work."

Smith later learned that by entering the construction zone, she and the other fence-jumpers had halted work on the site for the day. She and a young woman named Holly dodged a group of security guards and continued through the ninety-degree heat, reaching the Cannonball a couple hours later. On the swampy riverbank they had an experience which, like D'Angelo's vision on the Arctic Challenger, stretches the limits of what people schooled in Western thought patterns may easily understand.

"I heard crying," Smith said. "I asked Holly if it was her. She said, 'No, I thought it was you.' Then we heard it again. I said, 'It sounds like a grandma.' And she said, 'I know.' That's when the hair on every part of my body rose up. In that moment, I felt my Grandma was there with me and I wanted to cry, too."

The young women later consulted tribal elders, whose opinion was that they heard a water spirit weeping because she knew Dakota Access would eventually be built.[49] This is consistent with Indigenous views of resistance to unwanted fossil fuel projects as a spiritual undertaking.

"At Standing Rock, I saw a movement grounded in Native religion," said Eamon Ormseth, a recent University of Montana graduate and colleague from my Missoula activist days. He was working as an interfaith campus ministry organizer at UM when he carpooled to Standing Rock with a group of activists in October 2016. Ormseth told me that "the climate movement as a whole tends to downplay spirituality, partly because of understandable hostility toward organized Christianity and its history of conquest and genocide. But Standing Rock was rooted in Indigenous spiritual traditions."[50]

Ormseth was among the thousands of people who traveled to the encampments in the second half of 2016. For many climate activists, supporting the resistance there seemed like a chance to bring the opposition to fossil fuels to a new level. Yet, Standing Rock was a climate protest second, a defense of Indigenous sovereignty first. Participants left with memories of evening round dances, prayer songs used to wake campers in the mornings, and a road lined with flags of the almost 200 tribes represented.[51]

"There was constant coming and going," said Kiewsis Morsette, a young Chippewa Cree who visited in late November 2016. "Surveillance helicopters and planes would fly overhead throughout the day. At night law enforcement shown lights into the camp and illuminated everything."[52]

State surveillance and repression became part of life at Standing Rock. Police used chemical weapons and water cannons on nonviolent protesters. Morsette was caught in a rain of tear gas during a peaceful march.[53] At a separate incident, Smith and several others were bitten by attack dogs. "It was literally spiritual warfare between a peaceful, beautiful protest and a bloodthirsty government," Smith said.

Climate activists love to quote the latest findings of scientists, with good reason. Yet, it is noteworthy that some of the most inspiring acts of resistance to fossil fuel development have come from deeply spiritual people. It seems at least possible that the willingness for self-sacrifice required to face repressive violence is difficult to achieve from a purely secular mindset. If so, this challenges the assumptions those of us with Westernized worldviews, including myself, bring to climate activism.

"People can say I'm crazy," Smith told me. "But I know deep in my heart that my being at Standing Rock was in answer to a call from my grandmother and my ancestors. I can't even describe what I experienced. The closest I can come is undying commitment, loyalty, and love for the people."

Smith abandoned her city job and stayed at Standing Rock for the duration of protests that lasted into early the following year. "The most beautiful thing was in the face of all the violence against us, to see our people still standing there," she said toward the end of our conversation. "And we're still here today, with me on the phone with you right now letting you know we're still standing and still fighting."[54]

By the time our call ended, a few minutes later, I felt I'd come briefly into contact with a force outside the boundaries of what my Westernized mind could fully comprehend.

Being the carbon tax

After addressing the massive crowds at the New York City climate strike on September 20, 2019, Greta Thunberg set out on a U.S. speaking tour that included a meeting in Standing Rock with young leaders of the resistance to Dakota Access.[55] The moment underscored how opposition to fossil fuel infrastructure was inspiring the new generation of climate activists then flooding onto the streets in the hundreds of thousands. As I witnessed this unprecedented display of support for cutting carbon pollution, I realized Generation Z had taken the climate movement to levels my fellow Millennials and I never reached.

I had recently turned thirty, and no longer thought of myself as a youth climate activist. A few years earlier I'd left Missoula, where I had worked to build community opposition to coal. The campaign against Montana coal exports was a more soul-encompassing undertaking than anything else I've devoted myself to, before or since. Activists sometimes speak of their work as though it weren't just a job, paid or not, but an all-consuming way of life. Having lived this lifestyle myself, I believe them. But it was time to move on.

I had made the classic activist mistake of overextending myself until I became depressed and burnt out. At the same time, the climate movement was changing in ways I felt ill-equipped to navigate. My limited social skills made it difficult to facilitate the collaborative organizing spaces that were increasingly important. I lacked the theoretical framework for conversations around race, gender, and class which I sensed needed to happen. And with many more organizers on the scene, some far more skilled than I, my role as a leader even at the local level seemed less necessary.

I moved back to Oregon for a few months as I prepared to return to school again, this time for a master's in environmental education at Western Washington University. In the time I'd been away from Portland, local organizations had brought public participation in the climate movement to levels that would have seemed impossible several years earlier. A January 2016 hearing on oil exports in Vancouver, Washington drew over 400 people, numbers that would have stunned me and others at the start of the Boardman anti-coal campaign. In 2019, Portland's well-organized network of climate groups turned out an estimated 20,000 people for one of the largest U.S. climate strikes outside New York City.[56]

At the same time, grassroots opposition to fossil fuel infrastructure was achieving impressive results regionally and nationally. As of this writing, almost every major Northwest coal, oil, and gas export project proposed since 2010 has been defeated, including every coal terminal.[57] With the market for coal exports evaporating, Arch Coal abandoned attempts to build its Otter Creek Mine in 2016.[58] Beyond Coal has secured the retirement of hundreds of coal plants nationally,[59] and gas pipelines like the PennEast project in New Jersey[60] and Atlantic Coast pipeline in Appalachia[61] have gone down in defeat. In September 2015, Shell abandoned deepwater drilling in the Arctic—ostensibly because early exploration for oil turned up minimal reserves, but it was hard to escape the impression public protests played a role in the decision.[62]

Not every campaign against fossil fuel infrastructure has succeeded. Construction of the Dakota Access pipeline finished in 2017,[63] after being briefly and belatedly halted by the outgoing Obama administration.[64] However, the movement born at Standing Rock ensured almost no major oil project would go unchallenged in the future. From the Texas Trans-Pecos pipeline,[65] to the Bayou Bridge pipeline in Louisiana,[66] to Line 3 in Minnesota,[67] oil projects all over the U.S. have faced Indigenous-led direct action campaigns since Standing Rock.

A popular quote attributed to Gandhi urges listeners to be the change they wish to see in the world. Many climate activists believe in the need for a price on carbon to internalize the social costs of burning fossil fuels—and in the absence of government action, they can in effect become this tax themselves. Protests and direct action may not stop every pipeline, but they send a message that the costs of completing such projects in terms of litigation, extra security, and damage to a company's public image will be high. As some developers decide it's not worth it, the overall amount of carbon emitted into the atmosphere will go down.

When I started at WWU in 2016, the climate movement had already become something far bigger and more sophisticated than the one I knew as an undergraduate. I finished my M.Ed. just as Zero Hour and the school strikes were about to bring even larger crowds into the streets. Many of the largest rallies and marches took place in cities like New York, Portland, and Seattle, where the fossil fuel infrastructure resistance had given local activists years of practice mobilizing huge crowds. Without the vision and skills of Generation Z, the wave of climate activism that began in 2018 would never have reached such great heights. But like all social movements, it built on the work of earlier generations.

As the country entered a turbulent new decade, I was anxious to see where the youth climate movement would go next. And could it translate its goals into policy wins at the local, national, and international levels?

PART THREE

Preparing for the
Next Wave

9

The Challenge of Here and Now

YOUTH CLIMATE ACTIVISM IN THE NEW DECADE

In early September 2020, I spoke on the phone with a member of the original Energy Action Coalition steering committee while looking out at a smoke-obscured view of Northwest Washington's Bellingham Bay. I wasn't far from where Chiara D'Angelo suspended herself off Shell's Arctic Challenger five years earlier. To the north lay the site of a proposed coal export terminal that was killed by a legal challenge from the Lummi Nation and community opposition. Like so many communities, Bellingham's recent history has been shaped by more than one climate movement fight. As I strained to see through the smoke, I had a sense of looking back in time at the series of events leading up to this moment.

"It's surreal," said Nick Algee, the activist I was interviewing. "Here we are, talking about the climate organizing being done twenty years ago, while watching firsthand as the effects of the crisis unfold today."

Algee was part of the national youth climate movement almost since its beginning. As a student at Florida's Rollins College in the 2000s he got involved with the loose network of organizations that became Energy Action Coalition. Now, almost two decades later, he was in the small town of Brookings, Oregon, where ash from nearby wildfires rained from the sky. "Things look pretty apocalyptic here," he said.

I could relate, although smoke from the unprecedented wildfires raging up and down the West Coast was not yet as bad in Bellingham as it would soon be. Within days, it became hard to make out buildings just a couple blocks away. The world in 2020 felt like a different place from the one in which members of mine and Algee's generation joined the early climate movement.

Algee's path to activism began in earnest in 1999, the year he turned twenty while hiking the Appalachian Trail. "Those six-plus months on the trail helped me realize my work in this life was to inspire human reverence for nature and help us become better stewards of the land," he said. "We have this idea that we're dominant over other living things. But in reality, all life is interconnected."

In 2002, Algee received a student government grant to cover transportation expenses for a spring break tour of colleges across the South, where he made contacts with groups doing sustainability work and gathered ideas to bring back to Rollins. "In some cases, I had appointments set up with student organizations or environmental departments," he remembered. "On other campuses I literally just knocked on doors until I found people who wanted to talk about sustainability."

During this and a similar, longer tour that summer, Algee built a list of contacts that helped lay the foundation for EAC's work in the

South. He drove a Prius borrowed from a local Sierra Club chapter at a time when hybrid vehicle technology was new.[1] Few if any campuses he visited would have had detailed clean energy transition plans, so what he was doing seemed radical in a way it wouldn't today. The thought of divesting from fossil fuels wouldn't even have occurred to most universities or pension funds at the time, and hardly any policymakers were talking about retiring coal plants. The youth climate movement has come a long way since then.

Part I of this book examined this movement as manifested in campaigns like the climate school strikes, the push for a Green New Deal, and divestment. Part II considered how the surge of recent activism that began in late 2018 built on a foundation laid by years of organizing. Without all this work, the prospects for a stable global climate would be even worse than they are today.

At the same time, the increasingly severe drought and wildfire seasons that seem to grip the Western United States each year are one reminder of how far the climate movement still has to go, and the deadly costs of failure. This chapter will look at both the movement's major accomplishments so far, and where it still has much to do.

Changing politics

When President Biden moved to cancel the Keystone XL pipeline and re-join the Paris Climate Accords on his first day in office, he was acknowledging the reality that climate change occupied a place of prominence on the political agenda unprecedented in U.S. history.[2] Soon, government agencies were working to reinstate more than a hundred environmental regulations rolled back under the Trump administration, while Congress took up federal climate legislation for the first time in over a decade. There were also many times when Biden and Congressional leaders failed to live up to their own rhetoric and disappointed climate activists. However, by 2021, the climate movement had shifted the political narrative to a point where actions which once would have seemed unthinkable were taken almost as a matter of course in this by-no-means-radical administration.

Although Biden's highly public early moves on climate were among the most dramatic signs of how the school strikes and other strands of youth-led activism were affecting U.S. policymakers, climate protests were having an impact well before Biden and a new Congress took office in January 2021. In fact, almost a year earlier something extraordinary had happened: leaders in the Republican-controlled U.S. Senate began talking seriously about passing climate legislation. The proposals on the table, like temporarily extending renewable energy tax credits and banning the super-pollutants known as HFCs, weren't especially ambitious. Still, faced with an unprecedented wave of climate protests, even conservative lawmakers who normally opposed environmental action apparently felt pressure to show they were doing something. By the end of the year a package of renewables-focused energy policies made it into a sprawling COVID response and budget bill signed into law by President Trump.[3]

It wasn't that Trump, or Senate conservatives who repeatedly stifled other efforts to address climate change, had suddenly decided to take the crisis seriously. Nor did the budget bill's climate measures—a collection of policies Congressional moderates had long advocated for, but with little success—come close to the scale of what was needed. However, their passage suggests youth-led climate activism was having a real impact, even on Republican lawmakers.

The effect within the Democratic Party was far more dramatic. Within months of Sunrise Movement's first sit-in at Nancy Pelosi's office in 2018, every Democratic senator considered a serious contender for the presidency had signed onto the Green New Deal resolution.[4] Former Vice President Biden declined to explicitly endorse the Green New Deal during his campaign for the presidency, but called the concept "a crucial framework for meeting the climate challenges we face."[5] By the end of 2020, the House version of the resolution had over a hundred Democratic cosponsors.[6]

Nor was the increased focus on aggressive climate action limited to the federal government. By the end of 2021, eleven U.S. states, Washington, D.C., and Puerto Rico had legislation mandating utilities source 100 percent of their energy from renewables by 2050 or sooner. As recently as 2018, only California and Hawaii had such policies in place.[7] In April 2019, New York City passed an ambitious set of climate measures billed as a local "Green New Deal."[8] Los Angeles followed with a similar package weeks later.[9] Since then, cities from Seattle[10] to Austin[11] have used the concept of a Green New Deal to frame far-reaching climate plans.

These developments reflected shifting attitudes among voters. Pew Research Center polling results published in January 2020 showed 52% of the U.S. public felt climate action should be an urgent national priority, a sharp increase from a few years earlier.[12] In a separate study in the *Journal of Environmental Psychology*, researchers found a spike in internet searches for terms like "climate change" in the U.S. and other countries in 2019, as compared with previous years. The upticks were especially pronounced around that year's major deep strike days, suggesting the school strikes caused a measurable increase in public interest and attention to the climate crisis.[13] In short, strikes and other forms of climate activism had a detectable impact on both public opinion and lawmakers.

This book has focused on the U.S., but youth climate activism is international. Europe, where the school strikes started and where governments are less beholden to fossil fuel interests than in the

U.S., is where the climate movement has arguably seen its biggest wins so far. But sometimes, foreign leaders have latched onto rhetoric popularized in the United States—as when the European Union announced plans for a continent-wide "Green Deal."[14] The following year, South Korea unveiled its own Green New Deal and a plan to achieve carbon neutrality by 2050.[15] This set off a domino effect among major Asian economies as first Japan,[16] then China,[17] Indonesia,[18] and India[19] made carbon neutrality pledges. The timelines for curbing emissions were often longer than activists wanted, and how governments follow through remains to be seen, but the global trend toward more ambitious climate targets is clear.

Still, as I worked on this book's final edits in early 2022, the biggest prize U.S. climate activists sought—sweeping Congressional action to encourage a wholesale shift from fossil fuels to renewables —remained elusive. The 2021 Infrastructure Investment and Jobs Act included modest support for clean energy and electric vehicles,[20] but efforts to pass a much more comprehensive set of climate policies in the Biden-supported Build Back Better Act had failed. It appeared climate activists' best efforts might not be enough to overcome resistance from lawmakers like Joe Manchin, West Virginia's Democratic senator with deep ties to the coal industry. As Congress debated Build Back Better in late 2021, Sunrise activists staging a hunger strike outside the White House confronted Manchin over his opposition to key climate provisions.[21] Manchin responded with this extraordinarily inaccurate statement: "We've done more [on climate] in the United States of America than any country. All the emissions are coming from Asia."[22]

Fortunately for the climate and all life on Earth, things took a turn for the better in summer of 2022, when Manchin unexpectedly announced his support for a pared-down set of climate policies in what became known as the Inflation Reduction Act (IRA).

Although less ambitious than Sunrise's vision for a Green New Deal or even the Build Back Better Act, the IRA invested $369 in clean technologies and put the U.S. on a path to reduce emissions 40% below peak levels by 2030.[23] Sunrise's Varshini Prakash called it "a historic investment in climate action that would have been unimaginable just a few years ago," while acknowledging Manchin's support hinged on also including "massive handouts to fossil fuel millionaires," such as new incentives for offshore oil development in the bill.[24]

The IRA's concessions to polluters are real, and a reminder of the fossil fuel industry's waning but still-powerful political influence. Even so, President Biden's signing of the bill on August 16, 2022 marked the beginning of a new era for climate activists. For the first time, the world's biggest economy and historic emitter of carbon pollution has a law on the books meant to trigger society-wide movement away from fossil fuels. U.S. activists' work is far from over—but the challenges they face going forward will look more like those of their European colleagues, who are trying to make elected leaders follow through on and strengthen existing climate commitments, rather than commit to doing something in the first place. As Prakash said, "when our [Sunrise's] movement launched, climate was so off the map, most people wouldn't have believed that within years Congress would deliver a climate and jobs plan. But today, it's clear that young people have organized the impossible into existence."[25]

Perhaps more than anything, passage of the IRA represents an opportunity for the climate movement to continue building momentum for future, even farther-reaching wins. To do this, activists will need to find new, innovative ways of keeping climate at the forefront of the public consciousness. Because it's undeniable that, well before the final stages of the fight over federal climate legislation in the 117th Congress wound down, the huge climate protests of a couple years earlier had receded into the past.

Ebbing and flowing

Any discussion of the climate strikes' decline should be prefaced with the understanding that sustaining mass protests over the long term is exceedingly difficult—especially in a country like the U.S., where systemic barriers make it hard for movements to catch on in the first place. When street movements fizzle, the press and even organizers themselves tend to blame activists' real or imagined missteps rather than society-wide structural challenges. Still, activists hoping to usher in the next flood of climate mobilizations can gain valuable insights from analyzing why previous waves have subsided.

COVID certainly contributed to derailing the strike movement. Pandemic restrictions forced activists to cancel in-person protests, while school closures made striking from class moot for many students. However, even before the pandemic there were signs of the movement losing steam; a deep strike day in December 2019 saw actions across the U.S. and globe, but not the huge crowds of September.[26] This may have been partly a case of simple protest fatigue. However, conversations I had in my capacity as an environmental educator with Bellingham-area students who participated in early strike events suggest another contributing factor. At least some young strikers seem to have grown discouraged because their efforts did not quickly result in larger, more tangible changes in U.S. government policy. This frustration is certainly understandable, but also misplaced. The strikes *were* making a difference, albeit more slowly than activists wanted.

Unfortunately, the U.S. education system does little to help students understand what a slow, involved process creating social change is—a point the next chapter will address at length. As 350.org's Will Bates told me, "Movements have arcs. They have highs and lows. They're going to have perceived failures and need to build something new from there. At those moments you don't stop, you double down."[27] If readers of this book take away one message, I hope it is that the climate movement is a long-term project whose goals will not be completed by any one protest.

Some youth-led climate organizing continued apace in the COVID era. Chapter 2 discussed Sunrise Movement's work turning out voters in 2020, and the organization resumed holding Democratic lawmakers accountable after Election Day. In June 2021, hundreds of Sunrise members converged on the White House and blockaded all ten doors at a time when Biden seemed in danger of giving up on climate legislation.[28] Sunrise volunteers also worked the phones, asking voters in key Congressional districts to contact their representatives.[29] These and similar efforts were likely vital to getting the IRA over the finish line.

Just as importantly, two decades of climate movement organizing by young people had chipped away at the fossil fuel industry's power to the point where legislative goals that once appeared fanciful now seemed achievable. This progress toward transforming what is politically possible will likely far outlast any one campaign or protest, and may be the climate movement's single biggest accomplishment yet.

*

"In many ways, the fossil fuel industry is on its heels," longtime climate activist Matt Leonard told me in January 2021. "They don't have the political capital they once did, or the same degree of influence. People are realizing they aren't a viable long-term investment. That's a huge change."[30]

Climate activists have sometimes been told campaigning against fossil fuels would inevitably fail unless they first secured a major buildup of renewables. However, the opposite may actually be true. The main barrier to government investments in clean energy like those eventually included in the Inflation Reduction Act was always the political influence of polluting industries themselves. The last ten years of climate movement history have largely been a story of slow but steady progress toward the goal of dethroning big oil, coal, and gas, which paid off in the most visible way yet in 2022.

Fossil fuel companies are still influential, of course, especially within the Republican Party. But they no longer appear invincible. Keystone XL was just one of several oil and gas pipelines to suffer stinging political defeats by early 2021. By then, coal generated about half as much electricity in the U.S. as it did when I first became a climate activist. And while natural gas companies try to position themselves as a lower-carbon alternative, gas is increasingly being displaced by renewables, too. Incentives for clean energy in the IRA will only speed up these trends. All this has occurred against a backdrop of trillions of dollars in investments fleeing the fossil fuels sector. The concessions to polluters in the IRA are a reminder that the industry has not yet been defeated—but young people are finding new ways to push back.

"Divesting from fossil fuels should mean full, complete divestment in every sense of the word," said Harvard student Ilana Cohen, when I reconnected with her in September 2022. About a year had passed since Harvard announced it would allow existing fossil fuel investments in its endowment to expire, a major milestone for the divestment movement discussed at length in Chapter 3. Now, students like Cohen were building on this victory with the launch of Fossil Free Research, a new campaign focused on pushing schools not to accept fossil industry money for climate research and other academic endeavors. "True divestment means you separate yourself completely from the companies driving climate breakdown and do not allow them to have a role in work critical to our future," Cohen explained.[31]

Climate activists often talk about planetary "tipping points," beyond which certain effects of the climate crisis will become irreversible. However, it seems possible the world is approaching another kind of tipping point, where the political power of a vibrant climate movement will outweigh that of a weakened fossil fuel industry falling out of public favor. "The question is," Leonard said, "will we get there over such a long timeframe that the harm done to ecosystems and communities is truly devastating and irreparable, or can social movements make it happen fast enough to minimize the damage?"[32]

The answer to this question may depend, in part, on the climate movement's ability to spring back from COVID-19 and other challenges and usher in the next major wave of mass protests.

How movements endure

Every movement has fallow periods punctuated by surges of sometimes-frantic growth. As I write in 2022, the youth climate movement emerging from the COVID pandemic seems to be in one of its fallows. School strikes haven't disappeared, and may yet experience another resurgence, but the specific tactic of skipping class for the climate seems to have lost some of its freshness and ability to inspire. Greta Thunberg's influence as a movement figurehead has also likely peaked, at least in this country. This leaves fertile ground for the emergence of new leaders and approaches to activism.

The movement has been in comparable places before. In 2009, in the leadup to COP15, U.S. progressive groups threw their energy into organizing around climate in a way that had never happened previously. Much of this momentum dissipated after the failure in

Copenhagen, but what seemed at first like a fatal collapse of interest in climate organizing turned out to be an opportunity. Over the next several years, the climate movement rebuilt itself into something much bolder, more politically adept, and less willing to compromise than before. Chapters 6-8 recount these developments.

In 2016, climate organizing suffered another blow. The election of Donald Trump threatened to erase many of the gains made so far, while the progressive community's energy was consumed with countering new threats to immigrants, communities of color, and women's rights. However, Trump's ascendance galvanized a new generation of activists like the founders of Zero Hour. They led a resurgent climate movement into its most ambitious, impactful phase yet.

The resilience of the youth climate movement has been no accident. Hundreds of dedicated people spent years building the organizational and training infrastructure to foster new leadership and ensure that even when interest in climate advocacy temporarily subsides, a healthy core of organized activity remains. Movements lacking such built-in stamina have proven far less durable.

*

In September 2011, as the campaign against Keystone XL escalated, hundreds of people descended on Zuccotti Park in New York's Financial District, determined to occupy Wall Street. Their actions spawned one of the most widespread protests in history, with solidarity encampments springing up in public spaces all over the U.S. Occupy Wall Street was a rare example of a movement that really did seem to come almost from nowhere, growing at dizzying speed in response to a post from editors of the Canadian magazine *Adbusters*.[33]

U.S. progressives had long been pushing for goals sought by the protesters in Zuccotti Park, like financial reform and an end to money in politics. However, established organizations played only minor roles in what came to be called the "Occupy" movement. Over a very short period, thousands of people got involved in activism for the first time. This influx of new energy gave the movement much of its power, but a lack of organizational infrastructure to absorb and train new activists contributed to its downfall.

I was in Montana during Occupy Wall Street. I was excited by this fresh movement whose goals for curbing reckless corporate behavior overlapped with those of climate activists, and I attended the first Occupy Missoula gathering on the County Courthouse lawn. I also participated in the "general assemblies" that served as the local movement's decision-making body, and spoke with activists who visited Occupy encampments in New York, Portland, Washington, D.C., and elsewhere. These conversations convinced me the dynamics I observed playing out in Missoula were typical of the larger movement. When encampments throughout the country began shrinking in 2012, commentators tended to blame flaws in broader movement strategy, with a common critique being that Occupy never developed a clear set of demands.[34] But I believe a more important factor was that too many Occupy activists didn't know how to run meetings.

The huge numbers of activist neophytes flooding to Occupy gatherings were a double-edged sword. Inexperienced facilitators did their best to keep general assembly meetings on track, but lacked training in how to keep fringe elements from hijacking the agenda. Meetings veered into tangents while decision-making proceeded at a snail's pace. Participation declined as frustrated activists stopped showing up. If the movement had possessed the ability to quickly absorb and train thousands of new leaders, this could likely have been avoided.

Occupy Wall Street was no failure. The U.S. public's perception of the powerful billionaire class has never been the same since—but the movement might have lasted longer and accomplished more if better equipped to develop and retain new leadership. At the very least, it could have survived the decline in activity in 2012 and perhaps reemerged more powerful than ever. A lack of movement infrastructure prevented this.

There are two main ways social movements come into being. An exceptional few rise quickly and almost from nothing, as Occupy Wall Street did, due to an unusual alignment of circumstances. But far more typical are those that build power slowly, gradually involving larger numbers of people. The youth climate movement belongs to this latter category. From its early days, organizations like the Sierra Student Coalition and Power Shift Network put a premium on training and mentorship as they sought to expand the movement's ranks. When Jamie Margolin attended one of PSN's annual gatherings for leaders of member organizations in 2018, she developed connections that proved integral to the success of Zero Hour.

"Zero Hour first reached out to us because they needed a fiscal sponsor," said Dany Sigwalt, who joined PSN as its operations director in 2016. One of Sigwalt's early duties was to build a fiscal sponsorship program that allows new climate organizations to accept charitable donations by effectively "borrowing" PSN's tax-free status. While not the stuff of headlines, finding a fiscal sponsor is often a determining factor in whether an activist group gets off the ground. PSN sponsored Zero Hour and supported the fledgling organization in other ways. After Margolin attended the January meeting, Sigwalt recalled former PSN director Lydia Avila spending hours on the phone with the founders of Zero Hour, "coaching them on messaging, logistics, and how to organize large mobilizations."[35]

That July, Zero Hour's debut day of marches ushered in a new era of youth-led climate protests. "That was a realization of the kind of leadership development PSN tries to make possible," said Sean Estelle, PSN's national network coordinator during the time Zero Hour was getting off the ground. "I like to think we created space for mentorship and networking opportunities that helped Zero Hour skyrocket."[36]

It is possible to trace a domino effect backward in time from school strikes for the climate, to the launch of Zero Hour, to Power Shift Network, to the founding of Energy Action Coalition, PSN's forerunner, in 2004. However, while this thread of continuity is important, so are ways in which the movement has changed over time in response to ongoing, fundamental challenges.

What must be done

Sigwalt spent her student days at Macalaster College in the early 2000s, when the Minnesota school served as a hub for Energy Action Coalition's activity in the Midwest. "I was aware of the coalition's work, but didn't get involved then," she told me. "The climate movement's public image at the time didn't make it seem very accessible to me as a young, Black woman."

Instead, Sigwalt devoted herself to organizing around issues like drug reform and violence against Black communities. Only when Avila, EAC's first executive director of color, began steering the coalition in a new direction did Sigwalt feel drawn to apply for a job there.[37] In 2019 she became co-director of the organization alongside Nadya Dutchin, also a Black woman with a background in social justice activism. "My goal is to marry the youth climate and environmental justice movements into the same thing," Dutchin said when I spoke with the two of them in a March 2020 Zoom call.[38]

It may be tempting to see the increased focus on diversity, equity, and inclusion in the climate movement as a linear march from an unenlightened past to the relatively progressive present—

but this is misleading. The work of making youth climate activism relevant and accessible to young people of all backgrounds is on-going, and tensions which emerged early in EAC continue to play out at the national and local levels today. I encountered an especially compelling example of this dynamic when interviewing students from Clark University in Massachusetts.

"I was a typical, environmentally-minded kid who loved being outside," Ari Nicholson, a soon-to-be-graduated senior, told me in May 2020. Nicholson attended Sprog in high school, then became a Sprog trainer and attended COP21 in Paris. They started college at Clark the following year, joining the school's fossil fuel divestment campaign just as it prepared to escalate.

At a divestment rally outside a Clark University Board of Trus-tees meeting that fall, one of the few students of color present stood up and made an impromptu speech.[39] "I'm looking around, and there are a lot of white people here," the speaker said. "And it's no coincidence that this is a climate justice rally and the crowd is heavily white." The student pointed out that few rally participants had shown up to support intersectional efforts like an immigrant rights action on campus weeks earlier. For Nicholson this was illuminating.

"The speaker had not said anything that we [divestment leaders] had not already thought important to consider," Nicholson wrote in their senior thesis about Clark's divestment campaign. "[B]ut before the rally we did not see urgency to address the issue among the [many] other things we felt pressured to take on."[40]

Too often, campus climate campaigns let a seemingly endless list of priorities—meetings with administrators, volunteer recruitment, planning, and escalation—take precedence over systemic concerns about inclusion. The result is a movement unable to appeal to the very people most impacted by the climate crisis. "Every place I've lived has been affected by climate change," said Gari de Ramos, a

Clark student who was born in the Philippines, emigrated to the U.S. by way of Hong Kong, and grew up partly on New York's low-lying Roosevelt Island. "I would look around my community and think, this will all be underwater soon. In college I wanted to turn my anxiety about climate change into action."

Yet, after attending some Clark divestment meetings, de Ramos wasn't inspired to go back. "I believed in the mission," she said. "But the space was super white, with an aura of privilege. I didn't feel comfortable being the only person of color in the room."[41]

Prompted by feedback from students of color, Nicholson and other Clark divestment leaders embarked on an effort to "situate ourselves within the legacy of white supremacy in the environmental movement," and "move past our white guilt and understand how to act in solidarity" with marginalized groups.[42] This journey is ongoing at Clark and countless other schools with active climate campaigns.

At the national level, leaders of color have at times reported a disconnect between the inclusive image which groups like Sunrise Movement present to the outside world, and certain internal practices. In a 2021 open letter titled "Do What Must be Done," members affiliated with Sunrise's Black Constituency argued Sunrise "excels at pitching the radical story of *who we want to become* to millions of people and the political elite. But this leaves a disingenuous gap between the movement one thinks they're joining and the actual training and resources a new member receives."[43] In a collection of communications obtained by BuzzFeed News, Sunrise activists of color spoke of feeling tokenized and silenced when they brought up concerns about representation.[44]

The "Do What Must be Done" letter, published months after the largest uprisings for racial justice in recent U.S. history, argued that in 2020, "With most young people in the streets, we didn't just fail to absorb, we lost [activists]," and that Sunrise was "losing more active members than we gain, especially Black members." Problems identified by the authors included a power concentration at the top of the Sunrise organization, where white leaders wielded disproportionate influence, and a "conflict-averse culture" that eschews difficult conversations. Also significant was a feeling that efforts to build a diverse grassroots power base were being sidelined by attempts to replicate the "lightning in a bottle" moment of the 2018 Pelosi office sit-in.[45]

Sunrise's astoundingly successful early actions catapulted it into the political mainstream. In 2020, in a sign of the youth climate movement's growing political clout, Varshini Prakash was invited to help shape the Biden campaign's climate platform.[46] But as exerting influence over events in Washington, D.C. became a bigger focus, Sunrise's grasp on the real sources of its power sometimes appeared to slip. The early emphasis on actions in Congressional districts increasingly gave way to more targeted protests in the nation's capital that no longer seemed truly new or disruptive. Plenty of organizations engaged in comparable transitions have made similar missteps.

Re-focusing Sunrise, and the youth climate movement generally, on the work of mobilizing a diverse grassroots power base represents what the "Do What Must be Done" authors call "a massive opportunity to build power for the free society we all dream of." Changes Sunrise has made since the letter's release include putting activists of color in key leadership positions.[47] In July 2022 the organization also published "Sunrise 2.0," a blueprint for a more democratic decision-making structure and becoming a truly "multi-racial, cross-class youth movement fighting for a Green New Deal."[48] Meanwhile, some local groups took matters into their own hands. Sunrise Baltimore identified steps it would take as a "majority-white hub in [a] majority-Black city" toward "dismantling white supremacy and classism within our hub."[49] The former Sunrise Seattle chose a different approach, dissociating from the national Sunrise organization altogether.[50]

The work of building an inclusive climate movement is far from over. What has changed over the last two decades is that organizations on this journey now have access to resources and support from groups like Power Shift Network, who have already undergone dramatic transformations of their own. According to Sigwalt, over 60 percent of participants at PSN's annual meeting in 2020 were young people of color.[51] "Many organizations have a diversity strategy," Sigwalt's then-co-director, Nadya Dutchin, told me. "But we live that work every day."[52]

Periods of reduced movement activity create space for climate organizations to assess their own strengths and weaknesses and re-focus on their highest stated ideals. "I want to see a lot more political clarity from young people," Sigwalt said when I asked about her hopes for the youth climate movement's future. "There's a lot of messaging around how capitalism, patriarchy, racism, and colonialism are the root causes of the climate crisis—which is absolutely true—but not much discussion about how we reproduce these structures in our organizations. We need to be making that a focus, not just using sexy words."[53]

False starts

This book has mostly focused on youth-led efforts that successfully used grassroots organizing to attack the climate crisis. The people involved sometimes made mistakes, like all humans, but overall left the climate movement in a more powerful position than when they started. In contrast, some organizations attempting to influence the youth climate movement have never put serious resources into building a grassroots power base. Below, I consider a couple such cases with important lessons for activists.

In October 2004, an essay titled "The Death of Environmentalism" caused a stir in climate circles. Authors Ted Nordhaus and Michael Shellenberger, founders of the recently launched Breakthrough Institute, argued that "modern environmentalism is no longer capable of dealing with the world's most serious ecological crisis [climate change]," and that solutions like stricter pollution controls "provide neither the popular inspiration nor the political alliances the [environmental] community needs."[54] The re-election of oil-loving president George W. Bush the following month seemed to prove their point.

Nordhaus and Shellenberger proposed that environmental groups widen their circle of concern to include labor and trade issues, focus on "win-win" solutions like jobs-creating clean energy, and "build a true, values-based progressive majority" to attack the climate crisis.[55] "The Death of Environmentalism" provoked some much-needed soul searching among green groups and was even featured at a Middlebury College forum organized by the student founders of 350.org.[56] But although they made an important contribution to the climate dialogue, Nordhaus, Shellenberger, and the organization they led soon seemed to lose interest in creating the broad-based social movement they once claimed to support.

I read "The Death of Environmentalism" at age sixteen, and like many more experienced activists I was impressed. However, over the next several years I grew increasingly puzzled by the behavior of Breakthrough Institute's founders. Rather than working to bring together the "values-based progressive majority" they had called for, they seemed more and more focused on tearing down the ideas of other climate organizations.

The nature of Breakthrough's attacks varied widely. When criticizing climate activists for driving to protests, Nordhaus and

Shellenberger could sound almost like apologists for the oil industry.[57] Later, Nordhaus temporarily adopted the position of a hard leftist to suggest that if Green New Deal architects were serious, they should have pushed to nationalize automakers and utilities.[58] Still, there was a pattern visible in this scattershot approach. It seemed that any time a grassroots movement around climate began gathering real momentum, Breakthrough swooped in to play the naysayer as though it were the only role they knew.

Nor did the criticism often come in the form of constructive critique. Nordhaus and Shellenberger have often been scornful, sometimes sarcastic. They reserved a particular ire for the successful campaign against Keystone XL, wrongly predicting in 2014 that "no amount of marching and civil disobedience" would stop the pipeline.[59] Their contempt for grassroots organizing seemed matched only by their disdain for street protests and other staple tactics of large social movements. To the extent that Breakthrough had a political strategy, it appeared premised on the naïve idea that if climate groups just adopted its preferred messaging around "win-win" solutions, fossil fuel companies would sit passively by and let themselves be displaced by renewables. In a bizarre twist on the Breakthrough saga, Shellenberger finally left the organization in 2015 to launch a new career spreading false and misleading information about the severity of the climate crisis. In light of this development it seems fair to ask whether Breakthrough, at least to the extent that it was influenced by Shellenberger, ever really cared much about addressing the climate crisis at all.

Contrast Breakthrough Institute's approach with that of Sunrise Movement, whose vision for a Green New Deal attacks many of the same problems Nordhaus and Shellenberger identified in "The Death of Environmentalism." Sunrise has made missteps, but it recognized the importance of movement building and direct action from the beginning. The Capitol Hill sit-ins and other early Sunrise actions pushed transformative climate solutions into the political mainstream in a way Breakthrough never managed to do. The lessons here for activists are self-evident.

Breakthrough Institute's influence in the climate movement peaked soon after publication of "The Death of Environmentalism," and relatively few youth activists today are likely to have heard of it. The same cannot be said of the organization behind *Cowspiracy*, a 2014 film with a large social media following whose posts have sometimes been shared or retweeted by prominent youth organizers. *Cowspiracy* purports to shed a light on animal agriculture's large contribution to climate change and other environmental ills but, true to its name, spends more time spinning baseless conspiracy theories about green organizations.

The *Cowspiracy* plotline centers on the personal story of maker Kip Andersen, who it depicts asking leaders from climate and environmental groups loaded questions about their work. Throughout the film, Andersen implies without evidence that he is uncovering a vast plot in which green groups accept money or favors from meat and dairy companies in exchange for keeping quiet about the industry's carbon footprint. *Cowspiracy* uses inuendo and half-truths to make its point, in the process missing an opportunity to analyze the real, complex reasons why climate groups haven't focused more of their attention on animal agriculture. Whether the film is intentionally misleading or simply an exercise in shoddy journalism is hard to say.[60]

Perhaps more importantly, *Cowspiracy* never seriously examines the actual root sources of animal agriculture's political power. There is no in-depth discussion of how meat and dairy lobbyists influence policy, or of how the climate movement might challenge the industry using strategies that have worked against coal and oil giants. Instead, the film concludes with a call for viewers to end their own consumption of animal products (as I write, the "Take Action" page on Cowspiracy.com urges readers to "take the 30-day vegan challenge" and includes no appeal for any kind of political action).[61] If individual youth activists have managed to get something of value from the film while overlooking its weaknesses, so much the better for them—but the overall approach of *Cowspiracy* and the organization behind it remains problematic.

I have said little in this book about animal agriculture, a fact some readers may find frustrating. The reason is simply that, as of now, there is no politically oriented, grassroots movement confronting the U.S. meat and dairy industry on anything like the scale of the resistance to fossil fuels. Organizations who, like the makers of *Cowspiracy,* want to see more focus on animal agriculture from climate activists might do well to ask why they themselves have invested so little in grassroots organizing.

Although very different in some respects, Breakthrough Institute and the *Cowspiracy* organization have approached the climate crisis in ways that are problematic for similar reasons. Both correctly identified real blind spots in the climate movement, but failed to take seriously the need for an organized grassroots response. Both have seemed more interested in haranguing other environmental groups than in doing the hard work of movement-building themselves. These are not the actions of organizations genuinely committed to a stronger climate movement, and activists can learn much from their shortcomings.

The road ahead

In March 2022, I spoke again with Shiva Rajbhandari, whose involvement in protests against Chase Bank I discussed in Chapter 3. Rajbhandari, now a high school junior, reflected that he had "matured a lot as an activist" in the two years since our first conversation. "I've learned about becoming more inclusive and thoughtful with my words, stepping up and stepping back," he told me. "I've realized we're in this climate fight for the long haul, and the importance of rest along the way."

Rajbhandari had become a leader in the youth climate movement in Boise, Idaho and beyond. During sophomore year of high school, he got his first job as youth engagement coordinator for the Idaho Conservation League, where his primary task was building a network of students advocating for salmon habitat called Youth Salmon Protectors. "Salmon and climate are very related," he explained. "Salmon are going extinct because of dams obstructing their migration, but also rising water temperatures behind those dams." Rajbhandari's efforts led to Youth Salmon Protectors growing from a small group of students based mainly in Boise, to a Northwest-wide network of over 2,000 young activists.

Rajbhandari's participation in the global climate strike back in September 2019 led to getting involved in Extinction Rebellion, then becoming a leader in the groundbreaking effort to replace Northwest dams with sustainable energy. It struck me this would surely have pleased Jamie Margolin, who called the September mobilization "a point of entry" to the climate movement for young activists. It was also a good example of how the effects of the school strikes have rippled through our society.

In fact, my conversation with Rajbhandari helped me see that we may be only just beginning to realize the full impact of the surge of youth climate activism that began in late 2018. The decline in large protests is real, and presents a challenge for activists. However, it is only part of the story. "In Boise, we never stopped organizing, even during COVID," Rajbhandari told me. "The youth climate movement is more alive than ever—what's changed is the background music."[62]

*

"Everyone's freaking out right now over high gas prices. Everybody's stressed about it," said Anna Cerosaletti of New York Youth Climate Leaders, another young activist with whom I reconnected in the final months of my work on this book. "It reveals such a weakness in our energy system. If we weren't so dependent on oil and our own individual modes of transportation, the price of fossil fuels wouldn't be such a big deal. As a climate activist, I see all this as connected."

A couple of weeks earlier, Russia launched its invasion of Ukraine and the biggest European military conflict in over seventy years. The war in Ukraine joined COVID-19, a precarious economy, and an interminably tense political landscape in the United States as part of the background music against which developments in the climate movement play out. I was curious how organizations like New York Youth Climate Leaders were coping.

On the bright side, Cerosaletti told me, "We got to hold one of our first big in-person events since COVID at the State Capitol in Albany last summer." Since then, the Delta and Omicron COVID variants had again complicated local activists' ability to organize large rallies. However, Cerosaletti hoped they would be back to holding protests soon.[63]

As successive waves of COVID variants recede, the climate movement will have the opportunity to return to mobilizing large numbers of people in the streets—not just in New York, but everywhere. "Climate activists have found really innovative ways to protest during COVID, like doing car caravans instead of marches," Matt Leonard told me. "But driving by the Capitol building isn't the same as sitting in inside the doorway to prevent lawmakers there from doing business. The former can accomplish something, but it doesn't create the same political tensions as direct action."[64]

Climate activists in the future may need to be bolder and better organized than ever—partly due to the worsening state of the climate crisis itself, which demands bigger solutions the more it escalates, but also because of worrying trends in U.S. politics. A combination of voter suppression tactics, legislative district gerrymandering by Republicans, and a difficult U.S. Senate map over the next few election cycles means the political terrain ahead is likely to be challenging for progressives. A violent, right-wing fascist movement emboldened during the Trump presidency presents another kind of risk.

"As movements become more successful, they get more backlash," Tim DeChristopher, who helped spark the shift toward direct action in the climate movement, explained. "And as civil disobedience has become widespread in climate and other justice movements, we're seeing states pass laws protecting people who commit violence against protesters. We see people shooting protesters and getting celebrated by members of Congress. That doesn't mean we pull back, but it's a dangerous time."[65]

To imagine how climate activists might successfully meet the moment, it's helpful to think back to the final step in Sunrise Movement's original four-phase plan of action: mass disruption. Or, in the words of Varshini Prakash, "Marching, demonstrating incessantly. Even shutting our cities and schools down to halt business as usual if we don't get what we came for."[66] Such a truly nationwide direct action campaign would be nearly unprecedented in U.S. history, and even trying to picture how it could unfold may seem daunting. However, youth climate activists can turn for inspiration to smaller-scale examples from their own movement.

When student divestment organizers at the University of Michigan threatened to make it impossible for the Board of Regents to hold its regular meetings, as recounted in Chapter 6, they created an untenable situation which the administration could only resolve by divesting. "Part of our success was that we were unafraid to be antagonistic," said campaign member Jonathan Morris. "We treated the Board of Regents as—maybe enemy isn't the right word, but we weren't worried about keeping up a friendly relationship. It was only when students began getting arrested that they took us seriously."[67]

Similarly disruptive tactics at schools including Harvard and Columbia University led to divestment victories there, and many of the most impactful protests against fossil fuel projects likewise involved large-scale direct action. "Honestly, I want to see more youth in the climate movement risking arrest and pushing boundaries," Kiran Oommen, a twenty-two-year-old Rising Tide organizer in Washington State, told me in late 2019 as I worked on an early *Waging Nonviolence* story about the climate strikes. Weeks before, Oommen had chained themself to a landing dock on the Columbia River to prevent a vessel carrying Canada-bound oil pipeline parts from landing. "At some point we're going to need to escalate."[68]

Is it so implausible, from the vantagepoint of the early 2020s, to imagine a reinvigorated national climate movement eventually building the capacity to hold protests that nonviolently disrupt the activities of local governments, financial institutions, and large corporations in individual cities? Or from there, to picture similar actions unfolding in many places at once, until even the federal government finds its day-to-day operations impeded? It wouldn't be easy. But that doesn't mean it can't be done.

It is also possible the next major wave of climate organizing will take a different form, involving tactics and strategies most activists today have neither seen nor thought of. The task of creating conditions conducive to the rise of the next generation of climate movement leaders is the focus of the next chapter.

10

The Movement of the Future

THE NEXT GENERATION OF CLIMATE ORGANIZING

The trail to Mount Baker's Easton Glacier follows a steep incline along a ridge marking the edge of a valley carved by ice. On sunny days, the hike offers stunning views of alpine meadows and the snowy head of the mountain itself, which is increasingly known by its Indigenous name, Kulshan. Hoary marmots and pikas—plump, furry members of the rabbit family—inhabit boulder fields below the trail, which ends at an overlook above a mass of blue-hued glacial ice striated by crevasses. It is here that I pause with the groups of college students who accompany me on this hike each summer on backpacking trips led by the Bellingham-based nonprofit organization Reconnect Earth. We admire the glacier, whose gradual retreat has scraped the valley clean of vegetation. I hesitate before beginning the conversation we've come to have.

I always feel torn when traveling through landscapes like this, I tell students, between the desire to enjoy their beauty and the need to acknowledge threats they face. Much of Easton Glacier's retreat over the last couple centuries was a natural result of the planet coming out of the Little Ice Age—but it has sped up alarmingly in recent decades.[1] I hold up a photograph showing the glacier in 2003, with a line marking where it extended as recently as 1985. The disappearance of ice is shocking, and has worsened since the photo was taken.

I ask the group about other impacts of climate change they know of, here in Washington State or elsewhere. Many students have observed changes in their lifetimes, the worsening Northwest fire season among them. We talk about river flows reduced by shrinking snowpack and the impact on salmon and agriculture. We discuss the shrinking habitat of pikas and other alpine animals. The conversation turns to mass extinction, rising sea levels, and climate refugees.

I try to end on a positive note, asking what groups or individuals students know of who are taking proactive steps to address the climate crisis. Some mention organizations on their campuses or in the surrounding communities. National projects like Sunrise Movement, 350.org, and fossil fuel divestment come up. The list is far more extensive than any I could have made as an undergraduate during the climate movement's infancy.

By sojourning to Easton Glacier with students on Reconnect Earth's trips, I hope to help answer questions with which I have been increasingly preoccupied since I ceased identifying as a young activist myself: How can those who care about the planet's health ensure a vibrant future for youth climate organizing in the U.S.? And what roles can people of every age and background play in shaping that movement today?

An educator's journey

By 2015, I had been fighting fossil fuel companies in the Northwest for more than ten years. I found myself thinking increasingly often of the hours spent in nature as a child which inspired my love of the natural world in the first place—but it took longer than it probably should have to realize I couldn't sustain the exhausting lifestyle of a fulltime activist anymore. I finally began looking for other ways to contribute to the growth of the climate movement. I decided to go into environmental education. However, doing so required overcoming some prejudices.

Mainstream environmental education has long been a rather tame affair, eschewing hard examination of the root causes of environmental issues in an effort to appear "apolitical." One consequence has been a lack of crossover between organizations doing this type of education work and those involved in activism. If students inspired with a love of nature by the former sometimes find their way into the latter, it is usually by luck. This approach didn't appeal to me.

Could there be more to environmental education than what most mainstream nonprofits were doing? The hold my own early interactions with nature still had on me made me think such experiences must be powerful motivators for activism. In 2016, I began working on my M.Ed. at Western Washington University, where I learned education could indeed be a much more dynamic force for environmental change than I once supposed. I discovered the works of educators like Bill Bigelow and Tim Swinehart, editors of *A People's Curriculum for the Earth,* a captivating book full of lesson plans, role plays, and other ideas for educators who want to help students not only connect with the natural world, but act to defend it. Here was environmental education as I longed to see it practiced.

When I finished my M.Ed. in 2018, the youth climate movement to which I no longer belonged was about to enter its most exciting phase yet. Over the previous couple years I had watched youth-led activism reenergize social movements against gun violence and for gender equity. I hoped some of this energy might spill into the climate movement, but so far this was mostly wishful thinking. Then I began hearing through climate group email lists about a new organization called Zero Hour that was planning a day of marches that July.

Zero Hour's 2018 day of action, one of the first large climate protests organized almost entirely by members of Generation Z, makes as good a place as any to mark the boundary between two generations of youth climate organizing. It helped unleash a wave of climate activism unprecedented in history, while building on years of work by earlier leaders. This chapter will provide practical advice for readers of all ages who want to support and shape this ongoing movement's continued evolution and growth. First, though, will come a few observations about the factors that can help set a young person on the path to climate organizing.

How to make a climate activist

"I was always outside, growing up," said Jihan Gearon, whose work with the early climate justice movement I described in Chapter 4, of her childhood on the Navajo Reservation. "My family grew our own food and cared for the animals we ate. We had outhouses and not a lot of the conveniences most people experience. You're just more connected to the land with that kind of upbringing."[2]

It is important not to romanticize rural reservation life, with its real deprivations and poverty caused by centuries of colonization. Still, talking with Gearon helped me better understand the personal relationship with land she and many other Indigenous fossil fuel opponents have described. "This work is spiritual," Gearon told me. "It's a calling and responsibility you accept to protect your people, homeland, and the elements—water, earth, air, fire—and your spiritual knowledge of what those things mean."[3]

This book relates stories of many people whose work on behalf of a livable future is grounded in a deep, sometimes spiritual connection to land. Some, like Gearon and Enei Begaye of the Navajo, Evon Peter of the Gwich'in, and young defenders of Lakota Sioux lands against oil pipelines, have ancestral relationships with their homelands stretching back through millennia. I believe it is no coincidence that their work has been some of the most inspiring and effective in climate movement history.

For activists not indigenous to where they live, cultivating a powerful connection to the landscape is more complicated. In a 2014 special issue of the journal *Environmental Education Research,* scholars Eve Tuck, Marcia McKenzie, and Kate McCoy warned against "the seduction of claiming Indigenous land as 'our' (settlers') 'special places' where feeling connected the natural world is possible."[4] History is strewn with examples of Indigenous peoples being displaced by white conservationists who sought to "save" such places.

However, when paired with real understanding and respect for Indigenous peoples' long history in the landscape, a sense of affinity for place can inspire effective activism in non-Indigenous people. The snowy peaks of the North Cascades and sparkling waters of the Salish Sea helped prompt Jamie Margolin to found Zero Hour and Chiara D'Angelo to spend sixty-three hours chained to an oil vessel. Other young people featured in this book have drawn inspiration from Appalachia's hills and valleys, New England farmland, and the red rock country of Utah.

Then there are activists—usually immigrants or children of recent immigrants—who retain a deep connection with the country where some or all of their ancestors are indeed native. "My people [Indigenous Pakistanis] have an almost symbiotic relationship with the Earth," Extinction Rebellion University founder Ayisha Siddiqa told me. "Although I haven't lived in Pakistan most of my life, I too have a relationship with that dirt in that part of the Earth because my ancestors lived there."[5] A centuries-old connection to faraway places can be a powerful motivator even for young people who may barely remember or never have seen their family's homeland.

Some young activists I have talked with told stories that brought back memories of my own childhood. "I was always playing in the woods as a kid," said Ethan Wright of Zero Hour. In northern Virginia, where Wright grew up, nearby forests and a Park Service-maintained Civil War battlefield were sources of profound natural beauty to explore. His early experiences with nature primed Wright to be deeply affected the summer his family visited Glacier National Park, when a ranger told him that of the park's original 150 glaciers barely more than two dozen remained. "I realized climate change is ecological devastation and I needed to do anything I could to stop it," Wright said. However, he quickly acknowledged to me that he arrived at this insight from a place of privilege.

"My climate awakening comes from a very different place than people on the frontlines of extreme weather and climate disaster," Wright said. "One thing I love about Zero Hour is how intersectional, women of color-led, and centered on frontline youth it is."[6] Low-income youth, especially young people of color, may lack opportunities to safely explore outdoor spaces. This does not necessarily mean they don't have a deep relationship with nature. However, it may look different from that of the stereotypical child exploring in a park.

"My parents didn't want me playing outside, because there has been so much violence perpetuated against Black folks in outdoor settings," Amara Ifeji, a Northeastern University student and climate activist from Maine, told me in May 2021. "My family harbored a lot of intergenerational trauma around even being outside."

Ifeji immigrated to the U.S. from Nigeria with her parents and sister at age two, and grew up in a low-income household that at one point included fourteen people. "The best place to find time with my own thoughts was in our very small backyard," she said. "But although I felt drawn to the natural environment from a very young age, I didn't have many opportunities to explore it." When she was sixteen, Ifeji and a friend signed up for that year's Maine Environmental Education Association (MEEA) Changemakers summit. "I expected to learn about the environment and how we could help protect it," Ifeji remembered. "What surprised me was, we looked at everything through an intersectional, climate and environmental justice-focused lens. I was fascinated."

By the time I spoke with Ifeji, she had become MEEA's director of youth engagement.[7] That first experience at Changemakers represented, for her, another key ingredient which goes into the making of many young climate activists: the opportunity for formal training in how to translate concern about environmental issues into action. Many climate organizers have fond memories of the event where this first happened to them. For me, it was the Sierra Student Coalition's Northwest Sprog training in 2006.

"The SSC's greatest strength has always been that we trust young people to be leaders and seek to empower them at an early age," said former SSC director Jared Duval.[8] It was at Sprog that I realized there was a method to activism, and known procedures for things like identifying campaign targets or talking with elected officials. While my naivete seems laughable now, until Sprog I simply had no idea how much work experienced activists had put into developing templates for campaigning on behalf of the environment.

In combination, an early affinity for nature and later opportunities to develop grassroots activism skills create ideal conditions for a young person's transformation into a climate leader. Of course, there are also examples of youth with no formal training who plunge into organizing and succeed by learning through experience. Other young activists come to the movement having been directly impacted by pollution and environmental racism, and find ample motivation without necessarily feeling a deep connection to nature. However, absent some other concrete source of inspiration, climate advocates who lack meaningful experience with the non-human world may find it difficult to understand the gravity of a crisis that disrupts seasons and centuries-old weather patterns. This hit home for me when I heard Jihan Gearon describe taking a group of colleagues from a climate conference to visit a riverbank in the desert oasis of Sedona, Arizona.

"Someone commented that they'd never sat in a beautiful place like that and just taken it in before," Gearon said. "I was like, then why are you fighting so hard to be the one in charge of this work, when you don't have that understanding? The climate movement needs to be led by people with an actual connection to the environment, the climate, and Earth's natural cycles."[9]

Teaching activism: Advice for educators

When Solomon Duke—who later played a role in the Northwest fossil fuel export resistance—was in sixth grade, he and some friends sat on a street corner trying to drum up opposition to mountaintop removal coal mining. "We handed out pamphlets and asked people to sign a petition," Duke told me in March 2021.[10] This early induction into activism came partly thanks to Duke's education at the nearby Sunnyside Environmental School.

"At Sunnyside we weave activism throughout the curriculum," said Jan Zuckerman, a now-retired teacher and co-founder of the public K-8 school. "We incorporate service projects related to the issues students study. We want to involve students in actually taking action, not just make them feel depressed and overwhelmed about environmental problems."[11]

Duke belonged to a cohort of Sunnyside middle schoolers who started a project to educate their peers about fossil fuel exports. They testified in favor of Portland's fossil fuel infrastructure ban, a public schools climate literacy policy, and a plan to transition their city to 100 percent renewable electricity. By the time I interviewed Duke, he was studying renewable energy in college. What started as a middle school class project became a lifetime calling.

Sunnyside, with its curriculum organized around nature, environmental issues, and action, is an exceptional educational institution. That the wider Portland School District is recognized nationally as a climate education trendsetter is largely thanks to the work of Zuckerman, Lincoln High School geography teacher Tim Swinehart, and other teachers and students who pushed for adoption of a climate literacy curriculum in 2016. Swinehart, whose work on *A People's Curriculum for the Earth* impressed me in grad school, has long incorporated conversations about climate change into his own teaching. In early 2021, I got in touch to ask how he leveraged this experience during the push for Portland's groundbreaking climate literacy policy.

"A small group of educators, students, and community activists met in a church basement over the winter to draft a resolution we presented to the Board of Education," Swinehart said. "That spring at least a hundred people showed up at a board meeting to voice their support."[12] In response, the School District committed to providing "curriculum and educational opportunities that address climate change and climate justice in all Portland Public Schools."[13] However, supporters found getting their policy on paper was only the first step.

By early 2019, "we were struggling to make progress with the district," Swinehart said. The Board of Education had set up a Climate Justice committee, but its power was limited and key goals remained unrealized. Meanwhile, the growing school strike movement was inspiring an unprecedented wave of student activism globally—and Swinehart included information about these developments in his teaching. "My students were energized and wanted to take action."[14]

For the first global climate strike, on March 15, hundreds of Lincoln students joined thousands of other Portland high school and middle schoolers in staging class walkouts that converged for a rally outside City Hall.[15] Afterward some of Swinehart's students led a march to school district headquarters two miles away, where hundreds protested in the parking lot. It was the push the Board of Education apparently needed. Later that spring, the body allocated funds to hire a climate justice coordinator, support climate literacy professional development for teachers, and create a district-wide climate justice class modeled off one taught by Swinehart.[16] A small team of high school student climate activists assisted with developing the course.

"We built the class from scratch," Elliot Nopp, one of the students, told me in March 2021. The class launched as a pilot project at a subset of Portland schools, and Nopp and other students helped create lesson plans and even deliver parts of the curriculum on Zoom. "We have units on science, racial equity, clean energy solutions, and climate politics. Every day's been an adventure."[17]

Other students who were involved in the climate literacy fight went on to champion local government policies that have made Portland a climate action leader. A clause in the city's 100% renewable electricity policy, passed in 2017, established a Youth Climate Council to "provide regular support and advice to the city in meeting our climate goals."[18]

"The actual local policy outcomes from all this activism were important," Swinehart said. "But maybe even more important was the training in organizing students received along the way."[19] A takeaway for educators is that sometimes, engaging in activism is the best education of all.

*

"In the formative period of a person's life during late adolescence and young adulthood, if you combine the intellectual exercise of studying social movements with tactile, feet-on-the-ground experience in an activist campaign, you get a prime opportunity for leadership development," said George Lakey, whose work with students at Swarthmore College I discussed in Chapter 2.[20] This convergence of factors can occur in college, high school, or even earlier.

Not all teachers have the flexibility to design classes around climate and activism afforded in Portland, where the Board of Education was at least open to the idea. However, opportunities to slip relevant lessons into students' high school and college experiences abound and are not limited to environmental studies classrooms. Some of the most valuable courses I took as a budding activist in college dealt with the history of civil rights activism and other social movements. Educators teaching these subjects can seize the moment to show how grassroots movements build power, while correcting common misconceptions about the way social change happens.

After finishing my M.Ed. in 2018, I founded Reconnect Earth, a small nonprofit whose goal is to inject more critical thinking about activism into the education of college-age students outside the classroom. Reconnect Earth trip participants spend days backpacking through wild Northwest landscapes, learning about local ecosystems while participating in trainings and conversations that include an abbreviated version of a campaign planning workshop I first encountered at Sprog. I start that discussion by asking students:

What do they know about the Rosa Parks story, one of the most famous examples of activism in U.S. history?

We compare the story of Parks, as it's usually told, with what actually happened in the weeks and months preceding her momentous bus ride. I frame the discussion with information from *Huffington Post* contributor Paul Schmitz's illuminating article, "How Change Happens: The Real Story of Mrs. Rosa Parks and the Montgomery Bus Boycott." Students learn that, well before her arrest, Parks received training on nonviolent direct action from the Highlander Folk School; that Alabama NAACP President E.D. Nixon had been searching for a plaintiff to challenge segregation in a high-profile lawsuit, a role Parks later agreed to take on; and that the Montgomery Women's Political Council posted 15,000 fliers advertising the launch of a bus boycott the day of Parks' trial.[21] Far from being a lone individual spontaneously inspired to act, Parks was part of a well-organized community that worked over a long period of time to make the famous boycott a reality.

Climate change can be one of the most depressing topics students ever learn about, but not if it is handled in a way that leaves them feeling empowered. "Activism needs to be part of any meaningful climate education," Swinehart said. "Just teaching about the science can do more harm than good, because it's so overwhelming that students don't know how to engage with the information."[22] Placing iconic moments from historical social movements in context can help young people understand what making real change looks like.

Amara Ifeji of the Maine Environmental Education Association also emphasized the importance of helping students find a path to engagement. "For most young people, looking at graphs of CO_2 isn't going to make them feel passionate," she told me. "Youth want to be part of a movement that's making people's lives better by growing a more just and equitable future."[23] One of the most important things an educator can do is help young people see the climate movement as their own.

No more passing the buck: Advice for adult allies

In early 2013, I attended an activist house party in Missoula that served as the launch point for a local chapter of 350.org. The gathering drew an eclectic group of activists, from novice organizers to veterans of 1960s protest movements. At twenty-five, I was the youngest member of the organizing team that formed out of this first meeting. I was hovering in the grey area between "youth" and adult activist—and I felt some trepidation about the age gap between myself and most others in the group. Until then, my activism had been almost exclusively with students, and I feared older adults would be patronizing or dismissive toward people my age. I soon discovered what an overgeneralization this was.

Working with 350 Missoula's organizers, many of whom were of retirement age, turned out to be one of the most rewarding experiences I'd had as an activist. I learned from people who possessed much more worldly wisdom than I, but were very willing to hear my ideas. Many had more time to invest in activism than the college students I was used to interacting with. For the first time, I realized how powerful intergenerational organizing can be.

"Boomers are the number one group who come out to support us at our local climate strikes," said Hridesh Singh of New York Youth Climate Leaders. "Youth may be at the forefront of climate activism today, but to truly address the crisis we need individuals of all ages and walks of life."[24] People in their thirties, forties, fifties, and beyond can support or partner with young climate activists in countless ways. However, some basic rules for allyship should inform this work. First and foremost is the importance of not trying to take control.

In a message to social media followers on April 26, 2021, U.S. climate strike leader Alexandria Villaseñor warned about the "manipulation and toxicity that we [youth activists] sometimes experience in the environmental movement." A nonstop schedule of Earth Day events left her feeling pleased by the outpouring of public support for climate action, but exhausted by requests for collaboration with adult-led organizations that sometimes felt exploitive. Villaseñor's advice for adult activists was, "Listen to the youth and their message, and support them in speaking their truth authentically. Trust that we youth know our own movement, and don't tell us how our movement works or what it should look like."[25]

This doesn't mean adult allies can never offer their own ideas or challenge those of youth activists. Assuming young people cannot take constructive criticism would be patronizing in its own way, and adults can advise and even critique youth-led campaigns. The key is that the conversation be one between equals, with young people free to use or disregard feedback. In the end, it may turn out the youth know best.

If trying to control student-led campaigns is a mistake, so is being *too* hands-off. Jamie Margolin has spoken of being discouraged by adult platitudes about how kids will "save the world." "My power is limited to making you [adults] do something," Margolin told *Forward* in 2019. "...[A]nd now you're gonna sit here and point fingers at me?"[26] Her words brought back things well-meaning older activists would say to me as a student. I found it surreal when, in my late twenties, I began hearing my own peers talk of passing the mantle of leadership to a new generation who would hopefully fix problems we'd failed to solve. Surely it was too soon for that, I thought. When would this endless passing of the buck finally cease?

Not long after beginning work on this book, I reconnected with JP Kemmick, whom I met at Sprog back in 2006. We were both involved in the Cascade Climate Network during our college years, and when a creative writing master's brought Kemmick to University of Montana while I was still in Missoula, he became a core organizer of Blue Skies Campaign. He now lived in Seattle, where he and his partner were raising their young son.

"When I first joined the climate movement, older people would tell me, 'Our generation screwed up and yours has to fix it,'" Kemmick recalled saying in his testimony at a Seattle City Council meeting on a local Green New Deal. "Now, as a father, I refuse to say that to my son. Each successive generation has said, 'Sorry, we didn't get this right and now it's up to the young people.' But you can only keep doing that for so long before the planet's on fire."[27]

Older activists who talk of being inspired by young people sometimes forget their own actions can also be inspirational. "We have stood where you have stood," Cheyenne River Sioux member Jasilyn Charger told a crowd of activists, some still in high school, at an April 2021 rally against the Dakota Access and Line 3 pipelines. Five years earlier, Charger was among the youth who ran from Standing Rock to the nation's capital to deliver a message opposing Dakota Access. Now in her mid-twenties, she still fit many people's definition of a youth activist, but for the younger Indigenous youth in the audience she was already a role model. "Know you are not alone. We [older activists] are going to be beside you every step of the way."[28]

Adults who want to be good allies to the youth climate movement might take Charger's example to heart.

Transitioning from "youth": Advice for late twenty and thirty-somethings

In February 2020, I connected on Zoom with Morgan Goodwin, a leader of New England's early youth climate movement whose post about the Clipper pipeline featured in Chapter 7. Goodwin decided to dive into activism after Billy Parish spoke at an Earth Day event at his school, Williams College. He went on to work on national climate campaigns and ended up in the small town of Truckee, California. When we spoke, he had recently finished a stint on Truckee's Town Council.

"The idea of running for office terrified me at first," Goodwin said. "But it was a chance to have a new kind of impact and the political moment was right." The demographics of Truckee were changing with an influx of liberal voters from the Bay Area, and Goodwin—a younger candidate running on a progressive platform —came across as a fresh voice. He was elected in November 2014. "I loved being able to see an issue facing the town and instead of trying to organize people to sign a petition, just meet with other officials and change the course of the community's future within a couple of hours."[29]

Electoral politics is one of many paths open to former "youth" activists seeking new opportunities. "A lot of running for office is about talking with voters one on one, the same skills required to build a movement," said Christine Lewis, a climate organizer of my generation from Oregon. After the election of Donald Trump, Lewis was inspired to run for office and change politics for the better. She was elected to the tri-county body known as Oregon Metro, which makes land use and transportation policy for the Portland area, in 2018. "If you have grassroots organizing skills, you'll be able to serve your constituents in office," she told me. "Other official duties you can learn along the way, but not everyone knows how to connect with a community."[30]

Even a campaign for office that is not ultimately successful can have an impact. "It was clear to me Democrats and Republicans alike in Montana are subservient to fossil fuels and big money," said Daniel Carlino, who at age twenty-one ran for his state's

Public Service Commission. The University of Montana student had previously spoken at PSC hearings on the coal and gas-heavy energy plan of the state's main utility. He said that although public comments were overwhelmingly in favor of shifting to renewables, "I realized these officials, some of the climate change deniers, would make the wrong decision regardless. That's when I knew I wanted to run."

Carlino's all-volunteer campaign knocked on five thousand doors through early 2020, until COVID made in-person canvassing impossible. "For the first few months, people kept telling me I was too young or progressive to run," he remembered. This stopped when it became apparent his well-organized campaign had a real shot at victory. At a forum attended by most Democrats running for office in Montana, Carlino used his allotted speech time to challenge other candidates to join him in signing a Sunrise Movement pledge against taking money from fossil fuel companies. "Things like that got people's attention." In the end, a candidate with deep ties to the energy industry and backing from the state's political elite won the PSC race—but Carlino's candidacy helped re-shape the terms of debate.[31]

As important as electoral politics is, it isn't the only place where climate advocates can affect important policy decisions. "For any piece of legislation to be effective, you need the right people implementing it," said Juliana Williams, a former Midwest organizer for the SSC now employed at the National Renewable Energy Laboratory. "I used to resist describing myself as a bureaucrat because the word has negative connotations. But deciding how policy gets enacted is huge."[32]

I have talked with former student activists who now work as renewable energy entrepreneurs, legal professionals, artists, and teachers. Others never strayed from grassroots organizing, even as they transitioned from "youth" to adult activism. Early EAC leader

Kelly Lynch worked for organizations including Greenpeace, Avaaz, and Green for All before becoming a Sierra Club campaigner.[33] Kim Teplitzky, who spearheaded Campuses Beyond Coal, is now a United Steelworkers union organizer.[34] After leading Power Shift Network for three years, Lydia Avila joined the Climate and Clean Energy Equity Fund, an organization supporting grassroots organizing for equitable climate solutions in diverse communities.[35]

In any field, young professionals—especially young women and people of color—must be wary of workplace practices that exploit their labor while devaluing them as humans. This happens even in nonprofits, where workloads and time pressures often mirror the corporate world. "That's a familiar story for Black people," said Power Shift Network's Nadya Dutchin. "For centuries we lived on beans, rice, and vegetables when we couldn't afford anything else. That's not the future we're working for. I'm tired of fighting for scarcity."[36]

Sometimes, political groups want to elevate an activist's profile to advance an institutional mission in ways that may not align with the individual's interests or cultural values. So it was that Evon Peter, after becoming a nationally sought speaker, decided to pull back from this public role. "Around the time I spoke at Power Shift in 2007, being on that kind of stage started to feel a little much for me," he said. "It began to feel like the national progressive movement wanted to push me toward a more politicized path that would have magnified me on the national scene, but just didn't feel right. I've always trusted my heart, so I stepped back from giving speeches for about four or five years." Peter chose to focus on Indigenous youth suicide prevention in Alaska, later finding a role as an Indigenous Studies researcher and Vice Chancellor at University of Alaska in Fairbanks, where he and his partner Enei Begaye now live with their family.

The decision to have children is, of course, another of the most consequential a person can make in young adulthood. Climate organizers who are now parents often cite their children as a primary motivation for their activism. "Both [PSN co-executive director] Dany [Sigwalt] and I have beautiful Black children who will be affected by climate change and environmental injustice," said Dutchin. "I want a better future for them."[37]

At the same time, ever-larger numbers of young adults are choosing to forego parenthood. The Brookings Institute estimates the U.S. birth rate dropped 20 percent between 2007 and 2020—and although some of the recent decline was due to COVID, it is part of a longer-term trend.[38] Josephine Ferorelli, co-founder of the women-led organization Conceivable Future, wants people to understand that "a generation is balking at parenthood because the future is so frightening." Her organization highlights stories of women who struggle with the decision of whether to have children in a world of climate crisis. However, Conceivable Future is explicitly not an anti-reproduction or population control group.

"We try to help people move from just asking what harm their child might do to the environment, toward more essential questions like why it's so carbon-intensive to live or have children in the U.S. in the first place," Ferorelli told me in October 2021. "It's not that individual decisions to consume less aren't meaningful, but they don't change the system." More important is untangling the complex pressures, dreams, and fears that affect people's choices about whether to have children who will both impact and be impacted by climate change. "We encourage people to explore whether they're thinking of having kids because they truly want to, because of outside pressures, or because it's the cultural norm," Ferorelli explained. "This is an opportunity for self-inquiry that goes far beyond concerns about your child's carbon footprint."

Ferorelli believes the hope that you might raise the next Greta Thunberg is *not* a good reason to procreate. There are better ways to foster the next generation of climate leaders as an educator or adult mentor—and trying to sculpt one's offspring to follow a specific path rarely works anyway. "The point of having children is to love someone unconditionally. It can't be contingent on their being smart, successful, altruistic, or voting a certain way."

The final decision about whether having children makes sense is an intensely personal one. "My advice is, let go of the idea that there's a universally right answer," Ferorelli said. "What you can do is explore what considerations matter most to you."[39]

Thriving on the journey: Advice for youth activists

In Chapter 1, I discussed how mainstream narratives about climate activism usually focus on charismatic individuals and large, headline-generating events. Lost in that kind of telling is the work done behind the scenes by countless people who receive little recognition for their labor. Inspirational leaders like Greta Thunberg are influential because they are supported by much larger networks of organizers, just as Rosa Parks was during the Montgomery Bus Boycott. This means there are myriad ways to get involved in climate activism, not just through the roles typically associated with leadership.

For young people who are comfortable being a public spokesperson, there is no reason to hold back—provided stepping into the role doesn't take floor time away from someone with less privilege. Young activists also needn't assume this role isn't for them simply because it feels intimidating. "You can't let your fears stop you when much scarier things are at stake in the climate fight," said Isabella

Fallahi of Zero Hour, who addressed hundreds of thousands at the September 2019 New York climate strike. "You get into this work because it's a cause that's so important, you sacrifice parts of yourself for it. Fears are something you have to put to the back of your mind."[40]

Leadership doesn't always mean holding a microphone, though. "I'm the one always sending out annoying reminder emails, facilitating team projects, and who's just kind of there to make sure work gets done," said Audrey Watson, a New Jersey high school freshman and leader of her local Sunrise hub, in April 2020.[41] Sometimes the strongest leaders stay in the background while spurring others to reach their full potential.

The best advice I know of for young activists, gleaned from more than two decades of climate movement history, is to find ways to meaningfully engage that resonate with who you are as a person. This can mean pushing yourself to try new things. But it also requires taking a look at your authentic self and determining how you might contribute in a way that is personally sustainable. Trying for too long to do something not consistent with your personality is one way activists get exhausted. Working long hours without taking time for yourself is another.

"Sometimes you have to step back and re-evaluate your work/life balance," Jamie Margolin told me when she was a senior in high school. "I remind myself that activism is one thing I do, but it's not all there is to me as a person. The times I get burnt out are when I start thinking of climate organizing as my whole identity."[42] In college Margolin was even more explicit. "Pace yourself," she advised fellow youth activists in an April 2021 interview with the *Highlands Current*. "You don't need to sacrifice hanging out with friends and loved ones for the cause. You're going to burn yourself out several times and make yourself miserable if you don't learn to stop, smell the roses and be a kid sometimes."[43]

Other movement leaders I've talked to have offered similar wisdom. "Build your life in a way that fosters resiliency," said Lauren Ressler, who mentored future leaders of Sunrise Movement as an organizer with the Responsible Endowments Coalition. "Sometimes life happens, even when you're in the midst of campaigning. Those moments can be incredibly isolating if you don't have a support network of people who love you not just for what you produce, but for who you are."[44] Ultimately, self-care can create the space for reflection which activists need to recharge and come back ready to contribute to the movement in new ways.

A willingness to innovate has always been a hallmark of the youth climate movement. In the early 2000s, Energy Action Coalition's founders united behind their vision for student-led climate action in a way that had never been attempted before. In 2008, Tim DeChristopher galvanized fellow activists with an act of creative protest. Organizers of the school strikes, the push for a Green New Deal, and divestment campaigns employed equally innovative tactics with impressive results. Future leaders must be similarly willing to follow their instincts, even when that means disrupting ways of doing things entrenched by established organizations. "Youth have to decide for themselves who has the better strategy: grassroots organizations or big green groups?" said Cindy Spoon of the Tar Sands Blockade. "Never let yourself be run over by people wanting to co-opt your efforts."[45]

Training new activists so as to ensure the continuation of climate organizations is equally important. "There's so much burnout in college activist groups," Middlebury College senior Zoe Grodsky told me in June 2020. Few schools have played as pivotal a role in the climate movement as Middlebury, where students from Jon Isham's 2005 class launched the Sunday Night Group and went on to found 350.org. When Grodsky attended her first Sunday Night meeting, the organization was still going strong thanks to more than a decade of fostering new leadership. "A lot of student activists end up getting overcommitted in college and stop being involved once they become juniors or seniors," Grodsky said. "That's why it's important we help new people build the skills to lead. As someone who stuck it out and kept going, I know training is essential."[46]

The most durable activist groups tend to be those where members feel empowered by a supportive community. "Some of the deepest friendships I've made while in my PhD program have been with other organizers," Noah Weaverdyck of the University of Michigan divestment campaign told me.[47] "Take time to get know each other," Sasha Bishop added during the same conversation. "It's an important part of maintaining your organization, but also building the world we want to see where relationships are based on caring and support for people's mental and emotional needs."[48]

This kind of relationship building is important precisely because the work of building the next stage of the climate movement will sometimes seem exhausting. At times the end goal feels unreachable, the other side's capacity for petty cruelty limitless. Having the confidence and ability to advocate for oneself is therefore invaluable.

"I want young people to know you can stand up and not be afraid," said Morgan Brings Plenty, who coordinated social media for the run from Standing Rock to Washington, D.C. "Sure, there'll be backlash. Some people will say really awful things, especially toward women and members of the LGBTQ community. But you've got to look past that and say, 'Hey, this is my world, too. I live on this Earth and I have a right to be here like any other person.'"[49]

There are also real rewards that come from helping shape history for the better. When I spoke with Christine Lewis, by then of

Metro, she pushed back against the common narrative that depicts young activists as victims sacrificing their youth for a cause.

"Of course, young people shouldn't need to spend so much time fighting for their own future," Lewis said. "But youth activists have been at the forefront of every social movement in the U.S.—from women's rights, to voting rights, to the climate movement. Activism is part of the experience of youth in every generation, and the need has never been more urgent than now. My advice is to enjoy it, thrive on it, learn along the way, and use this opportunity to build power you can wield not just in the future, but here and now."[50]

Conclusion: As Smoky Skies Clear

The skies over large parts of the West Coast were still thick with smoke in September 2020, when about a dozen refugees from wildfires in the region arrived on twenty-three acres of Southern Oregon land where two young women were intent on revitalizing the connection to land shared by them and others with Indigenous heritage.

"We're trying to establish a community space and land back project," Bianca Ballará, one of the project organizers, told me later that month. "Our focus is on reuniting local Indigenous women with land, reclaiming Native plant and medicine practices, and re-learning traditional ecological knowledge about how to make a healthy forest." Ballará and her partner called the project Native-WomanShare.

The couple had arrived on the property—which they were in the process of acquiring from the lesbian feminist collective Woman-Share—a few months earlier. They wanted to honor the previous owners' commitment to creating a safe space for women to connect with land, but with an emphasis on the original inhabitants. They were in the process of making this vision a reality when the region was hit by a deadly fire season intensified by abnormally hot, dry conditions.[1]

In early September, the Almeda Fire blazed northward from the Southern Oregon town of Ashland, devastating the small communities of Talent and Phoenix and burning more than 2,600 buildings to ash.[2] To the east, the Slater Fire roared across National Forest lands and destroyed almost 200 homes on the Karuk Reservation.[3] NativeWomanShare was situated between the two blazes, and Ballará and her partner waited tensely to see if they would have to evacuate. In the meantime, they tried to help people already displaced by the flames.

"An amazing mutual aid network has blossomed in Southern Oregon over the last year, to help people during COVID," Ballará explained. "We plugged into that existing organizing base, which was now being used to coordinate fire relief. Being queer, Indigenous Latinx women ourselves, we were especially interested in providing a safe refuge for queer and BIPOC folks affected by the fires."

By the time I spoke with Ballará for a *Waging Nonviolence* article about West Coast climate groups' response to the wildfires, all the refugees who found shelter at NativeWomanShare had moved on to more permanent housing. But for a couple of weeks, those twenty-three acres provided them with safety.[4] It was an example of the kind of grassroots disaster response effort that has become an increasingly important responsibility for the climate movement in recent years.

*

One of the earliest interviews I conducted while researching for this book was with Juliana Williams, whose comments on the importance of government rulemaking processes appeared in Chapter 10. As was often the case when I spoke with activists of my own generation, there were moments when the conversation felt less like a formal interview than a chance to catch up with a colleague who I hadn't spoken to in years.

Williams was a founding member of the Cascade Climate Network, the group I joined as a college student which later helped bring Sunrise Movement to the Northwest. She became interested in clean energy as a student at Whitman College, and participated in the Sierra Student Coalition's Sprog. Williams took a job as the Midwest Organizer for the SSC after graduation, recruiting students to attend the first Power Shift. Because we'd been to some of the same activist events and knew many people in common, the two of us had plenty to talk about.

We spent over an hour reliving memories from the early youth climate movement and discussing Williams' current work with the National Renewable Energy Laboratory. But what stuck with me most was an anecdote Williams shared about attending a panel composed of youth climate activists at a conference a couple months earlier.

"As a former youth activist, I felt obligated to show up and support these young people," she said with a laugh. "But I didn't really expect to hear anything new." However, one panelist framed the climate crisis in a way that gave Williams pause. "She asked us, what kind of world do we want to have fifteen years from now? That's a span of time long enough to make major societal changes, but short enough to conceptualize mentally. How do we begin working toward it? It was such a different message from what I was used to from my years of climate organizing."

Williams came away with a renewed sense of hope that while it might be too late to stop some effects of the climate crisis, it is possible to find meaning in the work of rebuilding. "That's an exciting, interesting thing to plan for," she told me. "A lot of activists of our generation have gotten so used to playing defense and trying to stop the bad things, we never took time to consider what we would build in their place. That was a big mental shift for me."[5]

I concurred. When Williams and I were college students in the 2000s, much of the world had yet to experience tangible impacts from climate change. Most activists had not yet realized just how deeply entrenched fossil fuel companies' power was in our political system, and many of us naively believed the climate movement would only need to exist for a decade or so before packing up and declaring victory. We had yet to grapple with the reality that we were engaged in an undertaking which would extend well into our adult lives, perhaps beyond.

Today's young activists seem more realistic. Certainly, preventing future carbon emissions before things get even worse continues to be an urgent priority. But so is dealing with the harm already being done. Putting systems in place to respond in a just way to worsening climate disasters is a profoundly practical move, but it also sends a radical message. In an age of climate change, the simple process of planning for the future can become an act of resistance.

*

It is customary, in a book about climate change or climate activism, to end by warning that the window of opportunity for preventing disaster is closing rapidly, and the world must act within the next few years to prevent catastrophe. I have tried to stay away from such statements—not because there is anything misplaced about their urgency, but because of the unstated implication that if things don't turn around in the specified timeframe, there might almost be no more point in trying. This, I believe, is a flawed way of thinking about the climate crisis.

At a time when dystopian visions of the future are ubiquitous, the ability to set one's sights on building toward something more positive requires profound courage. It means taking a hard look at the challenges we face and the losses already sustained, then starting to work on healing the wounds and making the world a better place than it would have been without us. It calls for daring to spit in the face of dystopia and refuse to give into comforting nihilism, come what may. This is, increasingly, work today's young climate activists are taking on.

Barring the very worst climate change scenarios—some of which are admittedly still possible, but by no means guaranteed—a portion of humanity and an unknown number of other species are likely to survive well into the era of worsening extreme weather, rising sea levels, and other climate disruptions. Just how bad things get in terms of lives lost, animals and plants driven to extinction, and the collapse of societies and ecosystems will depend largely on how successful activists are at reining in future carbon emissions. But there will almost certainly be survivors tasked with rebuilding.

Will future civilizations that rise from the ashes of the climate crisis replicate the unjust systems under which most of us now live? Will refugees fleeing ever-worsening disasters encounter help and mutual aid, or violent xenophobia? In the wake of catastrophe, will dominant cultures finally achieve a less destructive relationship with the natural world? These are open questions, but the climate movement can play a role in determining the answers. In some interviews I conducted for this book, movement leaders shared their thoughts on what kind of future we should be working toward.

"I am absolutely interested in fighting to keep things from getting worse," said Dany Sigwalt of Power Shift Network. "I'm interested in saving lives. But I also want our collective struggles to be revolutionary in that they inherently challenge white supremacist culture, patriarchy, and the legacies of colonialism in our lives every day."[6]

Former University of Oregon student Zach Stark, an activist of my generation, told me of his vision for an equitable society based on anarchism. "Given current climate and resource depletion trends, our civilization is likely to become unsustainable and collapse sooner or later," he explained. "If that happened tomorrow, we'd probably have a patchwork of authoritarian warlords spring up in its place, because that's what society has been primed for. But we can start educating people now about alternative paths." Stark takes inspiration from the work of anarchists before and during the Spanish Civil War. "They spent decades teaching people what anarchism means and how it works. And when the government collapsed, workers and peasants were ready to start organizing collectives, redistributing land, and forming militias to fight the fascists."[7]

No one with a grasp on reality denies the gravity of the climate crisis, or that each year without major action from world governments brings us closer to tipping points beyond which certain catastrophic impacts become unavoidable. To take a clear-eyed look at this frightening situation and plan for a world where regeneration is possible requires not the blind optimism of climate science denial, but a commitment to rebuilding akin to that needed to help refugees in the wake of a wildfire.

"I hope for a recovery that leaves space for more equity, inclusion, and respect for diversity in our community," Bianca Ballará said when I asked about the path forward in Southern Oregon. "We also need to spread sustainable technologies, from forestry practices that take care of the land to urban architecture that serves everyone. I hope we learned, from 2020, how to survive and support each other through emergencies."[8]

If the youth climate movement is able to meet the challenges of a world where climate change is already a reality, it will be partly thanks to two decades and more during which activists have worked to build the grassroots power base needed to achieve societal transformations. Occasionally, progress has come in highly visible bursts. At other times it proceeded so slowly as to be barely noticeable, but the result was a stronger movement, nevertheless. The finest, most inspiring moments in this history came about when young people dared to challenge the status quo within and outside the climate movement. And the work is very far from over.

The leaders whose stories appear in this book are but a small sampling of thousands who have given time and labor to make youth climate organizing what it is today. My hope is that readers who think of themselves as youth climate activists—or who aspire to join their ranks—will be inspired by the movement's past, but not intimidated by it. Young people who started with little or no formal organizing experience have taken climate campaigns in innovative new directions before, and surely will again.

The activist who helps spark the next great wave of youth climate organizing might be a high schooler like Jamie Margolin, who dreamed of leading mass protests. It might be a college student like Tim DeChristopher, who challenged the movement to be braver. It might be a young person from reservation country, like Joseph White Eyes or Morgan Brings Plenty, who catapulted an inspiring battle against fossil fuel infrastructure into the national spotlight. It might be someone with an idea unlike anything climate activists have tried before.

It might be you.

Timeline

KEY EVENTS IN THE U.S. YOUTH CLIMATE MOVEMENT

2000

Evon Peter elected Chief of Arctic Village, Alaska.

2001

Environmental Justice and Climate Change initiative launched.

Young Navajo and Hopi organizers found the Black Mesa Water Coalition.

2003

Billy Parish, Kelly Lynch, and others organize the first youth-led national day of action on climate change.

2004

Energy Action Coalition (EAC) founded at a meeting in Washington, D.C.

Mountain Justice founded in Appalachia.

2005

Jon Isham teaches "Building the New Climate Movement" at Middlebury College.

EAC launches the Campus Climate Challenge.

Mohave coal plant and associated slurry line, opposed by Black Mesa Water Coalition, shut down.

2006

Rising Tide North America holds its first direct action at Virginia's Clinch River coal plant.

Fort Chipewyan community members approach Indigenous Environmental Network leaders about the tar sands at the Protecting Mother Earth Summit.

2007

First Step It Up national day of action.

Power Shift 2007 brings nearly 6,000 young people to Washington, D.C.

2008

Energy Action Coalition runs Power Vote campaign.

Tim DeChristopher arrested for disrupting an oil and gas auction in Salt Lake City, Utah.

2009

Power Shift 2009 attended by 12,000 young people.

Clipper pipeline approved by the Obama administration.

A climate-focused forest defense movement launches in Eugene, Oregon.

350.org holds its first international day of action in the leadup to COP15.

World leaders fail to agree on a binding climate treaty at COP15 in Copenhagen.

2010

Swarthmore students visit Appalachia and meet with landowners affected by mountaintop removal mining.

Beyond Coal Campaign secures retirement date for coal plant in Boardman, Oregon.

2011

First blockades of tar sands "megaload" shipments in Missoula, Montana.

The Tar Sands Action, two weeks of sustained direct action protests, unfolds in Washington, D.C.

2012

Tar Sands Blockade impedes construction of the southern leg of Keystone XL.

350.org and other organizations launch the national fossil fuel divestment movement.

2013

Forward on Climate rally, focused on opposing Keystone XL, brings 40,000 people to Washington, D.C.

2014

People's Climate March in New York City draws an estimated 400,000 people.

2015

Energy Action Coalition hires Lydia Avila, its first executive director of color, who leads the transition to becoming Power Shift Network.

Fracking trucks blockaded by activists in Denton, Texas.

Widespread protests against Shell's Arctic drilling plans unfold in Seattle, Portland, and other Northwest cities.

Paris Climate Accords struck at COP21.

2016

Portland, Oregon passes nation's first fossil fuel export infrastructure ban.

Divestment Student Network (DSN) organizes wave of sit-ins on college campuses.

Arch Coal cancels the Otter Creek Mine in Montana after years of community opposition.

Mass protests against the Dakota Access pipeline at Standing Rock.

2017

Jamie Margolin publishes the online call to action that leads to the formation of Zero Hour.

Divestment Student Network formally disbands, with some key leaders going on to found Sunrise Movement.

2018

Zero Hour holds debut day of marches in Washington, D.C. and elsewhere in July.

Better Future Project launches its national Divest Ed project.

Sunrise Movement holds its first sit-in at House Speaker Nancy Pelosi's office in November.

In December, U.S. students inspired by Greta Thunberg launch the country's first school strikes for the climate.

2019

First global "deep strike" day on March 15.

Extinction Rebellion University trains students throughout the Northeast in direct action skills.

Largest-ever week of global climate strikes kicks off on September 20.

University of Michigan students disrupt a Board of Regents meeting to protest fossil fuel investments.

Students interrupt Yale-Harvard football game to protest fossil fuel investments.

Strike movement organizers confront world leaders at COP25 in Madrid.

2020

Sunrise Movement members affiliated with the organization's Black Constituency release "Do What Must be Done" letter.

New York announces plans to divest its state pension fund from all fossil fuels.

2021

Northern leg of the Keystone XL pipeline rejected by President Biden.

Harvard announces it will let remaining fossil fuel investments in its $41.9 billion endowment expire.

Sunrise activists hold hunger strike outside the White House during negotiations over the Build Back Better Act.

2022

Congress passes the first comprehensive climate and clean energy bill in U.S. history.

Notes

Introduction

1. Lee, Rachel. Interview with the author, March 31, 2020.
Taylor, Lin and Sonia Elks. "Greta Thunberg's rise from teen activist to global climate leader." Thompson Reuters Foundation. https://news.trust.org/item/20190819233721-jaa90.

2. Sunrise Movement. "November 13, 2018—Sit-in at Nancy Pelosi's Office." Sunrise Movement. https://www.sunrisemovement.org/actions/pelosi-sit-in/.

3. Cohen, Ilana. Interview with the author, February 19, 2020.

4. Margolin, Jamie. Interview with the author, September 1, 2019.

5. Connelly, Joel. "Thousands join Climate Strike in Seattle: Networking for the planet." *Seattle Post-Intelligencer,* September 23, 2019. https://www.seattlepi.com/local/politics/article/Thousands-join-Climate-Strike-in-Seattle-14456503.php.

6. Schurman, Zoe. Interview with the author, November 15, 2019.

7. Price, Ian. Interview with the author, November 15, 2019.

8. Shalby, Colleen. "16 youth climate activists filed a human rights complaint to the UN. How the Paradise Fire inspired one." *Los Angeles Times,* September 23, 2019. https://www.latimes.com/california/story/2019-09-23/climate-activist-inspired-by-paradise-fires-un-complaint.

9. "Zayne Cowie Fridays for Future Climate Striker NYC." https://docs.google.com/document/d/1EKaaI27hyTQCTp2gVZDmZn-RrW1RrwOptG6ddb3ZEXHE/edit.

10. Benson, Kallan. "A Quaker Youth's Journey in Climate Activism." Quaker Earthcare Witness.
https://www.quakerearthcare.org/article/quaker-youth-s-journey-climate-activism.

11. Kalmus, Peter. "A few of the things I'm working on now." Peter Kalmus: Climate Scientist, Author. https://peterkalmus.net/now/.

12. Kalmus-Kunde, Zane. Email message to author, March 2, 2021.

13. Price, Ian. Interview with the author, May 7, 2020.

14. Price, Ian. Interview with the author, May 7, 2020.

1. Generation Climate

1. Doerer, Kristen. "Youth Climate Change Activists Marched on Washington, D.C. *Teen Vogue,* July 22, 2018. https://www.teenvogue.com/story/youth-climate-change-activists-marched-washington-dc.

2. Zero Hour. "Our Actions." This is Zero Hour. http://thisiszerohour.org/our-actions/#past.

3. Yoon-Hendricks, Alexandra. "Meet the Teenagers Leading a Climate Change Movement." *The New York Times,* July 21, 2018. https://www.nytimes.com/2018/07/21/us/politics/zero-hour-climate-march.html.

4. Doerer, Kristen. "Youth Climate Change Activists Marched on Washington, D.C. *Teen Vogue,* July 22, 2018. https://www.teenvogue.com/story/youth-climate-change-activists-marched-washington-dc.

5. Margolin, Jamie. Interview with the author, November 16, 2019.

6. Margolin, Jamie. Interview with the author, November 16, 2019.

7. Javna, John. *50 Simple Things Kids Can Do to Save the Earth.* Kansas City, MO: Andrews McMeel Universal.

8. Thompson, Caroline. "Earth Day 2015: 10 easy ways save money while saving the world." *The Christian Science Monitor,* April 22, 2015. https://www.csmonitor.com/Business/Saving-Money/2015/0422/Earth-Day-2015-10-easy-ways-save-money-while-saving-the-world.

9. Margolin, Jamie. "How I became a radical climate activist." *Vice,* June 17, 2019. https://i-d.vice.com/en_us/article/vb9q3m/jamie-margolin-youth-climate-activist.

10. Plant for the Planet. "Our Story." Plant for the Planet. https://www.plant-for-the-planet.org/en/about-us/who-we-are-2.

11. Margolin, Jamie. Interview with the author, November 16, 2019.

12. Blinder, Alan and Christina Caron. "Seattle Chokes as Wildfire Smoke From Canada Blankets the Northwest." *The New York Times,* August 7, 2017. https://www.nytimes.com/2017/08/07/us/wildfires-canada-seattle.html.

13. Margolin, Jamie. Interview with the author, November 16, 2019.

14. Margolin, Jamie. "Youth's futures are being stolen from us..." *Instagram,* July 3, 2017. https://www.instagram.com/p/BWE21Z1jqWQ/.

15. Margolin, Jamie. *Youth to Power: Your Voice and How to Use It.* New York, NY: Hachette Books, 2020.

16. Zero Hour. "This is Zero Hour." This is Zero Hour. http://thisiszero-hour.org/.

17. Manning, Andrea. Interview with the author, November 11, 2019.

18. Packer, Ashton. "National youth organization Zero Hour makes strides in Atlanta." *The Signal,* August 8, 2018. https://georgiastatesignal.com/national-youth-organization-zero-hour-makes-strides-in-atlanta/.

19. Eldeeb, Sohayla. Interview with the author, May 20, 2020.

20. Wright, Ethan. Interview with the author, November 1, 2019.

21. Democracy Now. "'We Are Striking to Disrupt the System': An Hour with 16-Year-Old Climate Activist Greta Thunberg." *Democracy Now,* September 11, 2019. https://www.democracynow.org/2019/9/11/greta_thunberg_swedish_activist_climate_crisis.

22. Urisman Otto, Alexandra. "Greta Thunberg in exclusive interview: 'The election of Trump was a turning point for the climate movement.'" *Dagens Nyheter,* December 16, 2019. https://www.dn.se/nyheter/varlden/greta-thunberg-in-exclusive-interview-the-election-of-trump-was-a-turning-point-for-the-climate-movement/.

23. Margolin, Jamie. Interview with the author, September 1, 2019.

24. Thunberg, Greta. Forward to *Youth to Power: Your Voice and How to Use It,* by Jamie Margolin, xi. New York, NY: Hachette Books, 2020.

25. Ernman, Malena and Greta Thunberg, Svante Thunberg, and Beata Ernman. *Our House is on Fire: Scenes of a Family and a Planet in Crisis.* Translated by Paul Norlen and Saskia Vogel. London: Penguin Books.

26. Taylor, Lin and Sonia Elks. "Greta Thunberg's rise from teen activist to global climate leader." Thompson Reuters Foundation. https://news.trust.org/item/20190819233721-jaa90.

27. Ivarsson, Daniel. "Full Speech: 15-year old Greta Thunberg at COP24 in Katowice 2018." December 15, 2018. YouTube video. https://www.youtube.com/watch?v=VbDnPj0G0wY.

28. Taylor, Lin and Sonia Elks. "Greta Thunberg's rise from teen activist to global climate leader." Thompson Reuters Foundation. https://news.trust.org/item/20190819233721-jaa90.

29. Plant for the Planet. "Felix Finkbeiner addresses United Nations with speech to open the International Year of Forests 2011." Plant-for-the-Planet. February 2, 2011. YouTube video. https://www.youtube.com/watch?v=Sur8coFE0tU.

30. Ernman, Malena and Greta Thunberg, Svante Thunberg, and Beata Ernman. *Our House is on Fire: Scenes of a Family and a Planet in Crisis.* Translated by Paul Norlen and Saskia Vogel. London: Penguin Books.

31. Crouch, David. "The Swedish 15-year-old who's cutting class to fight the climate crisis." *The Guardian,* September 1, 2018. https://www.the-guardian.com/science/2018/sep/01/swedish-15-year-old-cutting-class-to-fight-the-climate-crisis.

32. EURACTIV. "Greta Thunberg urges MEPs to 'panic like the house is on fire.'" EURACTIV. April 16, 2019. YouTube video. https://www.you-tube.com/watch?v=14w8WC1I3S4.

33. EKOenergy ecolabel. "Greta Thunberg's speech at the R20 Austrian World Summit, Vienna, May 2019." EKOenergy ecolabel. June 1, 2019. YouTube video. https://www.youtube.com/watch?v=FwptXauY2is.

34. Sawchuk, Stephen. "Students Swarm the Capitol Grounds to Protest Climate Change." *Education Week,* March 15, 2019. https://blogs.edweek.org/edweek/curriculum/2019/03/students_capitol_climate_strike.html.

35. Ruptly. "USA: Hundreds rally outside the US Capitol over climate change." March 15, 2019. YouTube video. https://www.youtube.com/watch?v=s6WEB50JFnY.

36. Carrington, Damian. "School climate strikes: 1.4 million took part, say campaigners." *The Guardian,* March 19, 2019. https://www.theguardian.com/environment/2019/mar/19/school-climate-strikes-more-than-1-million-took-part-say-campaigners-greta-thunberg

37. Weidgenant, Lana. Interview with the author, May 14, 2020.

38. Germanos, Andrea. "'Save Our Planet, Save Our Future': Youth Demand Action With Massive Climate Strikes Worldwide." *Common Dreams,* May 24, 2019. https://www.commondreams.org/news/2019/05/24/save-our-planet-save-our-future-youth-demand-action-massive-climate-strikes.

39. UN Environment Programme. "Climate Action Summit 2019: Schedule." United Nations. https://www.unenvironment.org/events/summit/climate-action-summit-2019.

40. Woodier, Jake. Interview with the author, September 4, 2019.

41. Watts, Jonathan. "Greta Thunberg sets sail for New York on zero-carbon yacht." *The Guardian,* August 14, 2019. https://www.theguardian.com/environment/2019/aug/14/greta-thunberg-sets-sail-plymouth-climate-us-trump.

42. Lee, Rachel. Interview with the author, March 31, 2020.

43. The 350.org Team. "7.6 Million People Demand Action After Week of Climate Strikes." 350.org, September 28, 2019. https://350.org/7-million-people-demand-action-after-week-of-climate-strikes/.

44. Sosa, Lorena. Interview with the author, May 28, 2020.

45. Wright, Ethan. Interview with the author, November 1, 2019.

46. Pressman, Jeremy and Erica Chenoweth. "Crowd Estimates September 2019." https://docs.google.com/spreadsheets/d/1Upkki9lu7vMjdtQ098m6tUsNIwva4ZHgrzkPKwLh1sI/edit#gid=1538635238.

47. United Nations. "Youth leaders vow continued pressure on governments and business for urgent action to address climate emergency at UN Youth Climate Summit." United Nations. https://www.un.org/sustainabledevelopment/blog/2019/09/youth-climate-summit/.

48. United Nations Framework Convention on Climate Change. "The Paris Agreement." United Nations Climate Change, United Nations. https://unfccc.int/process-and-meetings/the-paris-agreement/the-paris-agreement.

49. González, Erika, Sriram Madhusoodanan, Pascoe Sabido, "Meet the Big Polluters Sponsoring COP25," *Common Dreams,* December 3, 2019. https://www.commondreams.org/views/2019/12/03/meet-big-polluters-sponsoring-cop25.

50. Fallahi, Isabella. Interview with the author, December 22, 2019.

51. American Geosciences Institute. "Which states are the largest producers and consumers of coal?" American Geosciences Institute. https://www.americangeosciences.org/critical-issues/faq/which-states-are-largest-producers-and-consumers-coal.

52. United Nations Department of Economic and Social Affairs: Youth. "UN Youth Climate Summit, 21 September 2019." United Nations. https://www.un.org/development/desa/youth/news/2019/09/youth-climate-summit/.

53. Ahmadi, Mohammad. Interview with the author, March 30, 2021.

54. Angry Birds. "The Angry Birds Movie 2 & United Nations—ACT NOW." Angry Birds. July 10, 2019. YouTube video. https://www.youtube.com/watch?v=QbD5jI0CaL4.

55. Weidgenant, Lana. Interview with the author, May 14, 2020.

56. Yuan, Aurora. Interview with the author, March 17, 2020.

57. Worland, Justin. "Global Action on Climate Change Blocked by Political Disruptions." *Time,* September 25, 2019. https://time.com/5684533/un-climate-summit-action/.

58. United Nations. "An important opportunity lost as COP25 ends in compromise, but Guterres vows 'we must not give up,'" *UN News: Global Perspective, Human Stories,* December 15, 2019. https://news.un.org/en/story/2019/12/1053561.

59. Leonard, Nicole. "Protesters kicked out of COP25, stripped of badges." 350.org, December 11, 2019. https://350.org/civil-society-kicked-out-of-cop25/?akid=109819.129028.VvVfB1&rd=1&t=7.

60. Fallahi, Isabella. Interview with the author, December 22, 2019.

61. Hedberg, Claire. Interview with the author, May 11, 2020.

62. Rodriguez, Lena. Interview with the author, March 13, 2020.

63. Jarvis, Brooke. "The Teenagers at the End of the World." *The New York Times,* July 21, 2020. https://www.nytimes.com/interactive/2020/07/21/magazine/teenage-activist-climate-change.html?searchResultPosition=1.

64. Wright, Ethan. Interview with the author, November 1, 2019.

2 No Time for Small Ideas

1. Lawrence, Will. Interview with the author, July 23, 2020.

2. Santoro, Laís. Interview with the author, March 10, 2020.

3. Time. "Alexandria Ocasio-Cortez Joins Climate Change Activists In Protest At Nancy Pelosi's Office." *Time Magazine.* November 13, 2018. YouTube video. https://www.youtube.com/watch?v=puvQlVvhh2Y.

4. Stewart, Andrew. "Sorry Democrats, the Green Party Came Up With the Green New Deal!" *CounterPunch,* November 29, 2018. https://www.counterpunch.org/2018/11/29/sorry-democrats-the-green-party-came-up-with-the-green-new-deal/.

5. Kaufman, Andrew C. "What's the 'Green New Deal'? The surprising origins behind a progressive rallying cry." *Grist,* June 30, 2018. https://grist.org/article/whats-the-green-new-deal-the-surprising-origins-behind-a-progressive-rallying-cry/.

6. Lawrence, Will. Interview with the author, July 23, 2020.

7. Lawrence, Will. Interview with the author, July 23, 2020.

8. Firozi, Paulina. "The Energy 2020: Why climate activists stormed Nancy Pelosi's office again." *The Washington Post,* December 12, 2018. https://www.washingtonpost.com/news/powerpost/paloma/the-energy-202/2018/12/12/the-energy-202-why-climate-activists-stormed-nancy-pelosi-s-office-again/5c1004d11b326b2d6629d436/.

9. Olagbegi, Bolaji. Interview with the author, May 15, 2020.

10. Singh, Ananya. Interview with the author, April 2, 2020.

11. Witt, Emily. "The Optimistic Activists for a Green New Deal: Inside the Youth-Led Singing Sunrise Movement." *The New Yorker,* December 23, 2018. https://www.newyorker.com/news/news-desk/the-optimistic-activists-for-a-green-new-deal-inside-the-youth-led-singing-sunrise-movement.

12. Engelfried, Nick. "How young activists turned the old idea of a Green New Deal into a powerful movement." *Waging Nonviolence,* March 5, 2019. https://wagingnonviolence.org/2019/03/green-new-deal-sunrise-movement-climate-action/.

13. Elliott, Bee. Interview with the author, December 16, 2019.

14. Congress. "H.Res.109 - Recognizing the duty of the Federal Government to create a Green New Deal." Congress.gov. https://www.congress.gov/bill/116th-congress/house-resolution/109/text.

15. Engelfried, Nick. "How young activists turned the old idea of a Green New Deal into a powerful movement." *Waging Nonviolence,* March 5, 2019. https://wagingnonviolence.org/2019/03/green-new-deal-sunrise-movement-climate-action/.

16. Engelfried, Nick. "How young activists turned the old idea of a Green New Deal into a powerful movement." *Waging Nonviolence,* March 5, 2019. https://wagingnonviolence.org/2019/03/green-new-deal-sunrise-movement-climate-action/.

17. Schurman, Zoe. Speech at House on Fire Climate Demonstration. Seattle, WA, December 16, 2019.

18. Mahajan, Kimaya. Speech at House on Fire Climate Demonstration. Seattle, WA, December 16, 2019.

19. Lakey, George. Interview with the author, April 16, 2020.

20. Lawrence, Will. Interview with the author, July 23, 2020.

21. Swarthmore Mountain Justice. "Our Campaign." Swarthmore Mountain Justice. http://www.swatmj.org/ourcampaign/.

22. Lawrence, Will. Interview with the author, July 23, 2020.

23. 350.org. "Divestment Commitments Pass the $3.4 Trillion Mark at COP21." 350.org. December 2, 2015. https://350.org/press-release/divest-ment-commitments-pass-the-3-4-trillion-mark-at-cop21/.

24. Lawrence, Will. Interview with the author, July 23, 2020.

25. Divestment Student Network. Email to supporters list, July 31, 2017.

26. Lawrence, Will. Interview with the author, July 23, 2020.

27. Ptacek, Jamie. Speaking at Sunrise Seattle Orientation Training, August 15, 2020.

28. Watts, Jonathan. "Floods, storms, and searing heat: 2020 in extreme weather." *The Guardian,* December 30, 2020. https://www.theguardian.com/environment/2020/dec/30/floods-storms-and-searing-heat-2020-in-extreme-weather.

29. Ptacek, Jamie. Speaking at Sunrise Seattle Orientation Training, August 15, 2020.

30. Ptacek, Jamie. Speaking at Sunrise Seattle Orientation Training, August 15, 2020.

31. Yeo, Chloe. Speaking at Sunrise Seattle Orientation Training, August 15, 2020.

32. Lawrence, Will. Interview with the author, July 23, 2020.

33. Yeo, Chloe. Speaking at Sunrise Seattle Orientation Training, August 15, 2020.

34. Sunrise Seattle. "Orientation Training." PowerPoint Presentation, Orientation Training, August 15, 2020.

35. Vanden Heuvel, Katrina. "Progressives have a bold agenda. Biden should act on their priorities in his first 100 days." *Washington Post,* December 15, 2020. https://www.washingtonpost.com/opinions/2020/12/15/progressives-have-bold-agenda-biden-should-act-their-priorities-his-first-100-days/.

36. Sunrise Movement. "Sunrise Movement's General Election Impact." Sunrise Movement. October 31, 2020. https://www.sunrisemovement.org/press-releases/sunrise-movements-general-election-impact/.

37. Coopersmith, Emma. Interview with the author, September 25, 2020.

38. Sunrise Movement. Email to supporters list, January 6, 2021.

39. Wolfe, Shanté. Sunrise Movement supporters celebratory Zoom call, January 7, 2021.

40. Ptacek, Jamie. Speaking at Sunrise Seattle Orientation Training, August 15, 2020.

41. Prakash, Varshini. "NYC Sept 20, 2019 #ClimateStrike Speech." Medium.com. September 22, 2020. https://medium.com/sunrisemvmt/nyc-sept-20-2019-climatestrike-speech-varshini-prakash-be3e4118e4d8.

42. Meyer, Robinson. "Why Greta Makes Adults Uncomfortable." *The Atlantic,* September 23, 2019. https://www.theatlantic.com/science/archive/2019/09/why-greta-wins/598612/.

43. US Climate Strike. "The US Climate Strike Demands." Global Climate Strike. https://globalclimatestrike.net/the-us-climate-strike-demands/.

44. Prakash, Varshini. "NYC Sept 20, 2019 #ClimateStrike Speech." Medium.com. September 22, 2020. https://medium.com/sunrisemvmt/nyc-sept-20-2019-climatestrike-speech-varshini-prakash-be3e4118e4d8.

45. Mercado, Angely. "Why Go to School When You Have No Future?': A Q&A With a 13-Year-Old Climate Striker." *The Nation,* March 14, 2019. https://www.thenation.com/article/archive/interview-alexandria-villasenor-climate-striker/.

46. Bloch, Nadine. Interview with the author, August 28, 2019.

47. Ptacek, Jamie. Speaking at Sunrise Seattle Orientation Training, August 15, 2020.

3 *Money Talks*

1. McKibben, Bill. Divest New York virtual press conference, December 7, 2020.

2. Divest New York Coalition. "#DivestNY Supporting Organizations." Go Fossil Free. https://gofossilfree.org/ny/divestnewyork-copy/#coalition.

3. Dale, Jordan. Divest New York virtual press conference, December 7, 2020.

4. Singh, Hridesh. Divest New York virtual press conference, December 7, 2020.

5. Singh, Hridesh. Interview with the author, March 29, 2020.

6. DiNapoli, Thomas P. "N.Y. pension fund is one of the world's most responsible." *Times Union,* July 12, 2020. https://www.timesunion.com/opin-ion/article/N-Y-pension-fund-one-of-world-s-most-responsible-15403354.php.

7. Lee, Alyssa. Interview with the author, February 12, 2020.

8. Altemose, Craig. Interview with the author, May 13, 2020.

9. Lee, Alyssa. Interview with the author, February 12, 2020.

10. Collins, Sean. "Climate activists brought Harvard-Yale football game to a stop to protest fossil fuel investments." *Vox,* November 23, 2019. https://www.vox.com/2019/11/23/20979444/fossil-fuel-protest-harvard-yale-football-game.

11. Cohen, Ilana. Interview with the author, February 19, 2020.

12. New York City Recovery. "Impact of Hurricane Sandy." New York City. https://www1.nyc.gov/site/cdbgdr/about/About%20Hurri-cane%20Sandy.page.

13. Cohen, Ilana. Interview with the author, February 19, 2020.

14. Collins, Sean. "Climate activists brought Harvard-Yale football game to a stop to protest fossil fuel investments." *Vox,* November 23, 2019. https://www.vox.com/2019/11/23/20979444/fossil-fuel-protest-harvard-yale-football-game.

15. Cohen, Ilana. Interview with the author, February 19, 2020.

16. Cohen, Ilana. Interview with the author, February 19, 2020.

17. Siddiqa, Ayisha. Interview with the author, February 15, 2020.

18. Extinction Rebellion U.K. "About Us." Extinction Rebellion. https://rebellion.earth/the-truth/about-us/.

19. Extinction Rebellion U.S. "Day of Action." Extinction Rebellion. https://extinctionrebellion.us/day-of-action-january-26-2019.

20. Siddiqa, Ayisha. Interview with the author, February 15, 2020.

21. Huangpu, Kate. "CU Extinction Rebellion announces week-long hunger strike." *Columbia Spectator,* November 18, 2019. https://www.columbiaspectator.com/news/2019/11/19/cu-extinction-rebellion-announces-week-long-hunger-strike/.

22. Siddiqa, Ayisha. Interview with the author, February 15, 2020.

23. MacAskill, William. "Does Divestment Work?" *The New Yorker,* October 20, 2015. https://www.newyorker.com/business/currency/does-divestment-work.

24. UC Office of the President. "UC's investment portfolios fossil free; clean energy investments top $1 billion." University of California. https://www.universityofcalifornia.edu/press-room/uc-s-investment-portfolios-fossil-free-clean-energy-investments-top-1-billion.

25. McCartney, Kathleen and Deborah L. Duncan. "Fossil Fuels & the Smith Endowment." Smith College. https://www.smith.edu/president-kathleen-mccartney/letters/2019-20/fossil-fuels-and-smith-endowment.

26. Georgetown University. "Fossil Fuels Divestment Continues Georgetown's Commitment to Sustainability." Georgetown University. https://www.georgetown.edu/news/fossil-fuels-divestment-continues-georgetown-commitment-to-sustainability/.

27. Snyder, Susan. "Students are celebrating a small victory after Penn announced it won't invest directly in some fossil fuels." *The Philadelphia Inquirer,* February 4, 2020. https://www.inquirer.com/news/penn-fossil-fuels-divestment-climate-change-20200204.html.

28. Hamilton, Karen. "Antioch University Endowment to Go Fossil Fuel Free." *Common Thread: Antioch University News,* March 12, 2020. https://com-

monthread.antioch.edu/antioch-university-endowment-to-go-fossil-fuel-free/.

29. Dean, James. "Cornell announces moratorium on fossil fuel investments." *Cornell Chronicle,* May 22, 2020. https://news.cornell.edu/stories/2020/05/cornell-announces-moratorium-fossil-fuel-investments.

30. Creighton University. "Creighton Furthers Commitment to Sustainability with Modified Investment Policy." Creighton University, December 31, 2020. https://www.alumni.creighton.edu/controls/email_marketing/view_in_browser.aspx?sid=1250&gid=1&sendId=2058978&ecatid=73&puid=c6c6a67a-195b-45bc-9fe0-312841158133.

31. Wakefield, Jeffrey R. "UVM Divests From Fossil Fuels." *UVM Today,* July 13, 2020. https://www.uvm.edu/news/story/uvm-divests-fossil-fuels.

32. Columbia University. "University Announcement on Fossil Fuel Investments." *Columbia News,* January 22, 2021. https://news.columbia.edu/news/university-announcement-fossil-fuel-investments.

33. News Staff. "Tufts Enacts Investment Policies to Advance Sustainability." *Tufts Now,* March 5, 2022. https://now.tufts.edu/articles/tufts-enacts-investment-policies-advance-sustainability.

34. Polakovic, Gary. "USC ups commitment to sustainability with new, fossil fuel-free investment strategy." *USC News,* February 17, 2021. https://news.usc.edu/182493/usc-sustainability-fossil-fuel-free-investment-strategy/.

35. Rutgers University. "Rutgers to Divest From Fossil Fuels." Rutgers University. https://www.rutgers.edu/news/rutgers-divest-fossil-fuels.

36. Jordan, Don. "U-M shifts strategy for natural resources investments." *The University Record,* March 25, 2021. https://record.umich.edu/articles/u-m-shifts-strategy-for-natural-resources-investments/.

37. Nussbaum, Andrew J. "Amherst Formalizes Commitment to Phase Out Fossil Fuel Investments." Amherst College. https://www.amherst.edu/amherst-story/facts/trustees/statements/node/797137.

38. Princeton University. "Princeton Will Divest From Some Sectors of the Fossil-Fuel Industry." *Princeton Alumni Weekly,* July 2021 Issue. https://paw.princeton.edu/article/princeton-will-divest-some-sectors-fossil-fuel-industry.

39. Goodman, Jasper G. and Kelsey J. Griffin. "Harvard Will Move to Divest its Endowment from Fossil Fuels." *The Harvard Crimson,* September 10,

2021. https://www.thecrimson.com/article/2021/9/10/divest-declares-victory/.

40. Morris, Sadie. Interview with the author, February 17, 2020.

41. Georgetown University. "Fossil Fuels Divestment Continues George-town's Commitment to Sustainability." Georgetown University. https://www.georgetown.edu/news/fossil-fuels-divestment-continues-georgetown-commitment-to-sustainability/.

42. Morris, Sadie. Interview with the author, February 17, 2020.

43. Rajbhandari, Shiva. Interview with the author, May 5, 2020.

44. Palmer, Emma. Interview with the author, May 6, 2020.

45. Bleir, Garet. "JPMorgan Chase Will Halt Financing of Arctic Oil, Gas Drilling, Coal Plants." *Sierra,* February 25, 2020. https://www.sierraclub.org/sierra/jp-morgan-chase-will-halt-financing-arctic-oil-gas-drilling.

46. Stop the Money Pipeline. "Under Pressure, JP Morgan Chase Demotes Former Exxon CEO Lee Raymond from Board Leadership Role." Stop the Money Pipeline, May 2, 2020. https://stopthemoneypipeline.com/raymond-gets-demoted.

47. Rainforest Action Network and others. "Banking on Climate Change: Fossil Fuel Finance Report 2020." Rainforest Action Network. https://www.ran.org/wp-content/uploads/2020/03/Banking_on_Climate_Change__2020_vF.pdf.

48. Institute for Energy and Economic Analysis. "Finance is leaving thermal coal." Institute for Energy and Economic Analysis. https://ieefa.org/finance-leaving-coal/.

49. Institute for Energy and Economic Analysis. "Finance is leaving oil and gas." Institute for Energy and Economic Analysis. https://ieefa.org/finance-exiting-oil-and-gas/.

50. Institute for Energy and Economic Analysis. "Finance is leaving thermal coal." Institute for Energy and Economic Analysis. https://ieefa.org/finance-leaving-coal/.

51. Henn, Jamie. Interview with the author, February 5, 2020.

52. Holger, Dieter. "New York Banks Need to Brace for Climate Change, Regulators Say." *The Wall Street Journal,* October 29, 2020. https://www.wsj.com/articles/new-york-banks-need-to-brace-for-climate-change-regulator-says-11603988421.

53. Jackson, Felicia. "Is the Writing on the Wall for Fossil Fuels?" *Forbes,* April 28, 2020. https://www.forbes.com/sites/feliciajackson/2020/08/28/is-the-writing-on-the-wall-for-fossil-fuels/?sh=78000b1db55b.

54. Penna, Natalie. Interview with the author, April 15, 2020.

55. Bump, Bethany. "Crowd of 7,000 marches in Albany." *Times Union,* January 21, 2017. https://www.timesunion.com/local/article/Albany-activists-Inaugurate-Resistance-on-10873758.php.

56. Penna, Natalie. Interview with the author, April 15, 2020.

57. Divest New York Coalition. "Timeline of the #DivestNY Campaign." Go Fossil Free. https://gofossilfree.org/ny/divestnytimeline/.

58. Divest New York Coalition. "Majority of New York Senators Support Fossil Fuel Divestment Act." Go Fossil Free, April 8, 2020. https://gofossil-free.org/ny/press-release/majority-of-new-york-senators-support-fossil-fuel-divestment-act/

59. McKibben, Bill. Divest New York virtual press conference, December 7, 2020.

60. U.S. Energy Information Administration. "Short-Term Energy Outlook: U.S. Liquid Fuels." U.S. Energy Information Administration. https://www.eia.gov/outlooks/steo/report/us_oil.php.

61. Resist Line 3. "Breaking: 20 youth leaders blockade @Chase in St. Paul and deliver letter from Indigenous women to demand it defund tar sands and #StopLine3. The bank has locked its doors! @StopMoneyPipe." *Twitter,* December 11, 2020.

62. Stop the Money Pipeline. "Climate Activists Announce National 'Covid-Safe' Day of Action Push Back against Wall Street's financing of Keystone XL and Minnesota Line3 Tar Sands Pipelines." *Common Dreams,* December 11, 2020. https://www.commondreams.org/newswire/2020/12/11/climate-activists-announce-national-covid-safe-day-action-push-back-against-wall.

63. Singh, Hridesh. Interview with the author, December 10, 2020.

64. Carpenter, Caitlyn. Interview with the author, December 10, 2020.

65. Center for Information and Research on Civic Learning and Engagement. "Election Week 2020: Young People Increase Turnout, Lead Biden to Victory." Center for Information and Research on Civic Learning and Engagement. Tufts Tisch College. https://circle.tufts.edu/latest-research/election-week-2020#youth-voter-turnout-increased-in-2020.

66. Anand, Aditi. Interview with the author, May 12, 2020.

67. Stahl, Ava. Interview with the author, March 25, 2020.

68. Lee, Alyssa. Interview with the author, February 12, 2020.

69. Cerosaletti, Anna. Interview with the author, April 16, 2020.

70. Adler-Bell, Sam. "The Story Behind the Green New Deal's Meteoric Rise." *The New Republic,* February 6, 2019. https://newrepublic.com/article/153037/story-behind-green-new-deals-meteoric-rise.

4 News From the Front Lines

1. Peter, Evon. Interview with the author, April 28, 2020.
2. Gwich'in Steering Committee. "About the Gwich'in." Gwich'in Steering Committee. https://ourarcticrefuge.org/about-the-gwichin/.
3. Peter, Evon. Interview with the author, April 28, 2020.
4. Gwich'in Steering Committee. "Speaking with One Voice." Our Arctic Refuge. Gwich'in Steering Committee. http://ourarcticrefuge.org/gwichin-steering-committee/.
5. Shogren, Elizabeth. "For 30 Years, a Political Battle Over Oil and ANWR." *NPR,* November 10, 2005. https://www.npr.org/templates/story/story.php?storyId=5007819.
6. U.S. Department of Commerce. *1990 Census of Population, General Population Characteristics: Alaska.* Washington, D.C., 1992 https://www2.census.gov/library/publications/decennial/1990/cp-1/cp-1-3.pdf.
7. Peter, Evon. Interview with the author, April 28, 2020.
8. Palmer, Mark J. "Oil and the Bush Administration." *Earth Island Journal,* Fall 2002. https://www.earthisland.org/journal/index.php/magazine/entry/oil_and_the_bush_administration/.
9. Power Shift Network. "Evon Peter Power Shift 2007 Keynote." March 16, 2009. YouTube video. https://www.youtube.com/watch?v=0o50LMw0nbo.
10. Begaye, Enei. Interview with the author, April 30, 2020.
11. Nies, Judith. "The Black Mesa Syndrome: Indian Lands, Black Gold." *Orion.* https://orionmagazine.org/article/the-black-mesa-syndrome/.
12. Begaye, Enei. Interview with the author, April 30, 2020.
13. Nies, Judith. "The Black Mesa Syndrome: Indian Lands, Black Gold." *Orion.* https://orionmagazine.org/article/the-black-mesa-syndrome/.
14. Begaye, Enei. Interview with the author, April 30, 2020.
15. Lacerenza, Deborah. "An Historical Overview of the Navajo Relocation." *Cultural Survival Quarterly Magazine,* September 1988. culturalsurvival.org/publications/cultural-survival-quarterly/historical-overview-navajo-relocation.
16. Begaye, Enei. Interview with the author, April 30, 2020.
17. Sze, Julie. "Toxic Soup Redux: Why Environmental Racism and Environmental Justice Matter after Katrina." *Items: Insights from the Social Sciences,* June 11, 2006. https://items.ssrc.org/understanding-katrina/toxic-soup-

redux-why-environmental-racism-and-environmental-justice-matter-after-katrina/.

18. Delegates to the First National People of Color Environmental Leadership Summit. "Principles of Environmental Justice." *The Proceedings of the First National People of Color Environmental Leadership Summit,* April 6, 1996. https://www.ejnet.org/ej/principles.html.

19. Schlosberg, David and Lisette B. Collins. "From environmental to climate justice: climate change and the discourse of environmental justice." *WIREs Climate Change,* 2014. http://www.ssents.uvsq.fr/IMG/pdf/schosbergcollins_from_ej_to_cj_wire_cc_2014.pdf.

20. Gearon, Jihan. Interview with the author, April 24, 2020.

21. The Associated Press. "A look at coal-fired power plants set to close in the US West." *Federal News Network,* November 2, 2019. https://federalnewsnetwork.com/business-news/2019/11/a-look-at-coal-fired-power-plants-set-to-close-in-us-west/.

22. Wilson, Jamie. "Senate blocks attempt to allow oil drilling in Alaskan wildlife reserve." *The Guardian,* December 22, 2005.

23. Native Movement. "We are dedicated to building people power, rooted in an Indigenized worldview, toward healthy, sustainable, & just communities for ALL." Native Movement. https://www.nativemovement.org/.

24. Wood, Shadia Fayne. Interview with the author, February 27, 2020.

25. Karliner, Joshua. "Climate Justice Summit Provides Alternative Vision." *CorpWatch,* November 21, 2000. https://corpwatch.org/article/climate-justice-summit-provides-alternative-vision.

26. Schlosberg, David and Lisette B. Collins. "From environmental to climate justice: climate change and the discourse of environmental justice." *WIREs Climate Change,* 2014. http://www.ssents.uvsq.fr/IMG/pdf/schosbergcollins_from_ej_to_cj_wire_cc_2014.pdf.

27. Wood, Shadia Fayne. Interview with the author, February 27, 2020.

28. *Albany Business Review.* "Pataki signs brownfields bill." *Albany Business Review,* October 9, 2003. https://www.bizjournals.com/albany/stories/2003/10/06/daily39.html.

29. Wood, Shadia Fayne. Interview with the author, February 27, 2020.

30. Shabecoff, Philip. "Global Warming Has Begun, Expert Tells Senate." *New York Times,* June 24, 1988. https://www.nytimes.com/1988/06/24/us/global-warming-has-begun-expert-tells-senate.html.

31. Lynch, Kelly. Interview with the author, March 11, 2020.

32. Hamilton, Bruce. "Club Charts Direction for Next Five Years." *The Sierra Club Planet Newsletter.* https://vault.sierraclub.org/planet/200601/fiveyearplan.asp.

33. Duval, Jared. Interview with the author, February 21, 2020.

34. Gearon, Jihan. Interview with the author, April 24, 2020.

35. Wood, Shadia Fayne. Interview with the author, February 27, 2020.

5 *Moving the Elephant*

1. Parish, Billy. Interview with the author, January 24, 2020.

2. Lynch, Kelly. Interview with the author, March 11, 2020.

3. Parish, Billy. Interview with the author, January 24, 2020.

4. Parish, Billy. Interview with the author, January 24, 2020.

5. Lacey, Stephen. "Watt It Takes: The Origin Story of Mosaic With Billy Parish." *Green Tech Media,* May 9, 2018. https://www.greentechmedia.com/articles/read/billy-parish-mosaic-interview.

6. Cardwell, Diane. "A Bet on the Environment." *The New York Times,* September 2, 2013. https://www.nytimes.com/2013/09/03/business/energy-environment/a-firm-that-aims-to-match-environmental-values-with-financial-value.html.

7. Parish, Billy. Interview with the author, January 24, 2020.

8. Lynch, Kelly. Interview with the author, March 11, 2020.

9. Duval, Jared. *Next Generation Democracy: What the Open-Source Revolution Means for Power, Politics, and Change.* New York, Bloomsbury, 2010.

10. Lynch, Kelly. Interview with the author, March 11, 2020.

11. Duval, Jared. *Next Generation Democracy: What the Open-Source Revolution Means for Power, Politics, and Change.* New York, Bloomsbury, 2010.

12. Veazey, Liz. Interview with the author, February 20, 2020.

13. Lynch, Kelly. Interview with the author, March 11, 2020.

14. Veazey, Liz. Interview with the author, February 20, 2020.

15. Duval, Jared. *Next Generation Democracy: What the Open-Source Revolution Means for Power, Politics, and Change.* New York, Bloomsbury, 2010.

16. Duval, Jared. Interview with the author, February 21, 2020.

17. Duval, Jared. *Next Generation Democracy: What the Open-Source Revolution Means for Power, Politics, and Change.* New York, Bloomsbury, 2010.

18. Isham, Jon. Interview with the author, January 20, 2020.

19. Henn, Jamie. Interview with the author, February 5, 2020.

20. New Leaders Initiative. "May Boeve." Earth Island Institute. http://www.broweryouthawards.org/winner/may-boeve/.

21. Henn, Jamie. Interview with the author, February 5, 2020.

22. Bates, Will. Interview with the author, February 18, 2020.

23. McKibben, Bill. "Walk of Ages: How a Vermont March Helped Launch a Climate Movement." *Seven Days,* August 31, 2016. https://www.sevendaysvt.com/vermont/walk-of-ages-how-a-vermont-march-helped-launch-a-climate-movement/Content?oid=3633748.

24. Henn, Jamie. Interview with the author, February 5, 2020.

25. Kemmick, JP. Interview with the author, February 11, 2020.

26. Gearon, Jihan. Interview with the author, April 24, 2020.

27. Sierra Student Coalition. "FAQ for Sprog Participants." Sierra Club. https://www.sierraclub.org/youth/faq-for-sprog-participants.

28. Odeh, Amira. Interview with the author, April 20, 2020.

29. Kamenetz, Anya. "Climate Change Power Shift." *The Nation,* November 15, 2007. https://www.thenation.com/article/archive/climate-change-power-shift/.

30. Nuss, Ethan. Interview with the author, January 8, 2020.

31. Wood, Shadia Fayne. Interview with the author, February 27, 2020.

32. CSSCMathewEgan. "Nancy Pelosi @ Power Shift (2 of 2)." Sustainability Coalition. November 8, 2007. YouTube video. https://www.youtube.com/watch?v=1dOXotXRM3c&t=328s.

33. Nuss, Ethan. Interview with the author, January 8, 2020.

34. Veazey, Liz. Interview with the author, February 20, 2020.

35. Parish, Billy. Interview with the author, January 24, 2020.

36. Comer, Laura. Interview with the author, March 9, 2020.

37. Monahan, Kate. "Youth Voter Turnout Higher Than Ever." *CBS News,* November 12, 2008. https://www.cbsnews.com/news/youth-voter-turnout-higher-than-ever/.

38. Marx, Danny. "Great Work Power Vote, Now What?" *It's Getting Hot in Here: Dispatches from the Youth Climate Movement,* November 6, 2008.

39. Comer, Laura. Interview with the author, March 9, 2020.

40. Greenpeace. "Greenpeace Opposes Waxman-Markey." Greenpeace USA. https://www.greenpeace.org/usa/news/greenpeace-opposes-waxman-mark/.

41. Lynch, Kelly. Interview with the author, March 11, 2020.

42. Lynch, Kelly. "Kelly Lynch." *LinkedIn,* March 23, 2022. https://www.linkedin.com/in/kellyemlynch/.

43. Lynch, Kelly. Interview with the author, March 11, 2020.

44. Bates, Will. Interview with the author, February 18, 2020.

45. Schlickeisen, Derek. "Step It Up campaign leads national demonstration." *The Middlebury Campus,* April 17, 2007. https://middleburycampus.com/6084/news/step-it-up-campaign-leads-national-demonstration/.

46. Step it Up. "Blog." Step It Up. http://www.stepitup2007.org/article.php-list=class&class=20.html.

47. Henn, Jamie. Interview with the author, February 5, 2020.

48. Right Livelihood. "Bill McKibben/350.org." Right Livelihood. https://www.rightlivelihoodaward.org/laureates/bill-mckibben-350-org/.

49. Gracey, Kyle. Interview with the author, March 14, 2020.

50. Van der Zee, Bibi and Robin McKie. "Hundreds arrested at Copenhagen protest rally." *The Guardian,* December 12, 2009. https://www.the-guardian.com/environment/2009/dec/12/hundreds-arrested-copenhagen-protest-rally.

51. Comer, Laura. Interview with the author, March 9, 2020.

52. Veazey, Liz. Interview with the author, February 20, 2020.

53. Parish, Billy. "Billy Parish." *LinkedIn,* March 23, 2022. https://www.linkedin.com/in/billyparish/.

54. Lynch, Kelly. "Kelly Lynch." *LinkedIn,* March 23, 2022. https://www.linkedin.com/in/kellyemlynch/.

55. Veazey, Liz. Interview with the author, February 20, 2020.

56. Avila, Lydia. Interview with the author, March 19, 2020.

57. Avila, Lydia. Interview with the author, March 19, 2020.

58. Sigwalt, Dany. Interview with the author, March 25, 2020.

59. Isham, Jon. Interview with the author, January 20, 2020.

60. Margolin, Jamie. Email to the Power Shift Network supporter list, August 21, 2018.

61. Avila, Lydia. Interview with the author, March 19, 2020.

62. Lynch, Kelly. "Understanding Copenhagen." *It's Getting Hot in Here: Dispatches from the Youth Climate Movement,* December 24, 2009. https://itsgettinghotinhere.wordpress.com/2009/12/24/understanding-copenhagen/.

63. Lynch, Kelly. "Understanding Copenhagen." *It's Getting Hot in Here: Dispatches from the Youth Climate Movement,* December 24, 2009. https://itsgettinghotinhere.wordpress.com/2009/12/24/understanding-copenhagen/.

6 A Stand Worth Taking

1. *United States v. DeChristopher,* 11-4151 (10th Cir. 2012) https://law.justia.com/cases/federal/appellate-courts/ca10/11-4151/11-4151-2012-09-14.html.

2. DeChristopher, Tim. Interview with the author, October 14, 2020.

3. Democracy Now. "Posing as a Bidder, Utah Student Disrupts Government Auction of 150,000 Acres of Wilderness for Oil & Gas Drilling." *Democracy Now,* December 22, 2008. https://www.democracynow.org/2008/12/22/posing_as_a_bidder_utah_student.

4. DeChristopher, Tim. Interview with the author, October 14, 2020.

5. "Posing as a Bidder, Utah Student Disrupts Government Auction of 150,000 Acres of Wilderness for Oil & Gas Drilling." *Democracy Now,* December 22, 2008. https://www.democracynow.org/2008/12/22/posing_as_a_bidder_utah_student.

6. "Posing as a Bidder, Utah Student Disrupts Government Auction of 150,000 Acres of Wilderness for Oil & Gas Drilling." *Democracy Now,* December 22, 2008. https://www.democracynow.org/2008/12/22/posing_as_a_bidder_utah_student.

7. Gage, George and Beth Gage. *Bidder 70.* Telluride, CO: Gage & Gage Productions, 2012.

8. Russell, Joshua Kahn. "Direct Action." Beautiful Trouble. https://beautifultrouble.org/tactic/direct-action/.

9. TimDeChristopher.org. "About Tim DeChristopher." Tim DeChristopher.org. http://www.timdechristopher.org/about.

10. Russell, Joshua Kahn. "Direct Action." Beautiful Trouble. https://beautifultrouble.org/tactic/direct-action/.

11. DeChristopher, Tim. Interview with the author, October 14, 2020.

12. Skelton, Renee and Vernice Miller. "The Environmental Justice Movement." *National Resource Defense Council: Our Stories,* March 17, 2016. https://www.nrdc.org/stories/environmental-justice-movement.

13. DeChristopher, Tim. Interview with the author, October 14, 2020.

14. DeChristopher, Tim. Interview with the author, October 14, 2020.

15. DeChristopher, Tim. Interview with the author, October 14, 2020.

16. Nace, Ted. *Climate Hope: On the Front Lines of the Fight Against Coal.* San Francisco, CoalSwarm, 2010.

17. DeChristopher, Tim. Interview with the author, October 14, 2020.

18. TimDeChristopher.org. "About Tim DeChristopher." Tim DeChristopher.org. http://www.timdechristopher.org/about.

19. Williams, Terry Tempest. "What Love Looks Like." *Orion,* Winter 2011. https://orionmagazine.org/article/what-love-looks-like/.

20. DeChristopher, Tim. Interview with the author, October 14, 2020.

21. Veazey, Liz. "Blockade of Power Plant in SW Virginia." *It's Getting Hot in Here: Dispatches from the Youth Climate Movement,* July 10, 2006.

22. Frank, Brian. Interview with the author, May 15, 2020.

23. Earth First! "Earth First! blockades Virginia coal plant." *Cleveland Indy Media Center,* July 10, 2006. http://cleveland.indymedia.org/news/2006/07/20752.php.

24. Earth First! "Earth First! blockades Virginia coal plant." *Cleveland Indy Media Center,* July 10, 2006. http://cleveland.indymedia.org/news/2006/07/20752.php.

25. Frank, Brian. Interview with the author, May 15, 2020.

26. Dodson, Willie. "The Roots and Growth of Mountain Justice." *It's Getting Hot in Here: Dispatches from the Youth Climate Movement,* December 5, 2006.

27. Morello, Carol. "Child's death by mine boulder sets off avalanche of rage." *Chicago Tribune,* January 8, 2005. https://www.chicagotribune.com/news/ct-xpm-2005-01-09-0501090359-story.html.

28. Dodson, Willie. "The Roots and Growth of Mountain Justice." *It's Getting Hot in Here: Dispatches from the Youth Climate Movement,* December 5, 2006.

29. Frank, Brian. Interview with the author, May 15, 2020.

30. Veazey, Liz. "Blockade of Power Plant in SW Virginia." *It's Getting Hot in Here: Dispatches from the Youth Climate Movement,* July 10, 2006.

31. Zimmer-Stucky, Jasmine. Interview with the author, April 2, 2020.

32. Zimmer-Stucky, Jasmine. Interview with the author, April 2, 2020.

33. Anderson, Kiera James. "We Made the Change by Talking About It: Movement Narratives of Antiviolence Activism in the Radical Environmental Organization Cascadia Forest Defenders." *Frontiers: A Journal of Women Studies* 39, no. 2 (2018): 136–70. https://doi.org/10.5250/fronjwomes-tud.39.2.0136.

34. Frank, Brian. Interview with the author, May 15, 2020.

35. Rising Tide North America. "Principles." Rising Tide North America. https://rtna.tnotw.com/features/principles/.

36. Zimmer-Stucky, Jasmine. Interview with the author, April 2, 2020.

37. Associated Press. "Police arrest 27 protesters blocking logging." *KVAL,* July 9, 2009. https://kval.com/news/local/police-arrest-27-protesters-blocking-logging.

38. Zimmer-Stucky, Jasmine. Interview with the author, April 2, 2020.

39. Associated Press. "Police arrest 27 protesters blocking logging." *KVAL,* July 9, 2009. https://kval.com/news/local/police-arrest-27-protesters-blocking-logging.

40. Cascadia Forest Defenders. "The Elliott." Cascadia Forest Defenders. https://forestdefensenow.wordpress.com/the-elliott/.

41. Jones, Whit. "LIVE BLOG: Youth activists sit-in, refuse to leave until negotiators listen to 11 million voices calling for a fair, ambitious, and binding deal." *It's Getting Hot in Here: Dispatches from the Youth Climate Movement,* December 17, 2009.

42. Van der Zee, Bibi and Robin McKie. "Hundreds arrested at Copenhagen protest rally." *The Guardian,* December 12, 2009. https://www.theguardian.com/environment/2009/dec/12/hundreds-arrested-copenhagen-protest-rally.

43. Dewan, Amy. "The Twilight of Copenhagen." *It's Getting Hot in Here: Dispatches from the Youth Climate Movement,* December 17, 2009.

44. Newbold, Moey. Interview with the author, February 21, 2020.

45. Vulliamy, Ed. "Shell's battle for the heart of Ireland." *The Guardian,* May 28, 2011. https://www.theguardian.com/world/2011/may/29/shell-ireland-corrib-gas-project.

46. Wainwright, Martin. "In the shadow of Drax, not so much a fight as a festival." *The Guardian,* September 1, 2006. https://www.theguardian.com/environment/2006/sep/01/energy.activists.

47. Yeung, Louise. "The Youth is Starting to Change." *It's Getting Hot in Here: Dispatches from the Youth Climate Movement,* December 7, 2009.

48. Power Shift Network. "Tim DeChristopher: Power Shift 2011 Keynote." April 17, 2011. Power Shift Network. YouTube video. https://www.youtube.com/watch?v=81EZUkYzrxU.

49. DeChristopher, Tim. Interview with the author, October 14, 2020.

50. Power Shift Network. "Tim DeChristopher: Power Shift 2011 Keynote." April 17, 2011. Power Shift Network. YouTube video. https://www.youtube.com/watch?v=81EZUkYzrxU.

51. Parkin, Scott. "Climate Activist Tim DeChristopher Found Guilty." *It's Getting Hot in Here: Dispatches from the Youth Climate Movement,* March 3, 2011.

52. Goldenberg, Suzanne. "Tim DeChristopher Sentenced to Two Years for Making False Drilling Bids." *Inside Climate News,* July 27, 2011. https://insideclimatenews.org/news/27072011/tim-dechristopher-climate-change-sentenced-jail-false-oil-gas-drilling-bids/.

53. DeChristopher, Tim. Interview with the author, October 14, 2020.

54. Walsh, Bryan. "Despite Snow—and Irony—a Climate Protest Persists." *Time,* March 3, 2009. http://content.time.com/time/health/article/ 0,8599,1882700,00.html

55. Leonard, Matt. Interview with the author, April 27, 2020.

56. DeChristopher, Tim. Interview with the author, October 14, 2020.

57. Belalia, Henia. "Peaceful Uprising — supporting one man's right to protest." Peaceful Uprising. http://www.peacefuluprising.org/peaceful-uprising-supporting-one-mans-right-to-protest-20110217.

58. DeChristopher, Tim. Interview with the author, October 14, 2020.

59. Power Shift Network. "Tim DeChristopher: Power Shift 2011 Keynote." April 17, 2011. Power Shift Network. YouTube video. https://www.youtube.com/watch?v=81EZUkYzrxU.

60. Engelfried, Nick. "Coal Train Visits Bank of America and Wells Fargo." *It's Getting Hot in Here: Dispatches from the Youth Climate Movement,* May 15, 2011.

61. Engelfried, Nick. "Citizens Unite on International Day of Action Against the Tar Sands." *It's Getting Hot in Here: Dispatches from the Youth Climate Movement,* June 21, 2011.

62. Belalia, Henia. "This is what LOVE looks like." *It's Getting Hot in Here: Dispatches from the Youth Climate Movement,* August 12, 2011.

63. DeChristopher, Tim. Interview with the author, October 14, 2020.

64. Maffly, Brian. "10 years after he monkey-wrenched a Utah oil and gas lease auction, Tim DeChristopher is 'feeling demoralized' by 'the state of the world' but sees hope in humanity." *The Salt Lake Tribune,* December 15, 2018. https://www.sltrib.com/news/environment/2018/12/15/years-after-he-monkey/.

65. DeChristopher, Tim. Interview with the author, October 14, 2020.

66. Jordan, Don. "U-M shifts strategy for natural resources investments." *The University Record,* March 25, 2021. https://record.umich.edu/articles/u-m-shifts-strategy-for-natural-resources-investments/.

67. Morris, Jonathan. Interview with the author, May 4, 2021.

68. Morris, Jonathan. "How persistent student organizing forced one of the largest public universities to divest from fossil fuels." *Waging Nonviolence,* April 6, 2011. https://wagingnonviolence.org/2021/04/persistent-student-organizing-forced-university-of-michigan-to-divest-from-fossil-fuels/.

69. Weaverdyck, Noah. Interview with the author, May 4, 2021.

70. Bishop, Sasha. Interview with the author, May 4, 2021.

71. Jordan, Don. "U-M shifts strategy for natural resources investments." *The University Record,* March 25, 2021. https://record.umich.edu/articles/u-m-shifts-strategy-for-natural-resources-investments/.

72. Weaverdyck, Noah. Interview with the author, May 4, 2021.

73. DeChristopher, Tim. Interview with the author, October 14, 2020.

74. McNamara, Neal. *Patch,* February 5, 2020. https://patch.com/massachu-setts/worcester/30-activists-face-charges-after-harvard-coal-train-blockade.

75. DeChristopher, Tim. Interview with the author, October 14, 2020.

7 Tar Sands Wars

1. White Eyes, Joseph. Interview with the author, February 23, 2021.

2. Leonard, Matt. Interview with the author, April 27, 2020.

3. Union on of Concerned Scientists. "What Are Tar Sands?" Union of Concerned Scientists. https://www.ucsusa.org/resources/what-are-tar-sands.

4. Government of Canada. "Oil Sands: Water Management." Government of Canada. https://www.nrcan.gc.ca/energy/publications/18750.

5. Thomas-Muller, Clayton. "The Rise of the Native Rights-Based Strategic Framework." Honor the Earth. https://www.honorearth.org/the_rise_of_the_native_rights_based_strategic_framework.

6. Morin, Brandi. "Pipelines, man camps and murdered Indigenous women in Canada." *Aljazeera,* May 5, 2020. https://www.aljazeera.com/indepth/features/pipelines-man-camps-murdered-indigenous-women-canada-200412064302356.html.

7. Thomas-Muller, Clayton. "The Rise of the Native Rights-Based Strategic Framework." Honor the Earth. https://www.honorearth.org/the_rise_of_the_native_rights_based_strategic_framework.

8. Hollyhock. "Clayton Thomas-Muller." Hollyhock. https://hollyhock.ca/presenter/382/clayton-thomas-muller/.

9. Wood, Shadia Fayne. Interview with the author, February 27, 2020.

10. Thomas-Muller, Clayton. "The Rise of the Native Rights-Based Strategic Framework." Honor the Earth. https://www.honorearth.org/the_rise_of_the_native_rights_based_strategic_framework.

11. Thomas-Muller, Clayton. "The Rise of the Native Rights-Based Strategic Framework." Honor the Earth. https://www.honorearth.org/the_rise_of_the_native_rights_based_strategic_framework.

12. Braun, Joye. Interview with the author. January 25, 2021.

13. Goodwin, Morgan. "Clinton's Big Decision on Tar Sands." *It's Getting Hot in Here: Dispatches from the Youth Climate Movement,* July 24, 2009. https://itsgettinghotinhere.wordpress.com/2009/07/24/clintons-big-decision-on-tar-sands/.

14. U.S. State Department. "Keystone Pipeline Presidential Permit." Department of State Archive. https://2001-2009.state.gov/r/pa/prs/ps/2008/mar/102254.htm.

15. U.S. State Department. "Notice of Issuance of a Presidential Permit for the Proposed Enbridge Energy Alberta Clipper Pipeline Project." National Archives. https://www.federalregister.gov/documents/2009/08/26/E9-20598/notice-of-issuance-of-a-presidential-permit-for-the-proposed-enbridge-energy-alberta-clipper.

16. Hydrocarbons Technology. "Alberta Clipper Pipeline Project." Verdict Media. https://www.hydrocarbons-technology.com/projects/alberta-clipper/.

17. Leonard, Matt. Interview with the author, April 27, 2020.

18. Henn, Jamie. Interview with the author, February 5, 2020.

19. Bates, Will. Interview with the author, February 18, 2020.

20. *HuffPost.* "10/10/10 Global Work Party: People Across The Planet Work With 350.org On Solutions To Tackle Climate Change." *HuffPost,* October 11, 2010. https://www.huffpost.com/entry/101010-global-work-party-_n_757531.

21. Henn, Jamie. "White House Won't Put Solar on It...But We Will." *It's Getting Hot in Here: Dispatches from the Youth Climate Movement,* September 10, 2010.

22. Leonard, Matt. Interview with the author, April 27, 2020.

23. National Wildlife Federation. "Keystone XL Tar Sands Pipeline." National Wildlife Federation National Advocacy Center. https://www.nwf.org/~/media/PDFs/Global-Warming/Policy-Solutions/Keystone%20XL%20Fact%20Sheet_2.ashx.

24. Henn, Jamie. Interview with the author, February 5, 2020.

25. Henn, Jamie. "Bill McKibben, Naomi Klein, Wendell Berry Call for Civil Disobedience on Tar Sands." *It's Getting Hot in Here: Dispatches from the Youth Climate Movement,* June 23, 2011.

26. Graves, Richard. "70 People Arrested in Opening Day of Tar Sands Action." *It's Getting Hot in Here: Dispatches from the Youth Climate Movement,* August 20, 2011.

27. Leonard, Matt. Interview with the author, April 27, 2020.

28. *HuffPost.* "Tar Sands Pipeline Protests Continue (PHOTOS)." *HuffPost,* October 21, 2011. https://www.huffpost.com/entry/tar-sands-pipeline-protest-photo_n_932495.

29. Leonard, Matt. Interview with the author, April 27, 2020.

30. Henn, Jamie. Interview with the author, February 5, 2020.

31. Women's Earth & Climate Action Network. "Kandi Mossett of the Indigenous Environmental Network strongly speaking out against the Keystone XL." Women's Earth & Climate Action Network, International. https://www.wecaninternational.org/post/kandi-mossett-of-the-indigenous-environmental-network-strongly-speaking-out-against-the-keystone-xl.

32. Mackey, Kendall. Interview with the author, April 29, 2020.

33. Hance, Jeremy. "Climate test for Obama: 1,252 people arrested over notorious oil pipeline." *Mongabay,* September 6, 2011. https://news.mongabay.com/2011/09/climate-test-for-obama-1252-people-arrested-over-notorious-oil-pipeline/.

34. Nuss, Ethan. "Maggie Has Been Arrested After Sitting On a 40 Foot Pole to Delay Keystone XL Clear-Cutting for Two Entire Days." Tar Sands Blockade. October 4, 2012. https://tarsandsblockade.org/maggie/.

35. Tar Sands Action. "Spokespeople." Tar Sands Action. http://tarsandsaction.org/press/spokespeople/.

36. Spoon, Cindy. Interview with the author, March 9, 2020.

37. Kessler, Ben. "The Time Has Come: A Call to Action." Tar Sands Blockade. August 24, 2012. https://tarsandsblockade.org/the-time-has-come-a-call-to-action/#more-959.

38. Nuss, Ethan. "TransCanada Actively Encouraged Torture Tactics to be Used on Peaceful Protesters (Day 3)." Tar Sands Blockade. September 26, 2012. https://tarsandsblockade.org/transcanada-torture/.

39. Nuss, Ethan. "VIDEO: TransCanada Worker Attempts to Drop Tree on Peaceful Blockader (Day 4)." Tar Sands Blockade. September 27, 2012. https://tarsandsblockade.org/video-transcanada-worker-attempts-to-drop-tree-on-peaceful-blockader-day-4/.

40. Nuss, Ethan. "Texan Climbs 40 Foot Pole in Path of Keystone XL Clear Cut (Day 9)." Tar Sands Blockade. October 2, 2012. https://tarsandsblockade.org/tree-sit-day9/.

41. Nuss, Ethan. "Maggie Has Been Arrested After Sitting On a 40 Foot Pole to Delay Keystone XL Clear-Cutting for Two Entire Days." Tar Sands Blockade. October 4, 2012. https://tarsandsblockade.org/maggie/.

42. Spoon, Cindy. Interview with the author, March 9, 2020.

43. Zuckerman, Laura. "Nez Perce activists block Idaho highway over tar sands 'megaload.'" Indigenous Environmental Network. August 13, 2013. https://www.ienearth.org/nez-perce-activists-block-idaho-highway-over-tar-sands-megaload/.

44. *Lewiston Tribune.* "Nez Perce Tribe Omega Morgan Blockade." August 6, 2013. YouTube video. https://www.youtube.com/watch?v=b2ykSReO9Z4.

45. Porter, Zack. Interview with the author, March 18, 2020.

46. Ames, Michael. "Another Oil-sands Challenge: Transporting Equipment." *The New Yorker,* March 14, 2014. https://www.newyorker.com/business/currency/another-oil-sands-challenge-transporting-equipment.

47. Briggeman, Kim. "Megaload Test Module Hits Wire, Cuts Power to 1,300 Homes." *Missoulian,* April 13, 2011. https://billingsgazette.com/news/state-and-regional/megaload-test-module-hits-wire-cuts-power-to-1-300-homes/article_d1e3b732-65d2-11e0-8c5f-001cc4c002e0.html.

48. Porter, Zack. Interview with the author, March 18, 2020.

49. Porter, Zack. Interview with the author, March 18, 2020.

50. Parkin, Scott. "Montana Citizens Temporarily Block Tar Sands Megaloads." *It's Getting Hot In Here: Dispatches from the Youth Climate Movement,* March 10, 2011.

51. Porter, Zack. Interview with the author, March 18, 2020.

52. Ames, Michael. "Another Oil-sands Challenge: Transporting Equipment." *The New Yorker,* March 14, 2014. https://www.newyorker.com/business/currency/another-oil-sands-challenge-transporting-equipment.

53. Porter, Zack. Interview with the author, March 18, 2020.

54. Schneider, Keith. "Exxon and Imperial Oil Forced to Go Around Sensitive Idaho River Valley. Circle of Blue. May 23, 2012. https://www.circleofblue.org/2012/world/water-safety-concerns-force-exxon-and-imperial-oil-out-of-idaho-scenic-river-valley/.

55. Zuckerman, Laura. "Nez Perce activists block Idaho highway over tar sands 'megaload.'" Indigenous Environmental Network. August 13, 2013. https://www.ienearth.org/nez-perce-activists-block-idaho-highway-over-tar-sands-megaload/.

56. Engelfried, Nick. "Indigenous Organizing Drives Montana Tar Sands Opposition." *Waging Nonviolence,* February 12, 2014. https://wagingnonviolence.org/2014/02/indigenous-organizing-confronts-tar-sands-megaloads-montana/.

57. "Moccasins on the Ground Tour of Resistance Heads to the Cheyenne River Eagle Butte Sioux Reservation." Tar Sands Blockade. June 7, 2013. https://tarsandsblockade.org/motg_bridger/.

58. Brings Plenty, Morgan. Interview with the author, February 21, 2021.

59. Braun, Joye. Interview with the author, January 25, 2021.

60. White Eyes, Joseph. Interview with the author, February 23, 2021.

61. White Eyes, Joseph. Interview with the author, February 23, 2021.

62. Nordhaus, Ted and Michael Shellenberger. "The Environmentalist Need to Move On and Away From Keystone." *The New York Times,* February 12, 2014. https://www.nytimes.com/roomfordebate/2014/02/12/is-the-keystone-xl-pipeline-worth-the-fight/the-environmentalist-need-to-move-on-and-away-from-keystone.

63. Friends of the Earth. "Nation's largest environmental organizations stand together to oppose oil pipeline." Friends of the Earth. https://foe.org/news/2011-08-nations-largest-environmental-organizations-stand-to/.

64. Henn, Jamie. "Bill McKibben, Naomi Klein, Wendell Berry Call for Civil Disobedience on Tar Sands." *It's Getting Hot in Here: Dispatches from the Youth Climate Movement,* June 23, 2011.

65. Koch, Wendy. "Tens of thousands demand action on climate change." *USA Today,* February 17, 2013. https://www.usatoday.com/story/news/nation/2013/02/17/climate-change-rally-human-pipeline/1925719/.

66. Shelly, Deirdre. "XL Dissent: 398 Youth Arrested at Anti-Keystone XL Pipeline Protest at White House." *Democracy Now,* March 3, 2014. https://www.democracynow.org/2014/3/3/xl_dissent_398_youth_arrested_at.

8 Oppose All Pipelines

1. Engelfried, Nick. "Oregon Rallies for a Coal-Free Future at Public Utilities Commission Hearing." *It's Getting Hot In Here: Dispatches from the Youth Climate Movement,* June 24, 2010.

2. Karliner, Joshua. "Climate Justice Summit Provides Alternative Vision." CorpWatch. November 21, 2000. https://corpwatch.org/article/climate-justice-summit-provides-alternative-vision.

3. Colon, Mabette. Email message to the author, April 27, 2020.

4. Carmody, Steve. "Michigan State University commits to green energy (but not enough for some)." *Michigan Radio,* April 13, 2012.

https://www.michiganradio.org/post/michigan-state-university-commits-green-energy-not-enough-some.

5. Teplitzky, Kim. Interview with the author, August 28, 2020.

6. Tavor, Talya. Interview with the author, September 8, 2020.

7. Learn, Scott. "PGE's coal-fired Boardman plant gets approval to close in 2020, with fewer pollution controls." *The Oregonian,* December 9, 2010. https://www.oregonlive.com/business/2010/12/pges_coal-fired_boardman_plant.html.

8. Sierra Student Coalition. "Campuses Beyond Coal: The Sierra Student Coalition's Campaign for Clean, 21st-Century Energy." Sierra Club. https://content.sierraclub.org/creative-archive/sites/content.sierra-club.org.creative-archive/files/pdfs/0469-CampusBC_Fact_04_low.pdf.

9. Meng, Qingmin. "The Impacts of Fracking on the Environment: A Total Environmental Study Paradigm. *Science of the Total Environment* 580 (2017) 953 –957. http://dx.doi.org/10.1016/j.scitotenv.2016.12.045.

10. Malewitz, Jim. "Curbing Local Control, Abbott Signs 'Denton Fracking Bill.'" *The Texas Tribune,* May 18, 2015. https://www.texastribune.org/2015/05/18/abbott-signs-denton-fracking-bill/.

11. Baddour, Dylan. "Three protesters are arrested trying to block the state-order resumption of fracking in Denton." *Houston Chronicle,* June 1, 2015. https://www.chron.com/about/article/Three-protesters-are-arrested-trying-to-block-the-6299702.php.

12. Friends of the Columbia River Gorge. "Millennium Coal Terminal Litigation." Friends of the Columbia River Gorge. https://gorgefriends.org/protect-the-gorge/gorge-issues/millennium-coal-terminal-litigation.html.

13. Earthjustice. "Challenging the Otter Creek Coal Mine." Earthjustice. https://earthjustice.org/our_work/cases/2011/otter-creek-coal-strip-mine-challenged.

14. Chandler, Lowell. Interview with the author, July 9, 2020.

15. Schweitzer, Brian. Comments delivered at Montana State Land Board Meeting. Helena, MT, May 21, 2012.

16. Schweitzer, Brian. Comments delivered at Montana State Land Board Meeting. Helena, MT, May 21, 2012.

17. Braided Hair, Vanessa. "Why the Otter Creek Coal Mine Will Never be Built." *National Wildlife Federation Blog,* April 10, 2013. https://blog.nwf.org/2013/04/why-the-otter-creek-coal-mine-will-never-be-built/.

18. JC. "Big Sky High Students Stage Walkout over Otter Creek Coal." *4&20 blackbirds,* February 12, 2010. https://4and20blackbirds.wordpress.com/2010/02/12/big-sky-high-students-stage-walkout-over-otter-coal/.

19. Dickson, Rachel. Interview with the author, August 23, 2020.

20. Dennison, Mike. "Land Board approves $86M Otter Creek coal deal; Missoula protesters arrested." *Missoulian,* March 18, 2010. https://href.li/?http://www.missoulian.com/news/local/article_3fc5a006-32b4-11df-8cc5-001cc4c002e0.html.

21. OPB Staff. "Mayor Details Portland's Plans To Battle Climate Change Following Vatican Trip." *OPB,* July 28, 2015. https://www.opb.org/news/article/portland-mayor-charlie-hales-climate-change-plans/.

22. Columbia Riverkeeper. "Portland Makes History With New Protections From Fossil Fuels." Columbia Riverkeeper. https://www.columbiariver-keeper.org/news/2016/12/portland-makes-history-new-protections-fossil-fuels.

23. Johnson, Miles. "Fighting Fossil Fuel on the Columbia River." Columbia Riverkeeper. https://www.columbiariverkeeper.org/news/2015/6/fighting-fossil-fuel-columbia-river.

24. Earth First! News. "Portland Activists Blockade Columbia River in Symbolic Protest Against Fossil Fuel Shipments." *Earth First! Newswire,* July 28, 2013. https://earthfirstnews.wordpress.com/2013/07/28/portland-activists-blockade-columbia-river-in-symbolic-protest-against-fossil-fuel-shipments/.

25. Zimmer-Stucky, Jasmine. Interview with the author, April 2, 2020.

26. Zimmer-Stucky, Jasmine. Interview with the author, April 2, 2020.

27. Duke, Solomon. Interview with the author, March 24, 2021.

28. Theen, Andrew. "Mayor Charlie Hales 'urges' Pembina to withdraw plans for a North Portland propane terminal." *The Oregonian,* May 7, 2015. https://www.oregonlive.com/portland/2015/05/mayor_char-lie_hales_urges_pemb.html.

29. Zimmer-Stucky, Jasmine. Interview with the author, April 2, 2020.

30. Lawrence, Will. Interview with the author, July 23, 2020.

31. Ressler, Lauren. Interview with the author, January 17, 2020.

32. Lawrence, Will. Interview with the author, July 23, 2020.

33. 350.org. "Annual Report 2016." 350.org. https://350.org/2016-annual-report/.

34. Mujica-Steiner, Michaela. Interview with the author, May 13, 2020.

35. Sophie Cash interview, interview with the author, May 12, 2020.

36. Piserchia, Caitlin. Interview with the author, May 7, 2020.

37. Munguia, Hayley. "How Many People Really Showed Up To The People's Climate March?" *FiveThirtyEight,* September 30, 2014. https://fivethirtyeight.com/features/peoples-climate-march-attendance/.

38. The Columbian. "5 protesters who blocked oil train arrested." *The Columbian,* September 1, 2014. https://www.columbian.com/news/2014/sep/01/demonstrators-block-tracks-everett/.

39. Gaya, Ahmed. Interview with the author, July 2, 2020.

40. Knauf, Ana Sofia. "Activists blockade Seattle port to protest Shell's Arctic drilling plans." *Grist,* May 18, 2015. https://grist.org/climate-energy/activists-blockade-seattle-port-to-protest-shells-arctic-drilling-plans/.

41. Seattle Times Staff. "Kayaking protesters detained as oil rig leaves." *Seattle Times,* June 16, 2015. https://www.seattletimes.com/seattle-news/environment/polar-pioneer-oil-rig-may-be-moving-monday-morning/.

42. Greenpeace. "As It Happened: Activists Stop Shell Vessel as It Attempts to Leave Portland Harbor." Greenpeace USA. https://www.greenpeace.org/usa/breaking-activists-stop-shell-vessel-as-it-attempts-to-leave-portland-harbor/.

43. Whelan, Luke. "This Is What It's Like to Hang On to the Anchor of a Shell Oil Ship for 63 Hours." *Mother Jones,* June 6, 2015. https://www.motherjones.com/environment/2015/06/shell-protestors-arctic-challenger-oil-drilling/.

44. D'Angelo, Chiara. Interview with the author, August 26, 2020.

45. Smith, Tasina. Interview with the author, February 20, 2021.

46. U.S. Army Corps of Engineers. "Dakota Access Pipeline Environmental Assessment." U.S. Army Corps of Engineers Omaha District. https://www.nwo.usace.army.mil/Missions/Civil-Works/Planning/Project-Reports/Article/633496/dakota-access-pipeline-environmental-assessment/.

47. White Eyes, Joseph. Interview with the author, February 23, 2021.

48. Brings Plenty, Morgan. Interview with the author, February 21, 2021.

49. Smith, Tasina. Interview with the author, February 20, 2021.

50. Ormseth, Eamon. Interview with the author, September 24, 2020.

51. Solnit, Rebecca. "Standing Rock protests: this is only the beginning." *The Guardian,* September 12, 2016. https://www.theguardian.com/us-news/2016/sep/12/north-dakota-standing-rock-protests-civil-rights.

52. Morsette, Kiewsis. Interview with the author, September 25, 2020.

53. Morsette, Kiewsis. Interview with the author, September 25, 2020.

54. Smith, Tasina. Interview with the author, February 20, 2021.

55. Manning, Sarah Sunshine. "Thunberg and Tokata Iron Eyes Join Forces and Elevate Climate Justice Conversation." NDN Collective. https://ndncollective.org/thunberg-and-takota-iron-eyes-join-forces-and-elevate-climate-justice-conversation/.

56. Pressman, Jeremy and Erica Chenoweth. "Crowd Estimates September 2019." https://docs.google.com/spreadsheets/d/1Upkki9lu7vMjdtQ098m6tUsNIwva4ZHgrzkPKwLh1sI/edit#gid=1538635238.

57. McClure, Robert. "A Thin Green Line." *Grist,* January 31, 2021. https://grist.org/justice/washington-oregon-british-columbia-activism-lng-coal-exports/.

58. Frank, Matthew. "Coal's Latest Retreat: Arch Backs Away From Huge Montana Mine." *Inside Climate News,* March 15, 2016. https://insideclimate-news.org/news/15032016/arch-coal-retreat-montana-mine-otter-creek-valley/.

59. Sierra Club Beyond Coal. "America, Let's Move Beyond Coal and Gas." Sierra Club. https://coal.sierraclub.org/.

60. Hurdle, Jon. "PennEast opponents say community activism was key to beating pipeline." *NJ Spotlight News,* October 4, 2021. https://www.njspotlight-news.org/2021/10/penneast-pipeline-throws-in-towel-ends-quest-natural-gas-nj-public-private-land-grassroots-opponents-celebrate/.

61. Penn, Ivan. "Atlantic Coast Pipeline Canceled as Delays and Costs Mount." *The New York Times,* July 5, 2020. https://atlanticcoastpipeline.com/news/2020/7/5/dominion-energy-and-duke-energy-cancel-the-atlantic-coast-pipeline.aspx.

62. Shell. "Shell Updates on Alaska Exploration." Shell. https://www.shell.com/media/news-and-media-releases/2015/shell-updates-on-alaska-exploration.

63. Energy Transfer Partners. "Moving America's Energy: The Dakota Access Pipeline." The Dakota Access Pipeline. Energy Transfer Partners. https://daplpipelinefacts.com/.

64. Sierra Club Foundation. "Obama Administration Orders Environmental Review of Dakota Access Pipeline Easement." *Foundation News,* December 12, 2016. https://www.sierraclubfoundation.org/blog/obama-administration-orders-environmental-review-dakota-access-pipeline-easement.

65. Levin, Sam. "Native Americans fight Texas pipeline using 'same model as Standing Rock.'" *The Guardian,* January 9, 2017. https://www.the-

guardian.com/us-news/2017/jan/09/trans-pecos-pipeline-texas-protest-two-rivers-standing-rock.

66. Moore, Sheehan. "Indigenous and environmental water protectors fight to block Louisiana pipeline." *Waging Nonviolence,* July 16, 2018. https://wagingnonviolence.org/2018/07/indigenous-water-protectors-louisiana-pipeline/.

67. Engelfried, Nick. "Indigenous-Led Resistance to Enbridge's Line 3 Pipeline Threatens Big Oil's Last Stand." *Waging Nonviolence,* December 14, 2020. https://wagingnonviolence.org/2020/12/indigenous-water-protectors-enbridge-line-3-pipeline-big-oil-last-stand/.

9 The Challenge of Here and Now

1. Algee, Nick. Interview with the author, September 9, 2020.

2. Davenport, Coral and Lisa Friedman. "Biden Cancels Keystone XL Pipeline and Rejoins Paris Climate Agreement." *The New York Times,* February 19, 2021. https://www.nytimes.com/2021/01/20/climate/biden-paris-climate-agreement.html.

3. Powell, Rich, Mitch Kersey, and Spencer Nelson. "The Energy Act of 2020: A Monumental Climate and Clean Energy Bill." ClearPath. https://clearpath.org/our-take/the-energy-act-of-2020-a-monumental-climate-and-clean-energy-bill/.

4. Read, Bridget. "Alexandria Ocasio-Cortez's Green New Deal Resolution Gets Support From the Major 2020 Democratic Presidential Candidates." *Vogue,* February 7, 2020. https://www.vogue.com/article/alexandria-ocasio-cortez-green-new-deal-resolution-support.

5. Biden, Joe. "The Green New Deal is a crucial framework for meeting the climate challenges we face. It powerfully captures two core truths: This is an existential crisis requiring immediate, ambitious action. Our environment and economy are connected." *Twitter,* September 4, 2019.

6. Congress. "H.Res.109 - Recognizing the duty of the Federal Government to create a Green New Deal." Congress.gov. https://www.congress.gov/bill/116th-congress/house-resolution/109/text.

7. Gearino, Dan. "Inside Clean Energy: Here Are 5 States that Took Leaps on Clean Energy Policy in 2021." *Inside Climate News,* December 23, 2021. https://insideclimatenews.org/news/23122021/inside-clean-energy-states-2021/.

8. City of New York. "Action on Global Warming: NYC's Green New Deal." The Official Website of the City of New York. https://www1.nyc.gov/

office-of-the-mayor/news/209-19/action-global-warming-nyc-s-green-new-deal#/0.

9. Karanth, Sanjana. "Los Angeles Launched its Own Green New Deal." *Grist,* May 1, 2019. https://grist.org/article/los-angeles-launched-its-own-green-new-deal/.

10. Farrell, Jessyn. "Green New Deal." City of Seattle Office of Sustainability & Environment. https://www.seattle.gov/environment/climate-change/green-new-deal.

11. Thornton, Ryan. "Council Asks City Staff for Ideas on Local Green New Deal, EVs." *Austin Monitor,* May 15, 2019. https://www.austinmonitor.com/stories/2019/05/council-asks-city-staff-for-ideas-on-local-green-new-deal-evs/.

12. Pew Research Center. "As Economic Concerns Recede, Environmental Protection Rises on the Public's Policy Agenda." Pew Research Center. https://www.pewresearch.org/politics/2020/02/13/as-economic-concerns-recede-environmental-protection-rises-on-the-publics-policy-agenda/.

13. Sisco, Matthew R., Silvia Pianta, Elke U. Weber, and Bosetti Valentina. "Global Climate Marches Sharply Raise Attention to Climate Change: Analysis of Climate Search Behavior in 46 Countries." *Journal of Environmental Psychology* 75 (2021). https://doi.org/10.1016/j.jenvp.2021.101596.

14. Abnett, Kate. "Climate 'Law of Laws' Gets European Parliament's Green Light." *Reuters,* June 24, 2021. https://www.reuters.com/world/europe/climate-law-laws-gets-european-parliaments-green-light-2021-06-24/.

15. Think Tank. "South Korea's Pledge to Achieve Carbon Neutrality by 2050." European Parliament. https://www.europarl.europa.eu/thinktank/en/document/EPRS_BRI(2021)690693.

16. Japanese Ministry of Economy, Trade, and Industry. "Key Milestones on Japan's Roadmap." Ministry of Economy, Trade, and Industry. https://www.meti.go.jp/english/policy/energy_environment/global_warming/roadmap/.

17. Myers, Steven Lee. "China's Pledge to be Carbon Neutral by 2060: What it Means." *New York Times,* September 23, 2020. https://www.nytimes.com/2020/09/23/world/asia/china-climate-change.html.

18. Jong, Hans Nicholas. "Indonesia's Net-Zero Emissions Goal is Not Ambitious Enough, Activists Say." *Mongabay,* April 12, 2021. https://news.mongabay.com/2021/04/indonesia-net-zero-emissions-target-coal-energy-2070/.

19. Aljazeera. "India Targets Net-Zero Carbon Emissions by 2070, Says Modi." *Aljazeera News,* November 1, 2021. https://www.aljazeera.com/news/2021/11/1/modi-india-to-hit-net-zero-climate-target-by-2070.

20. The White House. "President Biden's Bipartisan Infrastructure Law." The White House. https://www.whitehouse.gov/bipartisan-infrastructure-law/.

21. The Majority Report w/ Sam Seder. "Joe Manchin Confronted by Climate Activists Outside of Capitol." October 27, 2021. YouTube video. https://www.youtube.com/watch?v=kyRkFlPcVIs.

22. The Majority Report w/ Sam Seder. "Joe Manchin Confronted by Climate Activists Outside of Capitol." October 27, 2021. YouTube video. https://www.youtube.com/watch?v=kyRkFlPcVIs.

23. Earthjustice. "What the Inflation Reduction Act Means for Climate." Earthjustice. https://earthjustice.org/brief/2022/what-the-inflation-reduction-act-means-for-climate.

24. Sunrise Movement. "The Sunrise Movement Celebrates the Inflation Reduction Act as a Down-payment on the Green New Deal." *Red, Green, and Blue,* August 13, 2022. http://redgreenandblue.org/2022/08/13/sunrise-movement-celebrates-inflation-reduction-act-payment-green-new-deal/.

25. Sunrise Movement. "The Sunrise Movement Celebrates the Inflation Reduction Act as a Down-payment on the Green New Deal." *Red, Green, and Blue,* August 13, 2022. http://redgreenandblue.org/2022/08/13/sunrise-movement-celebrates-inflation-reduction-act-payment-green-new-deal/.

26. Sunrise Movement. "December 6, 2019—Global Climate Strike." Sunrise Movement. https://www.sunrisemovement.org/actions/dec-global-climate-strike/.

27. Bates, Will. Interview with the author, February 18, 2020.

28. Sunrise Movement. Email to supporters list, June 28, 2021.

29. Sunrise Movement. Email to supporters list, December 20, 2021.

30. Leonard, Matt. Interview with the author, January 21, 2021.

31. Leonard, Matt. Interview with the author, January 21, 2021.

32. Komlik, Oleg. "The Original Email That Started Occupy Wall Street." Economic Sociology & Political Economy. https://economicsociology.org/2014/12/27/the-original-email-that-started-occupy-wall-street/.

33. Olen, Helaine. "Occupy Wall Street Won the Future." *Washington Post,* September 18, 2021. https://www.washingtonpost.com/opinions/2021/09/18/occupy-wall-street-won-future/.

34. Sigwalt, Dany. Interview with the author, March 25, 2021.

35. Cohen, Ilana. Interview with the author, September 14, 2022.

36. Estelle, Sean. Interview with the author, March 6, 2020.

37. Sigwalt, Dany. Interview with the author, March 25, 2021.

38. Dutchin, Nadya. Interview with the author, March 25, 2021.

39. Nicholson, Ari. Interview with the author, March 11, 2020.

40. Nicholson, Ari. "Seeking Autonomy in Student Organizing: A Case Study of External Influence on Clark Climate Justice." Clark Digital Commons. https://commons.clarku.edu/cgi/viewcontent.cgi?article=2637&context=asdff.

41. De Ramos, Gari. Interview with the author, March 10, 2020.

42. Nicholson, Ari. "Seeking Autonomy in Student Organizing: A Case Study of External Influence on Clark Climate Justice." Clark Digital Commons. https://commons.clarku.edu/cgi/viewcontent.cgi?article=2637&context=asdff.

43. Sunrise Movement members (unnamed authors). "Do What Must be Done: A Vision for Revolutionary People Power." https://docs.google.com/document/d/13Hiv5AK6lxHggg4J4uj5FjD9JBeobkuPv62YBNamM9k/edit.

44. Hirji, Zahra. "Inside the 'Very Secret History' of the Sunrise Movement." *Buzzfeed News,* August 12, 2021. https://www.buzzfeednews.com/article/zahrahirji/sunrise-movement-climate-change-black-activists.

45. Sunrise Movement members (unnamed authors). "Do What Must be Done: A Vision for Revolutionary People Power." https://docs.google.com/document/d/13Hiv5AK6lxHggg4J4uj5FjD9JBeobkuPv62YBNamM9k/edit.

46. Prakash, Varshini. "I'm Joining the Sanders-Biden Taskforce on Climate. Here's Why." Sunrise Movement. https://medium.com/sunrisemvmt/im-joining-the-sanders-biden-taskforce-on-climate-here-s-why-90a3dd0ff546.

47. Hirji, Zahra. "Inside the 'Very Secret History' of the Sunrise Movement." *Buzzfeed News,* August 12, 2021. https://www.buzzfeednews.com/article/zahrahirji/sunrise-movement-climate-change-black-activists.

48. Sunrise Movement. Email to supporters list, July 1, 2022.

49. Sunrise Movement Baltimore. "Sunrise Movement Baltimore: Public Reckoning and Reflections on White Supremacy within Our Movement." Sunrise Movement Baltimore. https://sunrisemovementbaltimore-11813.medium.com/sunrise-movement-baltimore-public-reckoning-and-reflections-on-white-supremacy-within-our-3d66270ed509.

50. Sunrise Movement Seattle. Email to supporters list, August 19, 2021.

51. Sigwalt, Dany. Interview with the author, March 25, 2021.

52. Dutchin, Nadya. Interview with the author, March 25, 2021.

53. Sigwalt, Dany. Interview with the author, March 25, 2021.

54. Nordhaus, Ted and Michael Shellenberger. "The Death of Environmentalism: Global Warming Politics in a Post-Environmental World." *Grist,* January 14, 2005. https://grist.org/article/doe-reprint/.

55. Nordhaus, Ted and Michael Shellenberger. "The Death of Environmentalism: Global Warming Politics in a Post-Environmental World." *Grist,* January 14, 2005. https://grist.org/article/doe-reprint/.

56. Isham, Jon. Interview with the author, January 20, 2020.

57. Nordhaus, Ted and Michael Shellenberger. "Environmentalists Made a Big Mistake by Focusing All Their Attention on a Keystone." *The New Republic,* February 5, 2014. https://newrepublic.com/article/116492/keyston-pipeline-focus-mistake-liberal-environmentalists.

58. Nordhaus, Ted. "The Empty Radicalism of the Climate Apocalypse." *Issues in Science and Technology,* Summer 2019. https://issues.org/empty-radicalism-of-the-climate-apocalypse/.

59. Nordhaus, Ted and Michael Shellenberger. "Environmentalists Made a Big Mistake by Focusing All Their Attention on a Keystone." *The New Republic,* February 5, 2014. https://newrepublic.com/article/116492/keyston-pipeline-focus-mistake-liberal-environmentalists.

60. Andersen, Kip and Keegan Kuhn. *Cowspiracy.* Santa Rosa, CA: A.U.M. Films and Media, 2014.

61. Cowspiracy.com. "Take the 30-Day Vegan Challenge!" A.U.M. Films & Media. September 18, 2022.

62. Rajbhandari, Shiva. Interview with the author, March 3, 2022.

63. Cerosaletti, Anna. Interview with the author, March 10, 2022.

64. Leonard, Matt. Interview with the author, January 21, 2021.

65. DeChristopher, Tim. Interview with the author, October 14, 2020.

66. Prakash, Varshini. "NYC Sept 20, 2019 #ClimateStrike Speech." Sunrise Movement. https://www.sunrisemovement.org/movement-updates/nyc-sept-20-2019-climatestrike-speech-varshini-prakash-be3e4118e4d8/.

67. Morris, Jonathan. Interview with the author, May 4, 2021.

68. Engelfried, Nick. "How Generation Z is Leading the Climate Movement." *Waging Nonviolence,* January 14, 2020.

10 The Movement of the Future

1. Pelto, Mauri S. "Easton Glacier." North Cascade Glacier Climate Project. https://glaciers.nichols.edu/easton/.

2. Gearon, Jihan. Interview with the author, April 24, 2020.

3. Gearon, Jihan. Interview with the author, April 24, 2020.

4. Tuck, Eve, Marcia McKenzie, and Kate McCoy. "Land Education: Indigenous, Post-Colonial, and Decolonizing Perspectives on Place and Environmental Education Research." *Environmental Education Research* 20:1, 1-23, DOI: 10.1080/13504622.2013.877708.

5. Siddiqa, Ayisha. Interview with the author, February 15, 2020.

6. Wright, Ethan. Interview with the author, November 1, 2019.

7. Ifeji, Amara. Interview with the author, May 17, 2021.

8. Duval, Jared. Interview with the author, February 21, 2020

9. Gearon, Jihan. Interview with the author, April 24, 2020.

10. Duke, Solomon. Interview with the author, March 24, 2021.

11. Zuckerman, Jan. Interview with the author, March 14, 2021.

12. Swinehart, Tim. Interview with the author, March 24, 2021.

13. Portland Board of Education. "Resolution No. 5272." https://drive.google.com/file/d/1-g7Uerfm0gHb2zT5qks2Rkjew-cRZEjX/view.

14. Swinehart, Tim. Interview with the author, March 24, 2021.

15. Campuzano, Eder. "Hundreds of Portland Students Stage School Walk-Out, Join International Climate Protests." *The Oregonian,* March 15, 2019. https://www.oregonlive.com/education/2019/03/hundreds-of-portland-students-stage-school-walk-out-join-international-climate-protests.html.

16. Portland Board of Education. "Resolution No. 5272." https://drive.google.com/file/d/1-g7Uerfm0gHb2zT5qks2Rkjew-cRZEjX/view.

17. Nopp, Elliot. Interview with the author, March 24, 2021.

18. Portland Youth Climate Council. "About PYCC." Portland Youth Climate Council. https://pdxclimatecouncil.wixsite.com/youth.

19. Swinehart, Tim. Interview with the author, March 24, 2021.

20. Lakey, George. Interview with the author, April 16, 2020.

21. Schmitz, Paul. "How Change Happens: The Real Story of Mrs. Rosa Parks & the Montgomery Bus Boycott." *HuffPost,* December 1, 2014. https://www.huffpost.com/entry/how-change-happens-the-re_b_6237544.

22. Swinehart, Tim. Interview with the author, March 24, 2021.

23. Ifeji, Amara. Interview with the author, May 17, 2021.

24. Singh, Hridesh. Interview with the author, March 29, 2020.

25. Villaseñor, Alexandria. "My letter to all youth climate activists and the climate movement." *Twitter,* April 26, 2021. https://mobile.twitter.com/AlexandriaV2005/status/1386868734107738113/photo/1.

26. Feldman, Ari. "This Teen Climate Activist is Done With Adults Saying 'Kids Will Save the World.'" *Forward,* July 1, 2019. https://forward.com/news/426568/climate-change-jamie-margolin/.

27. Kemmick, JP. Interview with the author, February 11, 2020.

28. Charger, Jasilyn. Speech at Frontlines to D.C. rally. Washington, D.C., April 1, 2021.

29. Goodwin, Morgan. Interview with the author, February 4, 2020.

30. Lewis, Christine. Interview with the author, March 15, 2020.

31. Carlino, Daniel. Interview with the author, April 29, 2020

32. Williams, Juliana. Interview with the author, January 31, 2020.

33. Lynch, Kelly. Interview with the author, March 11, 2020.

34. Teplitzky, Kim. Interview with the author, August 28, 2020.

35. Avila, Lydia. "Lydia D. Avila." *LinkedIn,* May 29, 2022. https://www.linkedin.com/in/lydia-d-avila/.

36. Dutchin, Nadya. Interview with the author, March 25, 2021.

37. Dutchin, Nadya. Interview with the author, March 25, 2021.

38. Kearney, Melissa S. and Phillip Levine. "Will Births in the US Rebound? Probably Not." The Brookings Institute. https://www.brookings.edu/blog/up-front/2021/05/24/will-births-in-the-us-rebound-probably-not/.

39. Ferorelli, Josephine. Interview with the author, October 14, 2021.

40. Isabella Fallahi, Isabella. Interview with the author, December 22, 2019.

41. Watson, Audrey. Interview with the author, April 16, 2020.

42. Margolin, Jamie. Interview with the author, November 16, 2019.

43. Cronin, Brian PJ. "5 Questions: Jamie Margolin." *The Highlands Current,* April 23, 2021. https://highlandscurrent.org/2021/04/23/5-questions-jamie-margolin/.

44. Ressler, Lauren. Interview with the author, January 17, 2020.

45. Spoon, Cindy. Interview with the author, March 9, 2020.

46. Grodsky, Zoe. Interview with the author, June 4, 2020.

47. Weaverdyck, Noah. Interview with the author, May 4, 2021.

48. Bishop, Sasha. Interview with the author, May 4, 2021.

49. Brings Plenty, Morgan. Interview with the author, February 21, 2021.

50. Lewis, Christine. Interview with the author, March 15, 2020.

Conclusion

1. Ballará, Bianca. Interview with the author, September 27, 2020.

2. Neumann, Erik. "A Hint of Future Fire Seasons, as Southern Oregon Emerges From the Ashes of 2020." *OPB,* January 13, 2021. https://www.opb.org/article/2021/01/13/oregon-almeda-fire-destruction-lessons/.

3. Ho, Vivian. "Fire Tore Through the Karuk Tribe's Homeland. Many Won't be Able to Rebuild." *The Guardian,* October 23, 2020. https://www.the-guardian.com/us-news/2020/oct/23/karuk-tribe-california-slater-fire-insurance.

4. Ballará, Bianca. Interview with the author, September 27, 2020.

5. Williams, Juliana. Interview with the author, January 31, 2020.

6. Sigwalt, Dany. Interview with the author, March 25, 2021.

7. Stark, Zach. Interview with the author, January 9, 2020.

8. Ballará, Bianca. Interview with the author, September 27, 2020.

Index

About Reconnect Earth

COME CHANGE THE WORLD WITH US!

Reconnect Earth works for a socially and ecologically just future by fostering and growing a network of empowered young leaders to sustain grassroots social movements for years to come.

Visit **reconnectearth.org** to learn about our experiential programs and trips for college-age students.

> *"I learned more about myself on this 9-day trip than in my 26 years on this earth. Reconnect Earth gave me the confidence to direct positive changes in this world."*
> **- 2021 Reconnect Earth trip participant**

Movement Makers is a publication of Reconnect Earth Action, which spreads information to further a more just, sustainable world. Views and opinions expressed in the book do not necessarily reflect those of Reconnect Earth.

Did you enjoy Movement Makers?

Keep the conversation going at
movementmakersclimate.com

Find resources for:

- Starting a *Movement Makers* book discussion group

- Getting involved in youth climate organizations

- Scheduling an author event

- *and more!*

www.ingramcontent.com/pod-product-compliance
Lightning Source LLC
Chambersburg PA
CBHW071138130626
46553CB00004B/1426